Middle Clash

Issues which will create a third party in the 21st Century

Martin M. Shinedling, Ph.D., L.P.

Writers Club Press

San Jose New York Lincoln Shanghai

Middle Clash
Issues which will create a third party in the 21st Century

Published by Writers Club Press
an imprint of iUniverse.com, Inc.

For information address:
iUniverse.com, Inc.
620 North 48th Street
Suite 201
Lincoln, NE 68504-3467
www.iuniverse.com

ISBN: 0-595-00467-9

Printed in the United States of America

To my wife, Teresa without whose constant help and support, this book could not have been written. And to my children whose confidence and trust have served as a constant source of inspiration. Michelle, Michael Martin, Jill, Bethany and Michael Joseph have been a great treasure to me.

Humans prefer the devil they know to the devil they don't know. This is why they pretend that each day will be like the day before. Eventually, they discover that quality of life is like a drop of dew on the tip of a blade of grass. And the devil they don't know will become a blessing, a curse or both.

Contents

Foreword ix

Acknowledgements xiii

Introduction xv

The Middle Class and the American Dream:
Myth or Reality? 1

The American Quandary: A Rebellious Nature,
the Struggle against "Control Freaks,"
and how Politicians Gain Power 19

The Ethics of Deceit 31

Does the "Health Crisis" Need Major Surgery? 43

The Drug War—Vietnam Re-Visited 55

N.A.F.T.A., International Trade and the Big Lie 69

Reducing the Cost of Government 89

TAXES—The Argument for a flat tax 101

WELFARE—Empowering the Poor—Abolishing Welfare Slavery 121

The Homeless—Dealing Appropriately with the Mentally Ill 137

Building the Infrastructure 147

Crime—Casting Politicians Aside and Returning 157

Power to the Judges and the People 157

Insurance and the Cost of a Suing Society 175

Education—Recognizing We Are All Equally Different 191

War and Its Manifestations 205

Political Parties—the Need for a Third Party 221

Living in the 21st Century 235

About the Author 247

Endnotes 249

Foreword

One of the first laws of human behavior is to avoid pain, usually at all costs. Children do this instinctively. However, as adults we sometime forget the lessons usually inherent in suffering. Benjamin Franklin noted "those things that hurt, instruct." Psychoanalyst Carl Jung added, "Neurosis is always a substitute for legitimate suffering." That is, humans often manufacture manageable pain so as to avoid real anguish. Perhaps that is why so many of us are distracted by the minor foibles of our current leaders and overlooking the vital fundamental changes that must occur if the middle class is to survive.

Those of us living on the brink of the 21st century know that our society is primarily motivated by pleasure, by an enhancement of "rights," and a frantic rush to live almost totally by the "pleasure principle,"—and ignore the "reality principle." One of Aesop's fables exclaims: "Oh foolish creatures that destroy themselves for transitory joy."

Dr. Shinedling, instead of running from the problems of the day, enthusiastically takes them on. He truly believes that each crisis he describes can be an opportunity for invigorating and expanding the quality of life in the "Silent Suburbs" and recapturing the American Dream. His solutions however, are not pollyannish but instead require thoughtful concentration and preparation. He believes as Dr. F. Scott Peck states "Without discipline we can solve nothing." Today we eschew discipline and insist on immediate gratification, which is ironically the hallmark of drug dependency: increased tolerance and demand for the opiate of choice.

Concentration on pleasure without responsibility has led us to the point of millions of unwed, teenage mothers, children without fathers and violent crime. The elderly are often forced to share their neighborhoods with drug addicts, alcoholics, and chaotic families. Each time they hear the sirens of the Emergency Medical Team rolling along their streets they wonder if it's a neighbor having a heart attack or stroke, a gang attack or a drive-by shooting. Both the cities and the suburbs want a better life. To seek solutions to "heal" these problems, we look to our elected leaders. But they offer no healing therapies.

To wallow in pessimism and cynicism only debases us and makes us fundamentally impotent. As an agent of change, I personally much prefer to look to ideas that are time-tested and pragmatic. If our age has unique and awesome problems, it also has unique and awesome opportunities. As the Chinese remind u, their ideograph for crisis is a symbol, which combines loss with opportunity. We can go forward or backward. Will we identify, hypothesize, and resolve the crisis, or instead deny the discipline of mind and resolve necessary to change? Will we continue to "tread water" nationally while emerging nations of the Pacific Rim and elsewhere use us and then out distance us? Surely the governments of the world are watching us with greater circumspection than we dare imagine. It is my belief that they have lost considerable respect for us and may simply watch us to learn from our mistakes.

Thus, I experienced an oasis of comfort when I read Dr. Shinedling's work on where we're at and where we could go. He is a practical author as well as an idealogue: he tells us what we might do. His volume is compelling as he builds us to awareness. To one who loves the American Dream, he asks only that we look, listen, and then—act.

If his solutions(s) may seem at times too simplistic or radical, bear in mind that he is trying to steer a realistic course between constitutionally limited government and individual liberty. Neither government nor freedom is the icon before which we can worship. If it is true that politics is "the art of the possible," what a shame if only moral expediency should be allowed to steer the ship of state. What an even greater shame if either fragmented "liberty" or government ever more dictatorial should presage our fall from grace.

Many will profit from thoughtful reading of this book, others may write if off as radical or impossible. Certainly it should serve as a stimulant to open-minded citizens and "leaders" of the most courageous, beautiful and prosperous nation this old globe of ours has ever seen born.

Joseph K. Miller, M.Div., Psy.D.

Acknowledgements

This book could not have been written without the support of my wife and partner Teresa Shinedling. She takes up the slack for me when I am not available at home or in the office. Needless to say, as I've spent time working on this book, she has increased the number of clients she sees to make up for my drop in client contact hours.

Another person I must recognize is Rush Limbaugh. I don't believe he would agree with what I have written. Rather, he was the impetus for writing this book. Rush became the motivator in an unusual way. My oldest son Michael has been a car fanatic since he was five years old. When he was 16, he acquired a 73 BMW and turned the sedan into a convertible. In the process, he came to love BMW's. So when he went to Brigham Young University, I was not surprised that he decided to major in mechanical engineering. What threw me for a loop was his decision to turn down an internship at BMW headquarters in Munich, Germany. When I asked him why he declined the internship, he told me that it would mean that he would not be able to listen to Rush Limbaugh every afternoon.

Michael was a fanatic 'ditto head.' He structured his life, his school schedule and his social engagements to accommodate Rush's broadcast time. His newly acquired fiance however, talked him into changing his mind about the internship by promising she would tape each of Rush's broadcasts and airmail them to him in Munich. Once Michelle agreed to supply him with his Rush tapes, Michael left for Munich and eventually started his own 'Rush Room.' In fact, he developed a small group of 'ditto heads' who when President Bush attended the G-7 conference in Munich, showed up with a big sign that said, Students support President Bush, G-7 and Rush Limbaugh.

Given my oldest son was so taken by Rush, I decided to listen to talk radio for the first time. I must admit that I enjoyed his music and his trenchant remarks about Liberal blockheadedness. Of course, I noted that he seemed to ignore the foibles of the Republicans. A fact he did not hide but instead insisted that there was so much Liberal bias in the media, that his program needed to provide balance. Once in a while however, a caller would call in and complain about something the Republican Party did or should have done. At that time, Rush would say something like, "Well if the Republican Party doesn't stand for something—mutter, mutter, mutter."

Rush responded in the same way several times. He never completed his thoughts. So I wondered what he meant, and then I started thinking. If the Liberals couldn't do it, and the Republicans wouldn't do it, then who would? Obviously, a third party. But no third party has successfully dominated politics since the Civil War. Then, I thought about what it would take for an independent third party to rise to a position of power. Hence my book. I've been working on this book for several years. During that time, Jesse Ventura was successfully elected to be governor of Minnesota using many of the strategies I had formulated in my book. This gave me some validation and also the impetus to continue the struggle of placing my thoughts on paper.

As I have worked on my book, I also have enjoyed the ideas and thoughts I have gleaned from Talk Radio and cable news personalities such as Don Imus, Michael Reagan, Shawn Hannity and Alan Colmes. I also have to thank the rebels who have contributed their dynamism such as Ross Perot, Pat Buchanan, John McCain, Alan Keyes and Bill Bradley.

Introduction

I am not a politician, economist, political pundit, historian or social scientist. My initial training was in clinical psychology—a discipline which specializes in helping people in trouble, i.e., divorce, loss of a loved one, addictions, loss of a job, depression, neurosis, etc. But, as I continued to practice, I eventually started working with head injuries, paralysis, chronic pain, and patients with serious medical problems. So I began to think of myself as a neuropsychologist or in a broader sense a medical psychologist. Finally however, I just decided to be a psychologist.

After obtaining my degree from Brigham Young University in 1971, I moved to Michigan after a brief stint with the C.I.A. and started taking postgraduate training at the University of Michigan. Luckily, my professor was Aaron Smith. Aaron was the former president of the International Neuropsychological Society. He had written hundreds of articles on the effects of trauma and medical conditions on the brain. But the first thing he taught me over and over was the dictum, if the patient disagrees with the book, throw the book away; not the patient.

The brain is wonderfully complex and has a vast ability to overcome trauma and disease in its own unique way. Every patient is equally different. No one is exactly like anyone else. Each new patient presents a marvelous opportunity to teach you something about how he or she copes and how he or she chose to overcome their problem. And none of them exactly fit into any book's description of a particular disease or condition.

During the course of my practice, I have learned again and again that every patient is equally different. And I have had to contend again and again with other professionals who refuse to acknowledge the simple fact that patients can't be fitted into nice tidy boxes.

No one patient tries as he or she might can escape the limitations of his or her particular physical/psychological constitution. They can make wonderful adaptations but not without accommodating their limitations. As I've helped each patient struggle with their unique problem(s), I have also had to face the fact that each patient has to live within their own environment with their own constellation of resources. Each is dependent on a support system, which varies from patient to patient.

Also, patients live within a political/economical framework, which sometimes affects them. For example, one patient who was in a coma for seven months, woke to a gradual awareness of experiencing extreme pain and muscle spasm that he could not obtain relief for because his physicians couldn't prescribe medication in sufficient doses. His attending physicians knew that they would come under scrutiny from state bureaucrats if they attempted to really help him. So they did what they could and he continued to suffer.

His experience drove home the point that just as each of us can't escape the limitations of our physical makeup, we also can't escape the political/social/economic milieu in which we live. I've written this book in hopes that it will contribute in its own small way to changing the growing pathology in our society that increasingly affects us all.

Societies wax and wane in terms of the amount of pathology they exhibit. If Aristotle, one of the early Greek Philosophers, were able to evaluate our present society, I am sure he would consider it to be sick and inflamed. Why? Because we have strayed and are straying farther and farther each day from his idea of a golden mean. Instead of an expanding, enriching and empowering middle class, we have a shrinking, impoverished and weakened middle class. While many in the middle class are finding themselves the beneficiaries of a 'software economy' others, the tens of millions that make up the majority of the intellectual/skill spectrum find their opportunities increasingly diminished as corporation down size and export their jobs to cheaper labor countries.

In this book, I will use for the most part Jeffersonian ideas to show you how the middle class can regain it's health and in the process produce a society that is healing for most of us and in particular for the patients I see. Some of my ideas are definitely not libertarian as they are defined now. That is why I have titled my book Post-Modern Libertarianism. Remember if the patient disagrees with the book, you through the book away; so too, if people disagree with an idea, you change the idea rather than destroy the people.

So as Rush Limbaugh ponderously pontificates to the tune of a comedic rock and roll beat and the G Man (G. Gordon Liddy) advocates carrying guns to protect yourself and the whining whimps of waffledom that inhabit the White House, Congress and National Media respond with images of starving school children and teenage mothers with new born babies abandoned and homeless, the silent suburbs carry on their own rhythm of life in quiet desperation.

Democrats and Republicans continually search for the magic potion or conundrum that will capture the imagination and devotion of the silent suburbs. But as Richard L. Berke of *The New York Times*[1] reports neither party has been able to succeed in attracting the loyalty of the silent suburbs. The power of the silent suburbs is awesome and has been felt before when they revolted against property taxes, expressed their anger toward politicians by imposing term limits and now are beginning to stir themselves up about affirmative action which is often the scapegoat for a real decline in middle-class jobs. So Democrats and Republicans seek unsuccessfully to assuage their anger. Newt Gingrich offered the carrot of the Contract with America, which laid an egg in the silent suburbs. *USA TODAY* (August 11-13, 1995) reports 62% of the suburbs see the need for a new party.[2] Jerry Nichols, a small business owner in Moreno Valley, California, puts it this way, "Unless something is done to take care of the economy in the next two years, there is going to be no middle class."[3] Clinton's own failure to heed his own admonition "Its the economy stupid" continues to cause him to lay many an egg in the silent suburbs.

Mike Pagan, a retired police officer said it well when he talked about a $259,000 home he purchased that he now can not sell for $184,000.[4] As Mike helplessly watches his savings wiped out, the "line item veto" or the screaming howls of the whining politicians do not amuse him as they seek to protect "liberal" programs.

Charles Johnson, an owner of a small ice cream parlor noted with disgust, "I just did my taxes yesterday. I made less and paid more in taxes."[5] The silent suburbs feel the effects of a society that rapes the middle class for taxes and speaks of programs that make no sense.

Imagine a pendulum in motion. Pretend the ball at the end of the string swings back and forth and contains the voting population of the United States. As the ball swings to the left the Democrats gain power and as it moves to the right, the Republicans attain control. But each time it moves in its arc, visualize more and more people getting off the ball. Till finally few people are on the ball and most are either ignoring it or watching indifferently. For a while the pendulum continues to swing, but since most voters have gotten off, the tendency to gravitate toward the center lessens. And with each election, more and more people are disgusted with the course of its track.

So disgusted in fact, that the Speaker of the House was defeated in the November, 1994 election (the last time a speaker was defeated was just prior to the Civil War). So disenchanted that the Democrats lost control of the House (the first time in forty years). So disenchanted that a President (Bush), with a ninety percent approval rating drops to less than forty percent in one year and is defeated for re-election bid. And so offended by our current President that many Congresspersons associated with him were also defeated for re-election in 1994. The defeat of Democrats and the empowerment of Republicans in no way however, portended a magic carpet of the good life for Republicans.

As the recent election of a liberal senator to Congress to replace Packwood shows, no party or person is safe, because none of them really understand a basic fact. The fact is that as long as politicians pretend they can help the populace and as long as they insist on ignoring the real problems and presenting pablum rather than soul nourishing food, the pendulum will continue to swing back and forth, throwing out Democrats, then throwing out Republicans and then back to throwing out Democrats.

It doesn't have to be that way! This book contains my view of a future. A future in which America has gained its second breath and is moving forward toward the mid-twenty-first century with renewed vigor, hope and confidence. It also describes the programs, which need to be put in place to attain this vision. My thinking is not politically correct. Nor is it politically incorrect. It is instead, middle-class radical. Some of my ideas may inspire you, others undoubtedly will offend you. I write not to inspire or to offend, but instead to challenge you to think and re-think the ancient philosophical question, "What course of life is best?"

Each decade is a decade of decision. But, as we approach the twenty-first century, perhaps this decade is more important. As never before, we must decide what we are willing to do to stop the negative train of events that threaten to destroy the middle class. Unless we take a stand to protect the middle class, our entire United States political, social, and economic climate will continue to disintegrate.

One way to gauge any country's problems is the health of its political parties. The last time both major parties lost the allegiance of the American people was just before the Civil War. At that time, the North and the South were fighting over who would control the West and the Slave issue. Because no one national party was able to accommodate a large enough portion of the population, the electorate fractured into a number of smaller parties.[6]

The Whigs, which had been a dominant party, was rapidly dying. The Democrats split into Northern and Southern sections. Know-Nothings (a group that attempted to deal with the conflict between North and South by refusing to discuss the issues) and a newly formed Republican Party surfaced. No one party was able to command the loyalty of the people, and with the election of Abraham Lincoln the fabric of American society ruptured. This bloody rupture enabled America to change from a slave nation to a free nation.

Freedom however, has to be constantly purchased in each generation. Sometimes, the cost of freedom is purchased with the blood of our youth and at other times it is bought with a radical change in how we live or think.

Today we stand poised on the brink of the 21st century. Dissatisfaction with the major political parties has continued to increase since 1973.[7] From 1864 to 1964, only three independent candidates commanded more than 6% of the vote (James B. Weaver in 1892, Theodore Roosevelt in 1912, and Robert La Follette in 1924). Yet in the last three decades, we have had three third party candidates that have garnered more than 6% of the vote: George Wallace with 13.5% in 1968, John Anderson with 6.6 percent in 1980, and Ross Perot in 1992 with 19% (Gordon S. and Benjamin D. Black: THE POLITICS OF AMERICAN DISCONTENT).

If we combined the number of Perot supporters with the number of independents their total would significantly outnumber either the Democrats or the Republicans. The Congressional Quarterly Weekly Reports (Vol. 50, No.44) indicated that 104 million citizens voted in the 1992 election. Over 15 million of them stated that they would not have voted if Perot had not been running. Perot's share of the votes ranged from 16% in the South to 22% in the West. Only 35% of our population are tied to the Democrats, and only 26% considered themselves

Republicans in the 1992 election (*1994 Vital Statistics In American Politics, 4th Ed*).

If we further breakdown the issue of party allegiance, we find that 17% consider themselves strong Democrats and 11% consider themselves strong Republicans. Despite the fact that the Democratic Party thus represents a minority of the population, it controlled both houses of Congress and the Presidency till the November, 1994 elections. Public opinion polls consistently show that most of us have a negative opinion about government. According to *Public Opinion Quarterly* (April, 1992) a bare 17% of the population approved of Congress.

Evidence shows that the American people regard politicians, the national media, and economists with suspicion.[8] Most of us would like to find public figures we can trust, but each time we elect a new leader (President, Senator or Congressperson), the result is the continuing destruction of middle class hopes and ideals.

Since 1973, the economic prosperity of the middle class has continuously declined.[9] The *1990 Bureau of the Census Reports, (Series P—60, No. 174)* shows that upper class has grown 43%, and the lower class has grown 4.7 percent, while the middle class has shrunk by 8.7%. Donald L. Bartlett and James B. Steele (Pulitzer Prize winning reporters, of *The Philadelphia Inquirer*) in their book, *America: What Went Wrong?* put it another way. They note that in 1952 the top four percent of the population earned as much as the bottom 35% of the population. And in 1989, the top four-percent is earning as much as the bottom 51%.

Let me state the real problem in another way. Suppose you are told that new and high paying jobs are being created in the United States; BUT, to qualify you must have education and skills which require an I.Q. of at least 110. That means for every 100 people, only 25 will qualify. So in this new burgeoning economy the prospects for 25 people out of a 100 will dramatically improve while the hopes of 75 out of 100 hundred will diminish as their jobs are exported to other countries and they are left with McJobs which do not pay enough to live on their own, buy a car or look forward to a happier future. So while the political parties and national media states that the economy is doing so well, the reality is, for most people, things are getting worse.

As the middle class plunges toward oblivion, the United States is becoming more like a third world country ruled by an oligarchy of the rich and powerful, while the rest of the population struggles to survive. Ask yourself this question, if the same people contribute to both parties, who do they really represent? If for example, a corporation contributes hundreds of thousands of dollars to the Republican and Democratic parties, does either party really care about the middle class or instead do they pander to the corporation that contracts for slave labor in China?

Being a medical psychologist, these statistics turn into reality for me when clients come into my office. No more do I hear parents talking about their sons or daughters joining their fathers and grandfathers in the plant. Instead, I hear comments such as, "I just hope it doesn't close before I have my time in for retirement."

More and more youth stay at home with their parents because they can't afford an apartment or car on McDonald's or Burger King salaries. A resigned pessimism and quiet hopelessness pervades them. Their view of government is that it is largely irrelevant or if they vote, it is because they want to empower the party that will hurt them the least. But I don't think it has to be that way. If the middle class were to use its power of numbers while its voting power still exists, it can recapture control of America in the 21st century.

In an excellent article published in the *Atlantic Monthly* (May, 1994) entitled "Who Speaks for the Middle Class?" author Jack Beatty noted how things have deteriorated for the middle class. He pointed out that real wages started declining from 1973 and hit a low point in the early 80's. He itemized several reasons for middle class decline: 1) the oil price shocks of 1973 and 1979, 2) insufficient savings and capitol investment, 3) shift away from high wage manufacturing to low wage service jobs, 4) decline in private sector union membership 5) Wall Street's hunger for bigger and bigger dividends, sooner and sooner and 6) America's love for imported products.

While Beatty was accurate in his summation of reasons, he ended his article the same way political leaders do, that is, "ain't it awful and there's nothing we can do about it".

That is where I differ. As a trained and experienced therapist, I specialize in challenging the assumptions that clients relate to me. Whenever they say, I can't or there's nothing different I can do, I automatically ask why or why not?

My clients reflect the heart of America's middle class. Working in areas that serve rural, urban, industrial, farming, professional, educational and service-oriented citizens, I have had a unique opportunity to learn what is important to people. In order to guide them to help themselves, I have learned to ask my clients to step out of the paradigm that controls their thinking.

Most clients seek therapy because they have a problem that offers no obvious answer. In truth, they are sitting on a spiked fence experiencing agony as the spikes bury themselves deeper and deeper into their body. They cannot get off the fence. On one side they see poisonous snakes, and on the other side rabid dogs.

Most human beings usually operate on a simple premise: better the devil we know than the devil we don't know. Since these people see danger no matter what decision they make, they usually elect to stay undecided despite the pain.

The abused wife stays in her marriage because she fears life without her husband would be worse. The man or woman who hates the job they are in, stays because they don't know what would happen if they quit. Politicians play on this fear of the unknown, characterizing their opponent as someone who can't be trusted and would hurt their interests.

My job as a therapist is simple: to make clients feel comfortable enough to widen their vision. When people are tense or angry, they narrow the cognitive vision that empowers them. By relaxing and releasing tension, fear, anxiety and anger, human beings become aware of other choices. They see a safe place to jump off the fence, a place free of hungry lions or lurking tigers.

Sometimes they even realize how much more enjoyable life is off the spiked fence. Unfortunately, many people never realize they are sitting on a spiked fence and rarely seek help. They know only that they are in pain, leading lives of quiet desperation, as Henry David Thoreau observed "we lack the bravery to depart from established paths and despair because we see no alternative but to follow the dictates of established norms in culture, government and society." Hopefully, today a growing number of Americans are ready to reclaim the pioneering spirit of America, to finally get off the spiked fence.

Some of you might be concerned that the ideas promulgated in this book could ruin America. Is America so easily destroyed? For too many years, our country has been for sale to the highest bidder; our Congress and our presidency have become sycophants to the public: saying in public what they think people wanted to hear; but in private, selling themselves to the special interest groups that finance elections.[10] Senator Bob Smith, who just recently quit the Republican Party in disgust said it all when he said, AI'm tired of political pollsters telling us what we can and can't do.@ The silence from the Democratic party was deafening as they didn't respond at all because they knew that the Clinton White House worshipped at the feet of the pollsters.

Special interest groups dominate political life. They include businesses that buy the products of slave-labor camps in China, foreign countries that sell their products in the United States while they bar our products from their shores, importers who purchase the products of three-dollar-a-day peasants in third world countries and have absolutely no concern for anything but the bottom line of their businesses, and bureaucrats who are so interested in building their power bases that they have no concern for the jobs they destroy.

Bureaucrats specialize in writing regulations, which increasingly infringe on the rights of American citizens, impede productivity, and hasten the flow of jobs out of our country. Unwilling to face the consequences of their actions, they are, in effect, allied with the special interest groups who destroy middle class jobs.

Politicians choose to protect their power base while they knowingly destroy middle class jobs. As Beatty said, "Democrats refuse to make the tax incentives that would increase investments which would enable corporations to build more plants while Republicans refuse to invest in infrastructure development."[11]

Both savings and infrastructure development are necessary to expand the middle class. But the politicians in Washington are too interested in fighting with each other to be concerned about the middle class.

Political gridlock is not particularly unique to Washington, D.C. In the late 1960's and early 1970's, middle class Californians were being taxed out of their homes. The elderly on fixed incomes along with much lower income Californians were getting tax bills that doubled each year. Ronald Reagan was elected to be governor of California partly as a reaction against huge increases in taxes.

But the public continued to be frustrated. State government, both major parties, and the media only suggested that things should be better, but offered no practical solutions. Instead, each party blamed the other and stopped each other's solutions.

Fed up, the middle class stopped accepting the lame excuses of the politicians and bureaucrats in Sacramento. They enacted Proposition 13 to control and reduce property taxes. Now I offer a national challenge: let us enact our own Proposition 13. This proposition suggests that until both political parties (and a political party), decide to truly represent the middle class, a vote will be cast against each incumbent, from the local school district board up to the presidency.

For example, if only a small portion of the electorate (for example, the 19% who supported Perot), concentrated their vote against the current politician in office, while the remainder of the population voted as normal, the vast majority of incumbents would be defeated. Such a fall would be exceedingly great! As a further example, if you assigned to George Bush or President Clinton all of the voters who voted for Perot, you would find that Clinton would only have carried Arkansas and Washington, D.C. and that Bush would not have carried any state.[12]

My premise is simple. Decide for yourself. After reading this book, if you agree with these ideas, vote against every incumbent in every level of government. But do not expect most people to agree with you. Most people would rather stay undecided. They remain undecided, although each year nine hundred thousand middle class jobs are lost, and each year the future looks grimmer for them and their children as real income continues to decline for both factory workers and white collar workers.[13]

President Clinton states we have to learn to live with job insecurity.[14] I don't believe that. And let us not forget that crime remains a problem that has not been solved nor will be solved by our incumbent politicians. Are we so afraid of change that we would rather sit on the spiked fence?

Those of us with enough courage to act can make a difference. We can change America for the better. How? By voting every elected official out of office. Do not listen to the hype of your elected politician, who says the other guy is bad, but I am good and I will listen to you and follow your wishes.

When you hear your Senator, Congressperson, or other politician who seeks to stay in office agree with you about "politicians" and promises to fight for your rights, I suggest you react with skepticism. When your elected representatives claim to have political influence with their colleagues, what does it really mean? It proves they have net-worked with other politicians who have hurt *you* by voting for schemes which resulted in increased government expenditures, or reduced middle-class jobs by increasing the cost of doing business in this country. There is a Middle-Eastern saying, "the enemy of my enemy is my friend and the friend of my enemy is my enemy!"

The fact those politicians can afford T.V. or radio advertisements is substantial proof that they have been bought and paid for by special interests. As more and more millions are poured into elections, is it a coincidence that the number of millionaires increased by 2,184 percent in the last decade while the number of poor rose to 56 million Americans.[15] Twenty-two percent of our population are now unable to earn enough to cover basic necessities and many of the rest of us are only a plant closing, divorce, illness or restructuring away from joining them.

You might argue that the challengers are also beholden to special interest groups. But remember, special interest groups donate their money with the expectation that "their" politician will continue to help their cause while in office. If the electorate challenges special interests, by continually defeating incumbents, their willingness to contribute large sums to one-term politicians will eventually decline. We ought ask ourselves this question: unless specific programs suggested in these chapters are established to directly help the middle class what does it matter whom we elect?

Once incumbents get the message it will matter. It does matter! We can be empowered to make a difference. Don't be a fence sitter. Test your resolve to change America for the better. Help recapture our country for the middle class! How? Again conquer the special interests by voting out all incumbents.

You have the opportunity to choose one of two Americas. The first is one that will occur if you do nothing. This is an America on the Latin American model where there is a huge class of barely surviving poor and a wealthy upper class. Or we can return to the American dream. A dream, which reasserts equality between the blue-collar factory worker and the white-collar salaried worker, is possible. A vision of America, which throws out the politics of poor versus rich and states that we can and will expand the middle class makes sense. Food on the table, a job, a car, and a home are not just wishes but are, in fact, a reality in this new second America. This book is written in the spirit of hope and renewal.

The results of the November, 1994 election tells me the middle class has finally begun to awaken. And the 1998 election of Reform Party Governor Jesse Ventura in a state known for supporting liberal democrats is an indication of just how shallow the support for both Democrats and Republicans is at this time.

The Middle Class and the American Dream: Myth or Reality?

Just before I started to write this last revision of Chapter One, I was in the barn cleaning out horse stalls. We have a Quarter Horse and an Arab. A couple of times a week, their stalls have to be cleaned and the old wet straw replaced with dry new straw. I don't mind the smell of horse manure. To me it has a sweet smell, something like overly digested hay. On the other hand, I've never been able to feel the same way about cow manure. Cow manure smells sulfureous and acrid. My father in law (who was a small dairy farmer), used to try to convince his children that the smell of cow manure was the smell of money. My wife never bought it. Every time she walked into the cow barn, she started spitting, because she hated the smell.

To my mind, American elections have always been a combination of horse manure (things we'd honestly like to do and would like to be) and bull manure (deliberate lies and deceptions to gain power and influence). Unfortunately, it seems to me that in each election, the amount of Bull Manure continually increases to the point that most Americans can't stand the smell and so don't enter the barn to vote.

Maybe that is why I'm writing this book. I'm not a politician. (I've never run for election for anything) And I'm not a philosopher. (I'm not comfortable with multi syllable words and fine points of verbal discrimination) I'm also not an economist. (I think most economists rarely if ever understand what they are talking about). I am a medical psychologist. I'm board certified in disability evaluation, forensic neuropsychology and medical psychotherapy.

I work with people who have just been injured or are suffering from a disease or condition, which is so painful that it causes them emotional problems. These are the people who have stepped into the abyss of misery that is created when they can no longer function the way they used to. In their new and uninvited situation, they discover their own strengths and weaknesses and the more often than not, the underside of our society. Many learn that to other people, they are just a number and a statistic. A number to be reduced and a statistic to be eliminated are a sad thing. Not wanting to, they reluctantly are forced to come to terms with society in ways they never dreamed they would.

My experiences with my patients led me to write this book. It's about applied political psychology and American Pragmatism. It represents my hope we can have a gentler society—but to do so—we have to re-think what is America and what we want it to be in the 21st Century. In the introduction of this book, I presented the idea that if the patient disagrees with the book, you should throw the book away and not the patient. Unfortunately, just the opposite usually happens. When the settlers first came to America, American Indians died by the tens of thousands because they didn't fit into the Western European idea of being "civilized." Years later, when the Communists took power in Russia, hundreds of thousands of land owners, small business owners, professionals and political dissidents died because they didn't fit into the Communist Conception of an ideal society.

Not to be outdone, when Germany became dominated by the racial purity ideas of the Fascists, millions of Jews, Gypsies, Slavs, Jehovah Witnesses and homosexuals died in Hitler's quest for a perfect society.

It seems to be the nature of man to constantly define others out of existence. While the Muslims and the Serbs carry on an uneasy truce in the Balkans and while Jews and Arabs try to find a way to accommodate each other in the Middle East, the American Middle Class seems to be facing its own struggle for existence. Each day thousands of middle-class Americans finds themselves closer to losing their job, home, health insurance, safety and hopes for the future. Scarcely a week passes without a notice that corporations are becoming much more profitable as they "downsize," i.e., cut middle-class jobs and employ slave labor, child labor or peasant labor in other countries.

The "global economy" has become the new in word for the destruction of the American Middle Class. So, when I originally started to write this book, I thought I had a great idea! My idea was to encourage middle-class voters to vote against each political incumbent until one of the major parties got the message and started to represent the middle class. However, with the substantial defeat of the Democratic Party in 1994 and its partial resurrection in 1996, and observing the current behavior of the Republican Party it is painfully clear to me that neither party represents nor can represent the middle class.

Unfortunately, it is the nature of humans to think of things in dryads, i.e., good vs. bad, hot vs. cold, comfortable vs. uncomfortable, peaceful vs. anxious, etc. But, when a monied elite controls both parties, dyadic thinking is no longer feasible. We need a triadic solution—a way to build a third party. I am not alone in my thinking. A poll published in *U.S.A. Today*, (August 17, 1995) reported that 71% of American voters want to be able to choose an independent third party. Throughout this book, I will propose triadic solutions to old problems. Solutions that are anathema to both parties but which make a considerable amount of sense to the middle-class. I've discussed them with many of my associates, now I would like to offer them to you.

My goal is to convince you we need to combine European Parlimentarianism with American Pragmatism. We need to stop voting for individuals and start voting a straight party ticket. I hope to show you that if we vote out *all incumbents* and then establish and/or support new parties, we can without a doubt resurrect the American Dream.

I am well acquainted with the American Dream. For the last thirty years I have lived and worked in Michigan's Tri-City area which comprises Midland (the headquarters of Dow Chemical and Dow Corning), Saginaw (home to thousands of General Motors employees, a community college, university, two hospitals and an area prison) and Bay City (an industrial, farming, fishing and recreational area).

The Tri-Cities encompass a wide spectrum of society: urban, suburban, rural, white, black, Latino, rich, middle class, and poor; and all the problems and hopes that define our society: crime, unemployment, drugs, a deteriorating life style, as well as holistic medicine, new age thinking, healthful living , born again Christians, and spiritual renewal. In short the Tri-Cities of Michigan represent a microcosm of America as a whole.

In my thirty years of practice, I have seen over ten thousand clients. Most clients saw me because they faced a crisis, a problem that offered no ready solution. They hoped I would help them find some answers and cope more effectively. As a specialist in short-term therapy, I had developed my own three-fold approach: 1) reframing their crisis into an opportunity, 2) teaching them about themselves and 3) helping them let go of the fears that stop them.

In this type of therapy, I have to get to the core of the problem, then teach that each crisis has the potential for loss or gain, depending upon their response. Clients learned that the more tense and concerned they became, the more they developed tunnel vision and were unable to consider alternative solutions. As situations become progressively more black and white, they lose the ability to see the shades of gray in their lives as well as hidden opportunities. As they learn to relax, they lower their tension level and discover new alternatives they had been unable to consider before.

Most of my clients sought therapy because they felt their lives were falling apart and they faced losing their dream. Many could not conceptualize their depression. But in time, they begin to talk about the loss of their goals and status. They reported feelings of depression, panic, anger, and insecurity. As they defined their problems, they seemed almost paranoid. It is easy to dismiss a truth by labeling it. But as they continue to talk about their problems, I realized the truth of the aphorism: "If they really are out to get you, it's not paranoia." It became more evident that what troubled them most was that the fear of losing their *hopes for the future.*

Hope is crucial thing for most of us. We can endure much if we have hope, if we believe things will improve in the future. But many felt convinced of just the opposite. They expected things to deteriorate not to improve. These expectations also affected how they viewed politics. To most, elections have become totally irrelevant or a chore of choosing the lesser of evils or, "who's going to screw me the least."

Surprisingly, clients often voiced their beliefs that whatever happened it would not help them personally. This pattern of loss of hope and increased cynicism affected many clients. I realized that the underlying mechanism had to do with their own beliefs; about who they were and how this related to their definition of being middle-class Americans.

More than ninety percent of my clients would identify themselves as middle class. But what is middle class? The popular media tends to define middle class according to job or income. But in my professional experience, most people reject the idea that your income or your job defines your class status. Unemployed clients who lived below the poverty line in terms of income, still felt middle class. Conversely, some of my millionaire clients also continued to identify themselves as middle class.

Many Americans seem to have adopted a sort of Lockean Liberalism as the signature of middle classness. Middle classness from this point of view, a right to "life, liberty and property"[16] would include a wide variety of Americans.

In Europe, the middle class is defined both by income/job and *behavior*. The petite bourgeoisie are expected to have certain common behaviors and attitudes, which tend to be law abiding, conservative and un-insightful. Americans, in contrast to Europeans, do not identify themselves so easily. Persons who describe themselves as middle class may be liberal, conservative, radical, employed, unemployed, insightful, un-insightful, etc. But whatever their differences, they up to now have "had a centrist, two-party post ideological politics."[17]

Thus, it has been the norm in politics that as each candidate captures the nomination of the party, the candidate races to the middle in hopes of being elected. But when society starts to fracture, racing to the middle becomes like standing on a white line in the middle of a busy highway. If the candidate stands there long enough, it will only be a matter of time before a passing vehicle will strike down the candidate. In a time of uncertainty and conflicting ideas, perhaps it is time we remind ourselves what America is all about.

American Dream

Americans are unique and different. To understand the concept of middle classness as Americans define it, we need to identify the glue that holds the middle class together. What is that glue? That glue is the American Dream.

Commenting on the lack of a true left wing party in America, the German political economist Werner Sombart wrote in 1906, socialism "foundered on roast beef and apple pie." Americans felt different from Europeans, they believed that they were exceptional and they believed in exceptionalism because they felt that their dream was just around the corner. If you don't understand this dream and the importance of freedom and hope (i.e., the myth of Horatio Alger), you simply haven't a clue as to what makes Americans feel middle class!

What is the American Dream? The American Dream is a practical, down-to-earth and common sense way to evaluate quality of life and, especially independence and freedom. Americans are at heart an odd soup of idealists, utilitarians and pragmatists. They simply are not in love with theory. There is an implied yard stick by which each middle class American says, "Yes I am middle class and I feel good about life and the future," or, "No I am in danger of losing my middle-class status and I feel scared/angry/fearful." If such self-evaluation, of the conscious or unconscious, is negative, the result impacts profoundly on the client's attitude and self-image.

Self-measurement by the middle class is neither complicated nor theoretical. Once said, it is black and white, simple and concrete, easily understood and obvious. Conversely, it is largely unconscious. Most of us are rarely able to define the term unless it's articulated. Then we exclaim, "Yes, I have always felt that way."

The American Dream for the middle class is a test, which consists of the following items:

1. Do I have a decent job with a reasonable expectation of security and status and/or income advancement?

Of course each American defines "decent job" in his/her own way. The blue-collar American factory worker may define the dream in terms of a decent paycheck, good benefits, and job security, while the nurse or health care worker may define it in terms of challenge and status.

2. Do I live in a decent home/apartment in a safe area?

Increasingly, members of the middle class define their class in terms of where they live, whether they live in a city or suburban area that is "safe". Crime and violence have had a profound impact on the attitudes of most American citizens.

3. Can I leave my present employment and, with minimal anxiety, find compatible work as good, and hopefully, better than my present job?

When the middle class American is told that his/her job is about to be terminated, the anxiety of job loss is tolerated better when there is a fall back position which surfaces in the statement, "Oh well, I was looking for a job when I found this one." The belief that there are other attractive jobs in other areas affords the middle class freedom—freedom to believe that they are choosing to stay in their current job rather than believing they are forced to stay due to a lack of other possible jobs.

4. Can I sell my present home in a reasonable amount of time and buy a new one, making a small profit or upgrading my living quarters?

Traditionally, most members of the middle class regard their home not only as a place to live, but also as a savings investment, an investment either for a better, future home or for a comfortable retirement.

5. Can I afford a decent car and effective transportation?

The freedom to travel and commute is essential to most members of the middle class. This freedom is often taken for granted. This attitude is one that the bureaucrats in Washington, D.C. and the political leaders of the Eastern Establishment fail utterly to understand when they talk about gasoline rationing or raising gasoline taxes.

6. Can I afford to send my children to a reasonably effective school or college?

Wanting their children to enjoy a decent future is one of the major priorities of the middle class.

7. Will my children have a better future than I did?

Middle-class Americans not only want their children to be safe and have a future, but to also have a better future than they did. Unfortunately, this is a major dilemma today. Most middle class Americans now believe that their children will not have a better future than they do. Why? Part of the reason is the continuing decline in the standard of living, which has affected the middle class since 1974.[18]

8. Can I anticipate a relatively problem free retirement?

As more members of the middle class age, the issues of importance increasingly are problems that confront the elderly. The elderly have been forced by unthinking politicians to often live in combat zones. Drug laws, which have contributed to deteriorating urban and suburban areas and increased crime, have contributed to destroying the infrastructures of many cities. The elderly citizen's reduced income, combined with declining property values, make it impossible for them to flee. So instead they resort to measures which affect their normal life.

As an example in Chicago, "housing-project residents are forbidden to have over night guests and, apartheid-style, are required to show security guards their "papers" to get into their own homes."[19]

9. Can I participate in religious/spiritual/social organizations with relative freedom?

Religion/spirituality is one issue that the middle class rarely agrees upon. But if I were to define it, I would have to use the definition that was voiced by the Canadian Supreme Court in its decision regarding Sheena B., a premature infant whose Jehovah Witness parents refused to let have a life-saving blood transfusion. The court removed Sheena from her parents and placed her under court custody to ensure that her life was saved.

When her case was brought before the court, the court stated, "While it is difficult to conceive of any limitations on religious beliefs, the same cannot be said for religious practices, notably when they impact on the fundamental rights and freedoms of others."[20]

The issue of religious belief vs. religious practice has plagued the middle class almost from the inception of our country. The Civil War, Prohibition, War on Drugs, tobacco laws and numerous other rules and regulations including abortion and birth control are often thinly disguised attempts of one group to enforce its values on another.

What is usually forgotten is that America was populated for the most part by rebels and each time a new restriction on behavior is made the law of the land, others step up to the plate to break the law. How else cans one explain the fact that America has the largest prison population percentage wise of any country in the world?

10. Can I go from point A to point B in relative safety?

Safety is a major concern for all individuals, but for the middle class it is one of the reasons why many urban centers have died or are dying, as more money is spent in the suburb's malls.

If all of the above questions are answered affirmatively, then the middle class *feels* middle class and hopeful and happy about the future. For each question answered negatively, middle class Americans become increasingly concerned about the future and more disenchanted with the system, political, economic or social.

The majority of my clients do *not* feel reasonably secure in their job. And they question the safety of the area in which they live. Most do not feel that they can easily leave their present employment. They can sell their home, but not for as much money as they once thought they could. Many report that new cars are increasingly out of their reach. Typically, their children have to borrow money to get through college, with no guarantee that they will land a good enough job to pay back their government loan.

Most of these people believe that the well-paying jobs are leaving America and that their children will not have a better future than they did. Retirement looks increasingly risky because of uncertainty about selling their home, where to live and the costs of medical care, the stability of Medicare and the continued existence of social security.

Even religion is increasing as an issue, as many feel forced to take a position on abortion, prayer in schools, pornography, R rated movies, single parent households, etc. Some complain about their childhood church being torn down or not feeling safe attending their old church that is now in an "unsafe" area. The ability to travel in and out of the city to attend services at the church of their youth is an important concern to the elderly.

Given the negatives listed above, it should come as no surprise that the middle class feels disaffected, disenchanted, and in the process of abandoning their traditional party. "President Clinton's pollster Stan Greenberg told the Democratic National Committee: "We need to understand that the Republican coalition collapsed in 1992, but we have not yet formed a new Democratic majority."[21] His words proved prophetic in 1994. And in 1996 perhaps Senator Dole and Speaker Gingrich have had to say the same thing to their associates.

The loss of political identity is becoming more pervasive throughout society. For instance, you would expect most General Motors employees that work the line to be strong advocates of unionism and the Democratic Party. Not so, as their lives have changed so have their loyalties. Many of the General Motors blue-collar workers that I see view their union and the Democratic Party negatively. Considering the rampant alienation evidenced in my clients, it's not surprising that Ross Perot did especially well in Michigan in 1992 (19% of the vote).

Despite being called paranoid and having no real platform, Perot and his Reform Party continued to get many votes in 1996. And let's not forget the stunning victory of Jesse Ventura and the Reform Party in Minnesota over two traditional candidates of the Democratic and Republican Party. If conditions continue to deteriorate for the middle class, the possibility of more extreme solutions becomes appealing. The middle-class gives up centrism when they lose their security. Once they have nothing to lose extremist ideology becomes an increasing fact of life rather than an oddity. Germany and Italy both lost their democratic institutions to fascism in the early part of the twentieth century.[22] Could fascism take hold in America?

Although Ross Perot did verbalize concerns echoed by millions of Americans about the American Dream, he did not articulate them with great clarity and he failed to present a feasible program to recapture the goals of the middle class. Also, he forgot a basic truth! It doesn't help to run faster if you're going in the wrong direction. Jesse Ventura, on the other hand moved the Reform Party to a program which emphasized social liberalism and economic conservatism as well as social realism and won a resounding victory.

On the other hand, Perot did suggest how the middle class could recapture this country. He recognized that there are enough disaffected middle-class voters to substantially impact both political parties. In 1999, Senator Bob Smith from New Hampshire, threw his hat into the presidential race by in essence saying the same thing—opportunists govern the major parties and pollsters and a third party is possible! Canada has already shown us one way. In a recent general election in Canada, the middle class essentially voted the majority party out of existence. The Progressive Conservatives had over a hundred and fifty members in Parliament, but after the elections only four member were re-elected.

Jean Chretien, the leader of the Liberal Party in Canada rose to power and there was no coordinated opposition in the Canadian House of Commons. Both of the other two major parties, the Progressive Conservatives and the New Democrats had been decimated in the national elections. While the Canadians at present, are supporting Chretien[23], there is still no real evidence that he is going to really make a difference for the Canadian middle class or if it is going to be another case of business as usual.

If it is another instance of deceiving the middle class, the Canadians know what they will have to do again and again until their voices are heard.

Empowering the Middle Class

The middle class can improve its position initially by exercising its voting power. Remember the old proverb, "he who can destroy a thing can control a thing." In other words, by consistently voting against the incumbent in each and every election—municipal, city, county, state or federal—the shock of removal will eventually have the effect of re-orienting politicians back to the interests and needs of the middle class! Theoretically, it sounds strange to suggest that tossing out one politician will cause the newly elected politician to consider the middle class. What if the same monied interests have supplied money for both campaigns?

Then what happen are new faces with the same agenda. Perhaps that is why most Americans want a third party! The answer is not only to vote out all incumbents a new third party will have to be formed.

In ensuing chapters, I will *show* how we can take this country back to true democracy, how we can again put America on the track of being the best world class vehicle for the middle class.

Before we can take this country back, we must identify the forces, which have led to the increasing destruction of the middle class? The enemy is the stark dependence of politicians on money! In the 1992 elections, politicians spent one billion dollars in their election bids. Our old friend Congress, spent $678 million dollars. And in the 1994 elections, over six hundred million dollars were spent in the congressional campaigns. The average house member spent $550,000 dollars and the average Senate victor spent $4 million dollars. Republican Senator D'Amato of New York, for instance, spent $11 million dollars while Senator Boxer of California spent $10 million. Both figures were eclipsed in the 1994 elections by senatorial races in California and Massachusetts. And in 1996, the numbers were even larger.

Clinton and his associates were adept at acquiring money from any and all including drug and gun runners, slave labor countries, spies for Communist China as well as making the White House a $100,000 bed and breakfast hostel.

The national media however, is surprised that Americans are not reacting. They seem not to care. Actually, I believe Americans are smarter than the media elite realize. They have known for some time that government is for sale. At least with the Clinton/Gore Administration, they know who is buying.

Martin L. Gross in his book, *A Call for Revolution* wrote, "Elections in the United States are not won. They are bought!" Since 1973, the enemy is and has been Congress...[24] (As well as the White House) The cost of campaigning has made Congress a collection of high-priced patricians who sell "access" to themselves to finance their respective campaigns. The purchaser of access can be any country from Austria to Zimbabwe or any business from A.A.A. to the Zoos of America.[25]

When the cost to win a Senate seat is millions of dollars, it is obvious that Congress has to have something to offer. That something is a pay-off in terms of tax dollars (your money) or special favors (your job). In truth, promising covertly to "rob" you of your money or your job can only elect a member of Congress! Despite the fact that they promise to deliver more jobs or to reduce governmental expenses, the very fact politicians can advertise on radio or T.V. is proof of the fact that they have already agreed to "listen" to special interest groups, those who hope their contributions turn their "access" into Congressional votes.

Despite what some skeptics might believe, Americans eventually wake up and "smell the roses". As an example, the *Saginaw News*[26] ran a ballot question about the G-7 conference in Detroit, Michigan. Economic ministers from the major countries met in Detroit to discuss ways of improving the job climate. The specific ballot box question, "Do you believe the job conference in Detroit will help the state?" The results of the poll: Yes: 16% and No: 84%.

Sample negative comments included the following: "Clinton wants the media to make him look good again for all his lies;" and "I don't believe it will happen in my lifetime and I'm only 44."[27]

As each year passes an increasing number of people no longer iden-tify themselves as Democrat or Republican? The Center for Political Studies, University of Michigan, Ann Arbor reported the following response to the question, "Generally speaking, do you consider yourself a Republican, a Democrat, an Independent, or what?" In 1992 over 40% considered themselves independents.[28] And in 1996, voter participa-tion continued to decrease. We see much evidence that regardless of whom gets elected, middle class interests are not served.

As Professor Peterson writes in his book *Silent Depression,* "Before the 1990's, the usual pattern in a recession was for workers to lose their jobs, suffer through a period of idleness, and return to work—often to the same jobs lost earlier—"…(Now) "workers lose their jobs, but the jobs they lost have often disappeared (into the morass of third world countries)."

Since the middle class comprises the bulk of society, the middle class will eventually pay for the election of each member of Congress. How? The middle class will pay through the jobs that go overseas, through reduced competition at home, through unnecessary personal constraints or restraints, and via an increasingly sparse and anemic economy.

The simple fact is that those who voted against Bush and Clinton or Clinton and Dole could unite with independents and "leaners" (voters who aren't sure about either party) to change America and triumph over Congress and special interests groups.

To take our country back from special interest domination, I am suggesting a two-fold method, which is absurdly simple and effective: First, simply vote against each and every incumbent politician who is up for re-election. No matter if the incumbent is young or old, black or white, Democrat or Republican, rich or poor, nice or nasty, concerned or distant, attractive or ugly, intelligent or stupid, vote him/her out and you will regain control of America! This process sounds extremely simplistic because the counter argument may be, "but the challenger is no sleeping beauty either!"

The elegance of voting against all incumbents is simple once you comprehend the implications of defeat. If politicians find that all they can anticipate for their future is one term of incumbency, it makes no sense for them to spend their time selling access. While amassing money for their next election campaign, they will fail if the electorate refuses to re-elect incumbents. Their only hope to stay in office is to play to the middle class. This means that they will have to "bite the bullet" and advocate programs which will result in *less governmental expense, a better quality of life and encourage the creation of more middle class jobs!*

The middle class is so large that if even a small percentage of them became consistently anti-incumbent, the complexion of government will change. The number of elections for Congress in which the winner beat the loser by more than ten percent of the vote can be counted on both hands. If even a small portion of the middle class votes against all incumbents, Congress will be vastly changed in the next election.

Don't be swayed by the argument that you will be giving the power to the Democrats, Republicans or new untried and unseasoned politicians. It doesn't matter. Two years hence, you will vote against every *incumbent* again. And again and again, until the party in power, Republican, Democrat or a new independent American party, finally wakes up and serves as advocate for the special interests of the middle class the majority of Americans!

My own estimation is that in as little as six years or three elections, the middle class could substantially retrieve control of America by decisively rejecting every local, state and national incumbent.

Destroying the power of special interest money and the reigning patrician politicians is only the first half of what has to be done to resurrect middle class interests. Second, we need to establish a new combination of European Parlimentarianism and American Pragmatism. Special interests obtain their power by providing individual politicians the money they need to campaign for election. If the middle class voted for a party and not for an individual, the power of special interests would be radically diminished.

For a party to convince the American people to vote a straight ticket and to ignore the vast and endless television sound bites sponsoring individual politicians, the party would have to have something meaningful to offer. Throughout the rest of this book, I am going to suggest programs that would define a party and allow it to upend the special interest politics that govern America. If Americans are willing to risk going back into the voting booth, I am going to suggest what we need to bring America into the 21st century.

I believe the countries which adapt these ideas will be the powerhouses of the mid 21st century. Think about each of these proposals.

Decide for yourself if you agree and can support them. Decide for yourself whether these suggestions can empower the middle class.

The American Quandary: A Rebellious Nature, the Struggle against "Control Freaks," and how Politicians Gain Power

"Government…controls almost every activity of common interest—fixing the pothole in front of the house, running public schools, regulating day care centers, controlling…the workplace, cleaning up the environment…" Philip K. Howard, *THE DEATH OF COMMON SENSE*[29]

To stir up voter interest and to gain an edge in a political campaign, a politician has to be both for something and against something. Pat Buchanan stirred up support by being for the average working man and against the "people who are sending jobs to third world countries." His approach was so effective that he won the primary in Louisiana and came in second in Iowa in 1996 and is now honing his rhetorical skills for the 2000 election. Bob Dole was so intimidated by Buchanan's success that he too suddenly became against the corporations who have increasingly "fat profits" and at the same time have let go thousands of workers.

The approach of "us against them" is not new. It's been going on for thousands of years. When the "us against them" involves citizens of the same country however, dire results often occur—civil war, genocide, political unrest, increasing crime, etc. Americans, in particular, having come from many countries and having ancestors who hated control, are prone to defy the efforts of the "us" to control them when they are the "them."

Politicians however, rarely are concerned with the long-term consequences of their bid for power. If being against alcohol (or for alcohol) will result in their election, so be it. This play of being against the "rich," "drug users," "liberals," "right wing conservatives," "baby killers," "doctor killers," "companies who are opposed to regulations," "environmental wackos," "smokers and second hand smoke," inevitably leads to more and more regulations and the empowerment of "control freaks."

In psychotherapy, the term "control freak" means a person who has a great need to control the behavior of others. In business, the term "micro-manage" describes a leader who is unable to release the reigns of control. In the same context, parents are told they are over parenting and psychiatrists may use the term "obsessive compulsive neurosis." Regardless of the terms, the behavior is the same—an unreasonable need to dictate how one should live, what freedoms we will be allowed to have, and what responsibilities one must shoulder.

The issue of freedom vs. control is not new. When the Puritans first came to America, they forgot that they had left England for freedom and instead decided their duty was to glorify the kingdom of God by ensuring that people attended Sunday services in an approved church and avoided sin—such as drunkenness, debauchery or profane language. Those Americans who did not like Puritanical rule, simply headed West and took their chances with the Indians and other like-minded rebels.

Now there is no West to head out to. But to make matters worse, we have over nineteen million government bureaucrats and tens of thousands of elected politicians, plus countless governmental boards and commissions. All of these entities seek to justify their existence by creating tasks for themselves or others. Often, however, their duties conflict with basic common sense. On the one hand, we hear that Vice President Gore wants to "re-invent government" and on the other hand we see the continued expansion of government into the private affairs of Americans—witness Food and Drug Administration's latest decision to define tobacco as a drug.

Consider for a moment the experience of the Nuns of the Missionaries of Charity[30]. They came to New York City in 1988 and wanted to provide a shelter for the homeless. They were allowed to purchase two abandoned buildings for one dollar each. The nuns wanted to provide a shelter, which would house 68 homeless persons. But they found that politicians could not assist them in getting around the numerous regulations that were already in place. Regulations, such as providing an elevator could not be bypassed. And so, regretfully, the nuns abandoned their project. Although there were several hundred thousand old buildings in New York that did not have elevators (pre-regulation), there was not room for one more for the homeless. Basically what the regulators said was rather than have a building that can't meet our standards, we would rather let the homeless continue to live on the streets and allow the building to stand empty—a menace to children and a haven to illicit drug dealers.

This kind of thinking increasingly pervades our society. It is in a real sense disguised religiosity. Although God is not allowed in the classroom or in community sponsored displays, a form of Godliness, i.e., laws and regulation, continues to expand. Community after community, in lockstep follows the regulations of other municipalities. The simple regulation of the width of roads in new subdivisions infuses our country from Boston to San Francisco. And with each new regulation, some members of our society choose not to conform. Thus, we have an ever-increasing number of scofflaws and outlaws.

Temporal sinners however, must be punished. While they cannot be assigned to some level of hell in a Dantesque inferno, other more temporal measures can be used such as fines, jail, confiscation of property, etc. And to be sure these temporal sinners are found out and punished, thousands, no tens of thousand, no better yet, hundreds of thousands of enforcers must be hired to ferret out the temporal sinners.

All of us pay a tremendous amount of our own limited resources so that "control freaks" can continue to not only exist, but to have almost unlimited power. As America enters the 21st century, we need to ask the same question asked twenty-four hundred years ago by Socrates, "What course of life is best?" The middle class's increasing disenchantment can not totally be explained by the loss of the American Dream. It is also due to the fact that a special elite has governed America. One that can afford the high cost of running for election. We have forgotten the dictum that Aristotle said was necessary for a just society—which is, the *middle class should rule.*

Our society is increasingly ruled by Machiavellian leaders, who pretend to be ethically and morally just while they engage in the deliberate manipulation of the electorate. Political leaders repeatedly remind United States citizens that they are the greatest democracy in the world. However, the fact is this great democracy has become ninth in average family income.[31] Further, we are no longer a democracy at all. In reality, we are a bureaucracy in that[32] forty-two cents of every United States dollar produced in 1994 will feed government programs at municipal, county, state, and federal levels. And this vast bureaucracy is so powerful that the current screaming by Clinton over the Republican's "heavy hand of budget cutting" amounts to less than one penny of every dollar being spent.[33]

To understand why the middle class has been increasingly frozen out of participation in America, let's first consider different systems of government worldwide. The basic systems in the last century have been Marxist Socialism, Socialism, Fascism, and Democracy.

Marxist Socialism has failed in Russia and other countries and is failing now in Cuba and China. Marxist Socialism is characterized by its excessive need for control, and for prohibiting free market economics to dictate allocation of resources. Governments which have attempted some form of socialism, including the United States, have also had to struggle with the problems of basic economic justice: job security, worker's compensation, unemployment compensation, health care, housing, and old-age benefits.

Each entitlement has a price, which often factors into the cost of products made in this country, and creates difficulties competing with third world countries. If money is allowed to flow where it will get the best return, those countries where labor costs the least, will garner more of the investments.

Fascism, which combines nationalism and socialism, basically doesn't function well because it is unable to relinquish control. Fascist countries concentrate power in one individual or a small powerful group. Fascists compensate for their inefficient economy by stealing the resources of other nations or groups, which then became the scapegoats of the fascist nation.[34]

Democracy, as an example of Lockean liberalism, asserts that each citizen is entitled to pursue life, liberty, and property ownership. This concept was accepted by the founding fathers of American democracy. Initially, the Republican Party of Abraham Lincoln stressed Lockean Liberalism. As the Civil War intensified, citizens lost their lives, liberty, and property. Despite the best intentions of parties and Presidents, democracy is a fragile commodity, which continually hangs like a drop of dew on a blade of grass.

Today, as government takes bigger chunks out of the economy, we again see government seizing property and taking citizens freedom. Government now takes property of citizens for not paying taxes, being accused but not convicted of crimes and astoundingly, there are over 200 different statues, which allow seizure of your property *BEFORE YOU ARE CONVICTED OF A CRIME!*[35]

Society's latest "war on crime" is not the only way innocent Americans can end up between a rock and a hard place. Since depressions and recessions tend to affect the emotional fabric of America, fail-safe mechanisms were devised to help those in need: i.e., the jobless, disabled, homeless, orphans, aged, and unwed mothers.[36]

Americans' inborn need to care and be fair, has allowed a large bureaucracy to develop. It now controls both parties of Congress and is growing at the rate of ten percent a year. What is the remedy? Vice President Gore's document *Re-Inventing Government,* is Machiavellian smoke and mirrors. We're are told we need to down-size government, yet politicians on both sides of the aisle constantly present new government sponsored proposals, such as increasing police, prisons, health care, etc.

Neither the Democratic Party nor the Republican Party can afford to alienate millions of bureaucrats and expect to have their support in the next election. Their solution? Pretend to save the taxpayer's money, while in reality you're planning to expand the bureaucracy in order to stay in power!

Is it any wonder that over seventy percent of Americans don't trust government? Or that most Americans don't believe politicians?[37] What's the answer? Do we allow conditions to continue as they are and run the risk that our country will plunge into chaos? Or, worse, possibly eventually becomes a type of fascist government? No! We must opt for programs that will empower the middle class!

As an experienced psychologist, I am used to offering therapeutic solutions. America is ailing and needs much healing. And I am not the first psychologist who has written about government.

In 1929, Sigmund Freud wrote about the need to reform government in his book, *CIVILIZATION AND ITS DISCONTENTS,* and he anticipated the vast disasters, which accompanied World War II. It seemed obvious to him that emotionally disturbed and dangerous men had to be prevented from taking power and becoming dictators. The world, of course, ignored his comments. as the middle classes of the Western World were already in the process of choosing leaders. The middle class of Germany, for example, having been abandoned by its leaders, became easy prey for fascism and Hitler's fanaticism.

If you, as a middle class citizen, are feeling progressively alienated contemplate abandoning your usual approach to politics, please consider a few central questions about the *American way of life.*

Initially, our country was organized as a Republic, and not a democracy. The Constitution was oriented toward a Republic because the founding fathers were, understandably, fearful about dictatorships. They had given their own blood and fortunes and those of family and friends to become free of the emotionally deranged King George of England. They certainly did not want to be subjected to their own "home-grown" dictator.

The founding fathers knew that dictatorship could arise not only from a hereditary king, but also from the alienated masses. When the bulk of society is morally, politically, or economically imperiled, they are vulnerable to being manipulated by a cunning, crafty leader. The so-called dictatorship of the proletariat fostered by the Communists represented a simple grab for power by a select group. This group was then able to seduce large portions of the population to followers.

The balance of powers between the Senate and the House of Representatives was clearly designed to limit both the development of a single dictator or a special class of oppressors. Unfortunately, the founding fathers could not foresee how the *intent* of the Constitution would be changed. Today, in America, we see what happens when special interest groups control elections, when they become despotic centers of power and callously use the resources of the United States and its citizens for their own selfish ends.

WE need to stop this nonsense…Now! We need to return to a PARTICIPATIVE democracy; One which fiercely protects *individual rights and freedoms,* including the freedom to make mistakes.

Each time we seek to control someone's freedom or right to engage in specific personal behaviors, certain costs have to be paid. Whenever we insist on controlling the behavior of others, we need provisions for its enforcement. Enforcement requires enforcers.

Politicians are quick to point to the need to deprive us of our freedom in the name of justice or societal order. But they are slow to list the price to be paid. What will be the fate of those who don't obey their new laws or regulations or caught in the crossfire between the enforcers and the violators. Politicians use grandiose terms such as the "War on Crime," but conveniently forget to mention all the byproducts of such a war, such as decaying city centers, abandoned neighborhoods, climates of fear and the loss of personal freedom and movement.

To illustrate some basic points, I'd like to relate the story of three clients: All innocent, law-abiding black citizens. These were hard working, tax-paying, decent people with no arrest record. Yet each one had their homes invaded and was torn out of their bed in the middle of the night. They had to stand naked against the wall or lie on the floor as police officers ransacked their home. When nothing was found, they received no apology.

When they sued, the circuit judge threw their cases out of court! Why? Because under the current interpretation of our laws, officers can invade anyone's home at any time with minimal justification. After the judge's decision, one of the families had their car impounded. Their teenage son and a companion were driving the family car when the police pulled them over and searched it. The son's friend had a marijuana cigarette, which he stuffed under his seat. When the officer's found it, they used this find as justification to impound their car.

The police said that unless they paid the court several thousand dollars for the car, their son would be charged with possessing a controlled substance with intent to distribute.

Similar stories are repeated tens of thousands of times across this "fruited land". Whenever you have a war, both sides become increasingly brutalized. As the war continues, the level of brutality, insensitivity and hostility inevitably increases. What is surprising is how we don't learn from the past. Yet each generation of politicians insists on re-inventing the wheel, much to the distress of all of us.

The present situation with the *war on drugs* is not the first time our society has been dealt a severe blow by politicians. Prohibition in the 20's is a classic example of the dictatorship of special interest groups. Politicians obeyed the first law of politics, (say whatever is needed to be elected or re-elected), and easily succumbed to an active and vocal prohibition-oriented minority. Thus, they voted into law that individuals had *no* right to consume alcohol in public or private. Being born-and-bred rebels, many Americans elected to avoid or ignore the law. The benefit of prohibition was supposedly to make us a "kinder gentler society." In fact, the costs of prohibition led to wide spread crime and disrespect of the law.[38] Organized crime obtained respectability by supplying the ordinary citizen with "Speak-Easies."

The problem of excessive control pervades our society. It ranges from detailing the conditions under which children's art can be displayed on school walls, to specifying how a ladder is to be constructed. In reality, these rules of living represent an underlying conflict about life. At one time, Vaclav Havel, President of the Czech Republic, noted that in a communist society people are not allowed to act unless specifically authorized.[39] But in a free society people are free to act unless *specifically* prohibited. This sounds almost too good to be true, and it is. America's political leaders, governmental employees, and administrative lawmakers

Lawmakers are trying to make us become a society in which *there is no room for judgement.* In a real sense, we ourselves become Machiavellian when we worship the law; we fear being criticized, fined, or exposed for violating the law; that we often fear to do what is right and complacently comply with what is wrong.

Inner cities and urban manufacturing centers have been particularly burdened with unnecessary regulation. Before a new factory can be built to replace an old factory, the ground underneath the factory must be cleaned. The cost of cleansing the ground often exceeds the cost of simply moving to virgin land. So the inner city is left to rot while new land is destroyed. Laborers are left to scavenge for pittances in the city while untrained rural residents are seduced into learning how to work in the "shop."

The real problem is that the minority of "control freaks" continually search for the good life and seek to build an alter of certainty. This altar of goodness must be constructed so as to protect the unwary from temporal sinners. It is not enough to make laws that address wrongs or correct past misdeeds, one must also attach to each law thousands of regulations so those temporal sinners can not evade the law.

As these self-described givers of righteousness, these "control freaks" assume that the average person lacks judgement. Even if they had judgement, it would be exercised improperly, i.e., to evade the law or regulation. Thus, we must have rigid laws and regulations that can not be compromised. We can't allow "old boy networks" or friendly relationship between town and business, government and industry, farmer and agricultural administrator to be tolerated. Accommodations and understandings may lead to a circumvention of the law.

What's the problem with this kind of thinking? Laws are made in state capitols or Washington, D.C. Isn't it the height of arrogance to assume that a rule in a state or federal capitol can be so written as to apply to *every* situation in every city and town in the United States (remember the 55 mile per hour speed limit?).

The increasing burden of government is not new to the 90's. For centuries, politicians have run on the plank of "getting government off of our backs." Since government is still safely perched on our homes and workplace, politicians can continue to run on "making government more efficient," or "reduce the waste in government," etc.

In considering the problem of "over control," we must remember this need to control is a disguised form of religiosity. It is an example of law minus a divine lawgiver. This type of religiosity can become a false idol to which hundreds, thousands or millions may be sacrificed. We need to free ourselves from the burden of excessive law and regulation. Attempts to do so will elicit howls of anger and dire warnings. Many false "Messiahs" will howl in the press and cry "doom."

As we move into the 21st century, we must strive to become a participative democracy; one in which the *freedom to choose* is not so easily destroyed. Can we not enforce simple prescriptions, such as to make governmental bureaucracies itemize the cost of each new regulation, and provide budgeting and thorough airing before implementation? Why not enact an ongoing review process to continually evaluate and discard unnecessary or unproductive rules? Why not state every agency must devote a certain percentage of its budget to evaluate, revise, and discard counter-productive rules and regulations?

We must acknowledge all rules and regulations are temporary not sacred and eternal. This is the first step toward freedom and a true participative democracy!

The second step? Establish a third Independent American Party and have an honest and searching dialog with newly elected political leaders about changing America back from a bureaucracy of over 18 million practitioners to a true democracy; one in which each of us have the right to pursue our own life, liberty, and property. American citizens and voters must set strict limits on how much of our life the politicians and bureaucrats are allowed to control. How much of our freedom is open to infringement? How much of our income can they co-opt in confiscatory taxes?

My own rather pessimistic belief is that unless we vote out most of the politicians, this dialog will not occur. Why? It did not happen yet in Canada, where the dominant party was recently overthrown. But if the Canadians in a second election continue to vote out the incumbents, a realistic dialog will doubtlessly occur. And if the Canadians can do it, why not us? Once Americans deliver the message, a dialog will and must happen. The famous psychologist, Carl Rogers, firmly believed that as we gained confidence in our own personal power, we'd face the necessary risks needed to change our government for the better.

The Ethics of Deceit

"For if everything is considered carefully, it will be found that something which looks like virtue, if followed, would be government's ruin; whilst something else, which looks like vice, yet followed brings government security and prosperity."[40]
Nicolo Machiavelli 1469–1527

Machiavelli's *THE PRINCE*, published in 1513 ushered in a new era in politics. Before his work, it was politically correct to assume that ethics and politics were intertwined. Governments were *expected* to be ethical. With Machiavelli's break from the past, a new philosophy upheld deceit as not only necessary but also laudable. This enabled governments, modern day politicians and rulers to look to Machiavelli for guidance and justification. And his influence extended to the 20th century. Stalin, for instance, kept a copy of Machiavelli on his nightstand.

The founding fathers however, wanted America to be a democratic republic, and they also wanted this country to be different in quality from the machinations and manipulations of dictatorial and royal governments of Europe and Asia. They wanted to return to a republic where ethics and politics were in harmony. This led to many an election, which revolved around who we are versus what we want to do.

This melding of ethics and politics has caused the ruin of many a leader in our own time. To name a few recent disasters: President Nixon with Watergate, Sen. Ted Kennedy with his disastrous party and subsequent death of his female companion, Sen. Hart with the picture of a girlfriend sitting on his lap while he was campaigning for President and the present day character attacks on Clinton, Buchanan, Dole, Forbes, and Perot. And now it is starting on George Bush for flying in the Texas National Guard and Al Gore for being in a cushy behind the line position, in Vietnam.

Congressional Representatives also, have not escaped unscathed. Gingrich was investigated for his supposed sweetheart book deal, Gephardt has also raised calls for an investigation because of mysterious profits on land acquisitions and how can we forget the past penchant of many Congresspersons writing checks on accounts in which there were no funds.

Our penchant for examining the actions and character of politicians doesn't play well in many parts of the world. To this day, Europeans have a terrible time understanding Americans. They saw Watergate as a simple mistake, which President Nixon committed and coverups as the norm, and not a reason for threatened impeachment or his resignation. They threw up their hands in Europe when so much uproar was made over Clinton's denial of an affair with Monica. After all what gentleman admits to something of that kind. And doesn't everyone who is anyone have a least one affair.

In Europe and Asia deceit is a way of life; and America's insistence on ethics seems naive at best and insane at worse.

Despite this worldly view of separating ethics from politics, America continues on its unique course. Although the American people increasingly yawn when character attacks occur. In the past, conservative newspapers exploited the story of "Whitewatergate." This play on words was an attempt to make a psychological connection between the criminal actions of President Nixon, which led to his resignation, to that of President Clinton.

Equating Watergate and Whitewater may seem a stretch to many people, even ridiculous to some, (the Democratic response continues to be a variation of so what), others however, seem to think the link makes perfect sense. Connecting ethics and politics, as interrelated and demanding politicians are ethical all their lives, we then can make a comparison between Clinton and Nixon. But such an ideal standard would put anyone at risk that dares to enter the political arena. To a great extent, such a standard of perfection ignores the basic Christian tenet of "let he who is without sin cast the first stone." Clinton's response to Bush's aspersions about his character were successfully defeated by the rejoinder, "It's the economy, stupid."

If President Clinton continues to allow the middle class to decline however, his place in history will meet defeat for the same reason Bush's did. No matter what he says or doesn't say, the voters will continue to state with their votes, "It's the economy, stupid."

Many columnists and reporters either defend or attack the Clintons, but how many have commented upon the essential hypocrisy in those who attack? Hypocrisy means the game of "let's pretend" which pervades politics. Consider for a moment, a little discussed fact. An acquaintance of mine is in management with Amway and recounted how a few years ago, South Korea would not allow Amway into their country. But pressure from the United States under the Bush Administration forced South Korea to open its doors to Amway.

After President Bush's defeat for re-election, he was invited by Amway to speak at a conference, and received a six-figure speaker's fee. What great pearls of wisdom did President Bush have to offer worth six figures? Or was this a payoff for opening up South Korea? Of course, it was a legal payoff! But, did anyone care?

So why should the media and others attack President and Mrs. Clinton for any action that has become routine behavior with most members of Congress and most former Presidents? The answer is relatively simple. As Americans, we have allowed ourselves to be maneuvered into the position of pretending to have moral, ethical politicians when we really know that they are little more than sellers of the "illusion of ethics."

When ex-House Ways and Means Chairman Dan Rostenkowski was indicted, members of Congress trembled in their boots. They feared that his defense would be some form of "business as usual" in court. Even though he had stepped down from the chairmanship, he openly stated he would continue to be an "influence in the managing the health and welfare agendas of President Clinton." He also ran again for his seat in Congress. But his constituents decided enough was enough and they had more than enough of him.

It is obvious that Congressman Rostenkowski either believed in the essential nobility of his position or was confident that he has paid off enough of his constituents with "our money" that he need not fear any opponent's effort to unseat him. The voters in his district proved otherwise when he was defeated in his re-election bid. Cunning and deceit however, are not an exclusive Democratic commodity. Consider what David Bonoir, House Minority Democratic Whip said about Newt Gingrich the former Republican Speaker of the House, "I see him as a very bright man, very skillful with people and ideas. And I'm always on my guard when he's speaking—because he has a way of bringing you in, telling you what you want to hear and then acting in a different way when the conversation is over. It's easy to be romanced by his ideas and his tone. But his actions are what counts."[41]

Machiavelli, a sixteenth century philosopher, would have been proud of our Congress and Presidency. In the year 1513 he wrote about the illusion of ethics:

"…The vulgar are always taken by what a thing seems to be…and in the world there are only the vulgar, One prince of the present time…never preaches anything but peace and good faith, and to both he is most hostile, and either, if he had kept it, would have deprived him of reputation and kingdom many a time."

I would like to offer you a challenge. At your local library check the microfilms for newspaper accounts of each of the last modern-day presidential elections. I guarantee you the issue emphasized most often were directly violated once in office! For example, in 1928 Hoover ran on a prosperity plank and ushered in the Great Depression. Roosevelt ran on a peace in our time plank and presided over the Second World War. Eisenhower ran on a "I have a secret plan to end the Korean War." He did, it was quietly threatening to nuke the North Koreans. Johnson ran on a peace plank and immediately escalated the war in Vietnam. Nixon ran on an "Honesty Plank" and ushered in Watergate. And we could go on and on. Bush said, "Read my lips, no new taxes." Clinton defies description in that he changes his mind so often, no one bothers to remember his promises.

Because of the continual "change of mind of politicians" Americans are seasoned to be skeptical. How else do you explain the general low opinion of politicians prevalent today? Personally, I believe that Presidential elections have degenerated into a grand metaphorical "football contest." On any one day in the National Football League, any one team is said to be able to beat any other. The league is designed that way so as to increase the urgency and excitement of each game and distract all of us from looking at substance rather than froth.

For many years during the presidential elections most people have felt that on any one day any Republican candidate can be exchanged for any Democratic candidate. Hence the saying, "Twiddle dum vs. twiddle dee." Each candidate after receiving the nomination of their party ran to the center and tried to portray his/her opponent as an extremist of low repute and awful character. Obviously, in 1996, we got this litany from Clinton, Alexander, Dole and Buchanan. The only really reputable candidate (Keys) doesn't even figure in the polls. And in the 2000 election, unless a credible third party candidate surfaces, the same will happen.

In reality, candidates must primarily appeal to the power base that has propelled their election. Electoral bases develop by a general belief that the political party they support promises to improve their position or attack their enemy, i.e., the rich, the communists, the socialists, the liberals, the right wing extremists, the religious nuts, etc. But to improve the position of their respective power bases, politicians must take away something from other groups to be able to give something to their supporters. Whom do you suppose they are taking from?

When the Democrats talk about improving the lot of the poor, the blacks, the unemployed, the discriminated against, they do so for a specific reason. As political scientist John Bibby points out in his book *POLITICS, PARTIES AND ELECTIONS IN AMERICA,* the power base of the Democratic party in the past rested with blacks, low income, blue collar and union workers.[42] Implied, but not specifically stated was that for the Democrats to stay in power, they had better pretend to help Blacks, ethnic minorities, blue collar and union workers while at the same time, making sure they didn't become upwardly mobile.

Consider for a moment some other salient facts. Columnist, Hanna Rosin[43] quotes Jesse Jackson in *THE NEW REPUBLIC,* who said that there is no crime problem in the United States unless you are black. If you're black between 1968 and 1984, the murder rate increased 65 percent. Jackson adds, "A black person is seven times as likely to be murdered, four times as likely to be raped, three times as likely to be robbed and twice as likely to be assaulted or have a car stolen."

Ms. Rosin's article did not cite the sources of Mr. Jackson's statistics. Assuming his statements are true, one would have to ask what benefit has the black community received by supporting the Democratic Party? Democratic Party leaders like their Republican counterparts have become masters of Machiavellian behavior. They promise everything and deliver worse than nothing.

Not only do they not help the black population but they also avoid assisting the middle class. As good Machiavellian manipulators, they understand that helping the middle class do better will not directly benefit the Democratic Party. Conversely, alienating the vast middle class will not allow them to be elected. So the Democratic candidate has to *pretend* to help the middle class, while in fact, their power base has to be assuaged so as to maintain the substantial allegiance of the blacks, poor, alienated, lower income, elderly on Medicare and blue collar worker.

Is it any wonder that the Democratic Party thunders against "trickle down economics?" But as they thunder, they continue to support programs, which do more to support bureaucrats than help the disenfranchised groups. They know that helping these groups move up the economic ladder will only create more Republican votes. It is against their better judgement to create a larger middle class. The trickle down theory, they claim, has not worked. Which is true. But their answer is to as quietly as possible take from the middle class and give to their power bases—in other words, destroy the middle class. This is no solution. Imbalance and a weakened democracy will continue to prevail!

Republicans, on the other hand, have their power bases among the boardrooms of the Fortune 500, the corporate powers of America, the college-educated and nonunion small business owners.[44] Fortune 500 companies are becoming increasingly international and downsizing in the United States. They are not in the process of creating more middle class jobs. In fact, their "truth" is that the more middle class jobs they can cut and still function, the more profitable their companies. Is it any wonder that the moment A.T. and T. announced they were cutting 50 thousand jobs, the value of their stock went up?

Each major political party has a stake in downsizing the American middle class. Not because they are intrinsically hostile to the middle class or crassly evil. The answer is much simpler. They simply have to *feed* their power base. Though both parties are hurting the American middle class for different reasons, the results are substantially the same.

The truth is that the major political parties have become like twiddle-dum and twiddle dee. Although they pretend to be different, they are alike in that their basic policies have disastrous effects on the lives of the middle class.

I was struck by this fact when I saw President Clinton stand next to Presidents Bush, Reagan, Carter and Ford in a T.V. news photo op. All of them advocated the North American Free Trade Agreement (N.A.F.T.A.).

Why would political leaders of both the Democrat and Republican parties support N.A.F.T.A? By endorsing this treaty, Mexico has access to all of our markets; this allows many of our factories, which now employ millions of people to relocate to Mexico. Mexico is a land where there is no minimum wage, no social security; no worker's compensation, no unemployment insurance, no clean air bill, and rampant access through bribery to corrupt the federal agencies they do have. (We only allow our Congressman to be bribed. It is called P.A.C. contributions).

The Democrats continually claim to have worked so hard to gain benefits for the "common person" in America. Why would they now turn their back on middle-class jobs and endorse exporting them to Mexico? Why would they push to accept a bill to allow factories that have no minimum wage, no working conditions (such as a 40 hour work week and minimum age laws), no labor unions and substantially none of the benefits the Democrats say they have worked so hard to get?

Why would they do that? The Democrats found out after the "New Deal" realignment of the 1930's that when lower-class workers gain middle class status and jobs, they become more conservative and vote Republican![45] One might argue that they have taken the high road in N.A.F.T.A. and be hoping that while in the short run middle-class jobs will suffer, in the long run the huge new trading block will benefit all of us.

Or could it be that Democrats "quietly" believe that the worse people do, the more likely they are to vote Democrat? One of the side-benefits of endorsing N.A.F.T.A. will be to force millions of now middle-class workers back onto welfare, early retirements, or McJobs. Their hope may be that these newly disenfranchised workers will vote Democrat because the Democratic Party is of course, the party of the poor, the disenfranchised, and the neglected. In other words, the Democrats have learned well the wisdom of Machiavellian manipulation!

Thus it is no surprise that the Clinton Administration advocates new and expensive regulations and programs, and at the same time encourages factories and businesses to move South of the border, where they do not have to pay a health care premium tax or worry about all of the other social benefits Democrats fought for. When you realize that the Democrats stand to gain the most from the impoverishment of the middle class, it is not surprising that they are simultaneously raising the cost of doing business in the United States while lowering the cost of doing business in Mexico.

What about the Republicans? In their case the logic is not quite so devious and manipulative. It is a simple matter of greed, plus the hard facts of competition and the infamous bottom line. The M.B.A.'s that populate the upper management of the Fortune 500 assert simply and confidently that if you can hire someone to work for 58 cents an hour with no benefits and little taxes, do so. If you can make millions of dollars off of the sweat of poorly educated Mexicans who will be shot by government soldiers if they try to protest or form a union, do so. If you can farm out your textile production in a slave labor camp in China, do so! And if this destroys hundreds of thousands of American jobs? No matter, the corporation will be rich! If worse comes to worse, the administration can move corporate headquarters to Austria or Switzerland while the United States goes to "hell in a hand basket."

This explains why substantial numbers of the leaders from both political parties back N.A.F.T.A. Of course, one wonders, maybe President Clinton and Vice President Gore might have been focusing on something else. Maybe they believed hundreds of thousands of the middle class would become unemployed, but in the end, we would

create the largest trading block in the world and high-paying jobs
would return to the United States. Three years later however, the
United States is still hemorrhaging jobs. But if you believe the official
line of Clinton and the Republican leadership, continue to vote
Republican or Democrat. Either way, it won't make a bit of difference
that you vote for. Because, as will become clearer as you read further,
the difference between the parties is like "smoke and mirrors."

Americans intuitively understand that our present political parties
no longer represent the vast majority of middle class workers. This is
reflected in the continual decline in "class based voting" since 1952.[46]
There really isn't a difference between the Democrats and the
Republicans when it comes to shafting the middle class. They just pretend there is.

Of course this wasn't always true. Once upon a time, both parties
attempted to help the middle class or at least not hinder them. But we
live in a time of increased greed, stronger special interests, addiction to
T.V. election commercials, and the excessive costs of election campaigns. Both the Democrats and Republicans feed at many of the same
special interest money troughs.

The point for most politicians is they have to obey the first law of
politics, "Get elected or re-elected!" To do that, they must have money
to campaign. So they have to pander to their contributors and also distract or disguise what they are doing. The easiest way to get elected is to
distract the public. So the candidates run on a soak the rich and provide
government programs at no cost to the voter, or fight crime or fight
Communism, etc. But as I have shown, the Democrat's claim to be for
the poor only serves to increase the poor, and the lie that the
Republicans are against Communism seems somewhat specious when
you observe them pandering to North Vietnam and China.

Enough! Consider the 1996 election. Clinton runs on a "I stood up
and protected Medicare platform." At the same time, however, he resists
making any changes to Medicare that could make it more viable, he

resists making any changes to Welfare (which could provide more money for Medicare), he resists fighting illegal immigration and insists illegal immigrants have a right to have welfare, spends money on unwinnable wars in Europe and Africa and fights reducing government or making it easier for businesses to operate in America. With a friend like this Medicare does not need any enemies!

Bush on the other hand is an excellent example of "Country Club Politicians." He stands for Conservatism without really defining what it is or who he is. He criticizes Forbes for being rich and trying to buy the election but avoids facing the fact that the rich are paying for his election also. Buchanan runs on a populist plank but was also a strong Nixon supporter, who was owned by the wealthy, so who is the real Buchanan?

After reading all this you might feel discouraged. Please don't. Remember this simple fact: Eighty percent of Americans classify themselves as middle class. A minority of us, even a small minority, can radically change the course of political life in America. Those of us who see the writing on the wall can stop the smoke and mirrors— *the practitioners of deceit can be removed from power.*

You have the might to change the process. How? You guessed it, simply vote out of office every incumbent. Would you really be that surprised, if within six years, the political parties suddenly discovered that middle class interests are important? Or if they didn't, that a new independent American party was formed to represent the interests of the middle class? We simply have to change the process of election from money dominated personal contests to issue oriented party politics. And, we can do it! This is not as hard as you might think. Most Americans for instance don't know the name of their Congressional Representative. So what is the big deal about voting against someone you don't even know?

Wouldn't you eventually be better off voting for a party that represented your interests rather than for a money-fed, bought and paid for politician who can afford unlimited T.V. commercials? Think about it!

Does the "Health Crisis" Need Major Surgery?

Is there truly a "health crisis" in the United States? And, if so, do we need major surgery, that is, more giant insurers or legions of bureaucrats that will require an employer mandate or a general health tax? Or is the "health crisis" another golden opportunity for "Control Freaks" to have their way. The fact is we have to protect ourselves from "Control Freaks" and we do need major surgery on our health care but not in the way the Clintons propose.

The four major reasons the Clinton Administration used to support the fact that a health crisis exists are: 1) skyrocketing health costs, 2) the lack of portability of insurance (i.e., if you lose your job, your new insurance may not cover a pre-existing condition), 3) discrimination by insurance companies that set rates which encourage employers to discriminate against employees on the basis of health, age or life style choices and 4) the fact that an increasing number of employers and citizens can not afford health care. And since Hilary's proposal went down the tubes, the increasing power of health maintenance organizations to destroy your opportunity for treatment.

These are legitimate complaints. But do they require major surgery? Instead of depriving us of choice or a voice in our coverage, I suggest Congress consider the following: 1) require all health insurers to cover pre-existing conditions, 2) make insurers provide a single rate to employers which does not take into account the specifics of a particular employer's work force and 3) provide a mechanism for citizens who cannot afford insurance to qualify for a basic no frills policy.

We are told that health care costs will climb to 20 percent of our national income, one in every five dollars the economy generates will go to health care. William Cox, vice president of the Catholic Health Association, warned: "Sometime in the next thirteen years we're going to be spending 22 to 25 percent of our income on health care. At that rate, if you want to go out for dinner and a movie, you're going to have to check into a hospital."[47]

Is this really true? No. In fact, in 1994, private medical insurance costs increased only 5.8 percent, the lowest since 1974. Further *decreases* are on the horizon. The reason for the decrease in the price of health care is that major players, i.e. corporations and health care insurance pools, are challenging medical bills as well as forming associations of providers. The insurance costs that continue to rise at a dizzying rate are those of Medicaid and Medicare.[48]

What exactly is this "health-care crisis"?

One of the major problems in health care in America is that politicians and bureaucrats have gained control of health management and personal-decision making. Medicare and Medicaid are the prime sources of health-care inflation. Our society has become so obsessed with control, and equality and fear that hospitals or doctors will "rape" the system, that politicians/bureaucrats create rules which result in stepping on "dollars to pick up pennies."

The underlying threat to participative democracy (in this case basic health care) is the refusal to recognize the *legitimate right of each citizen to make his or her own choice*. One example of controlling choice is to prevent many medications from becoming over-the-counter drugs, which keeps prescription drugs costs high and creates disastrous economic consequences. The "control freaks" at the Food and Drug

Administration have become so obsessed with regulation that many drug companies are moving to Europe and fewer and fewer drugs are being approved in the United States.

Thousands of patients suffer in the United States due to lack of drugs that are readily available in Europe.[49] Like a typical psychopath, the government pretends to be concerned about health-care costs on the one hand (protecting our back pocket) while at the same time making it more and more difficult for new drugs and products to come on the market (stealing from our front pocket).

If the government could really control costs, why are the biggest cost increases in the Medicare and Medicaid programs? When "free" services are provided, hospitals, doctors, and insured providers can charge what they will![50] Once there is no cost to walking in a doctor's office, many patients come more frequently, as they have in Germany and Japan (where doctor visits occur three to six times more often than here). Despite what you may hear, "free" services increase national health care expenditures. Or, if a cap were put on health-care spending, inflation would take another form, waiting lines for medical care, as it has in Canada."[51]

Forget for a moment the politicians and bureaucrats and consider instead a historical perspective. Twenty-five years ago 7.6 percent of the gross domestic product went to health care, 6.8 percent went to education, and 9.7 percent to defense. Today both defense and education costs are at 6 percent and health costs have climbed to 14 percent. They promise to increase to 18 percent by the end of the 90's.[52]

What fundamental steps can the middle class take to curb costs? Will insuring another 38 million uninsured cut costs? Having the working middle class pay more taxes or lose more jobs as business downsizes won't cut costs. To effect change in curbing health-care costs requires courage and fundamental discussions about *ethics and choice.*

At this point, I would like to relate the simple story of Pauline V. Pauline's husband died when she was 30. She was left with four children. Pauline hated the idea of going on welfare. So she rented an old farmhouse and worked three jobs to provide for her children and put them through school. When I first saw Pauline she was 55. Pauline had worked all of her life until she was disabled from Lupus at 53. Her physician referred her to me because she was a "difficult" pain patient. Remember the first day after you seriously exercised. How you were stiff and achy in every joint. Multiply the pain four fold and you would know the struggle Pauline faces every day.

Pauline looked me right in the eye (she was a straight shooter), and said, "My doctor thinks I abuse pain medication. All I want to do is take a Tylenol 3 with Codeine once a day so I can have four hours a day pain-free. He says I am becoming an addict. I know what an addict is. I threw my daughter out of my house when she started using crack. He wants me to use Moultrin. They make my stomach hurt! He says eat when I take the medication. Then he says I should take hot tubs and use hot packs. What does he think I am? A pickle?"

Pauline's insurer pays several thousand dollars a year for her treatment—treatment Pauline views as useless. She has her blood work—takes her Moultrin—takes over the counter pain medication and suffers and struggles through each day.

If Pauline were allowed however, to decide for herself what medication to use and then could be licensed to purchase it. The several thousand dollars, which is spent to no practical effect, could be reduced to several hundred dollars. And Pauline's story is duplicated a million times over throughout the land.

We need to seriously re-think our approach to health care. But an open discussion is the last thing politicians want. President Clinton suggested at one time we enact a seven-percent health-care premium payroll tax. He would have established health-care alliances to control drug companies, insurers and doctors, as well as reduce the cost of defensive medicine by reducing the frequency of malpractice lawsuits.

Let's consider the real health-care problem and what must be done. It is simply not possible to divorce the cost of health care from the nature of the American population.[53] First, the United States population is becoming older. Seventy-seven million "baby boomers" are now approaching middle age. The older a population, the higher health-care costs. The 1980's and 1990's have become the age of kidney machines, heart bypasses organ transplants, and aggressive medical treatment. Because of advances in medical technology, more people live longer today.

In fact, many of my head-injured clients would not be alive if they had been injured thirty years ago. Some of these people have been through rehabilitation programs costing over $300,000 for a year's treatment. Rehabilitation followed acute treatment in an intensive neuro-center and step-down unit, which also cost several hundred thousand dollars.

Other patients with heart disease or certain types of cancer are alive today, at tremendous cost, which would not have survived their illness thirty years ago. But all of these advanced treatments are expensive. Eventually, we must face the fact that there are limits and confront critical questions. Can we afford to provide heart bypasses to persons who are over 70, 75 or 80? Should dialysis be provided for as long as a person is alive to any and all patients? Should any person in the United States be given the most excellent care, even illegal immigrants?

Should the citizens of California, for example, be forced to pay for high-tech care for illegal Mexican immigrants? Politicians in Washington say that Californians must pay regardless of the citizenship of the patient or the legality of his/her residency.

Another significant source of health-care inflation is the ability of medical scam artists to provide "free care," "free diagnostics," and "free evaluations" to the public. Unions originally and with good intentions negotiated contracts, which enabled their members to obtain medical care without cost. The problem with this approach is that the patient that doesn't pay is not aware of what is being charged and less likely to be discriminating in what he or she asks for. Simple five percent co-pay, which could not be waived, would quickly drive the costs of many of these services down.

But do not expect defensive medicine to decrease. A close doctor friend of mine quit medicine after a distressing incident. He elected not to use a M.R.I. on a patient of his. He believed the patient's situation did not justify this expensive procedure. Three months later the patient developed symptoms which on further examination was due to a cancerous tumor. But my doctor friend had not been treating the patient for cancer. However, normal medical procedure indicated a M.R.I. could have been ordered. He had to pay $150,000 while the H.M.O. had to pay over $700,000. The message to physicians and H.M.O.'s? Order *every* test or else!

This is not an entirely wrong approach. Many of my colleagues order tests because they sincerely want to save every patient they can and check for every possibility. And if you were the one in one thousand that is saved, you would be the last to criticize this approach. Nevertheless, as more and more tests are developed, at what point should we set limits?

Another important issue is *free* universal health care. From experience it's clear that health care utilization decreases when patients have to pay some of the cost. Consider this question. Why should the elderly and the taxpayer pay for surgery to improve vision when eyeglasses would also correct the same problem? The real question is, who decides—and how—and what are valid, necessary medical procedures and what are not? This is not a medical or legal question. It is primarily a political issue, which has to be resolved through countrywide dialogue.

Another huge cost of insurance is the simple requirement "control freaks" have put into law, which governs our ability to manage pain. Why should taxpayers pay because the state refuses to allow citizens to make their own decisions about how to deal with their unique health situation, anxiety, or chronic pain? Let me give you a practical, real example of the nonsense that currently afflicts our current political/health system. A client of mine was a window washer. His scaffolding anchor broke and he fell off his three story perch. Following a five-month coma and several months of hospitalization for numerous injuries and broken bones, he was released to his family's care.

This patient is in pain twenty-four hours a day. To cope with his chronic and sometimes intense pain, his doctor prescribed a medication three times a day. This medication helps him sleep. For several months he was on a Striker Frame. This is an apparatus, which turns the patient without having to move him within the bed. While he did not develop bedsores and was able to maintain his circulation, the downside was that he could rarely sleep for more than a few moments. His sleep patterns were destroyed and he now can not sleep unless he takes medication. One of the few medications that work for him is the medication the doctor prescribed.

He needs triple the normal dose of the medication. But the standard dose of the medication is one a day. So an investigator from the state is investigating the pharmacy that serves him and the doctor that prescribes the medication. Message? Don't do anything out of the ordinary, even if it leaves a patient in acute distress.

My client became so distraught on learning about the investigation; he had to be hospitalized. At several hundred dollars a day, one can see what it costs our country to "make sure that citizens don't abuse pain killers, muscle relaxers and mood altering drugs." Steven B. Duke and Albert C. Gross estimate in their book, *AMERICA'S LONGEST WAR* that it costs over two hundred billion dollars a year to wage the war on drugs. But when you consider patients like mine, I believe their estimate is far too low.

Another example of patients between "a rock and a hard place" is chronic arthritic pain, a malady that affects millions and increases with age. The doctor recognizes arthritis as a chronic pain problem and tries to meet the patient's needs by prescribing anti-inflammatory medication.

The anti-inflammatory medicine reduces the pain but may cause the patient to develop other problems. A simple check of the *PHYSICIANS'S DESK REFERENCE* lists numerous disorders that can occur with prolonged use. Should the patient develop a disorder, the patient would have an iatrogenic disease (a secondary disease which was created by his physician's treatment of the original condition). Several years ago an article in the *HARVARD MEDICAL NEWSLETTER* indicated that 80 percent of the diseases now known are incurable and half of them caused by physicians who treated patients for *another* condition.

The window-washer that needed the medication to sleep developed ulcers taking anti-inflammatory drugs. He discovered on his own that smoking marijuana markedly relieves his chronic pain. Now he only has to worry about jail, prison or continuing to be able to pay for his illegal drugs.

In a 1912 *Sears Catalog,* there was an advertisement for laudanum, a morphine-based mixture. Back then, the elderly and patients with chronic pain could order from the *Sears Catalog* as much laudanum as they felt they needed, thus managing their own pain.

Today many doctors and citizens will express shock at the idea of having unregulated access to painkillers. Millions of others would be vastly relieved. The common argument is that people might use painkillers to mask a condition that can or should be treated. The other argument is that they would abuse drugs to the point of becoming addicted and/or ruin their health.

"Control freaks" lead us to believe the unlimited use of painkillers would encourage and abet rampant universal addiction. The reality is that the General American population had unlimited access to painkillers in the 17th, 18th and 19th centuries. But, no more than four percent of the population of the United States became regular users of painkillers.[54] In effect, 96 percent of citizens have to suffer to protect four percent of citizens.[55] Each and every one of us, the great majority, pay the cost of providing unwanted and uninvited protection for the four percent of the population who might abuse drugs.

When "control freaks" assert that all of us will become addicts, it implies a general contempt for the judgement of the public and a need to control each citizen's actions. As our population ages and our medical needs increase, we must either choose to give up control over something we never should have attempted to limit, or face some very grim alternatives.

What are the alternatives?

1) We can continue our present expensive system which forces many citizens to have no medical insurance, thus either being treated by hospital emergency centers (which by law have to take everyone, even the uninsured), or be untreated.

2) We can pretend to adopt a version of national health care, which will result in one or more of three patterns of utilization:

A) The rich will continue to purchase their own private insurance or fund their own health care through their personal financial resources.

B) The middle class will be increasingly given health insurance with invisible benefits i.e., coverage for problems, but the government will provide such low payment that most providers will elect to not accept your insurance (witness Medicaid). Limitations may also exist such as preventing you from getting a second opinion or even paying for your own M.R.I., C.T. or blood test.

In a front-page column of *The New York Times* (February 15, 1994), Elizabeth Rosenthal reports that many doctors dissatisfied with their payments from Medicare now require the elderly to sign contracts to allow them to charge the patient for services Medicare doesn't cover, or charge for phone calls, or charge for certain office calls. Other doctors are simply refusing to accept Medicare patients. Clinton's plan proposed to deal with this issue by making it a felony for the doctor to engage in such practices. Should a version of Clinton's ideas occur in the Republican Congress now or a future congress, many doctors may simply slow down and create even worse delays for patients who want to obtain and receive treatment.

C) Some medical procedures will simply be denied.

As a medical psychologist, some of my research interests have allowed me to develop contacts with physicians in other countries. In Canada, for example, physicians constantly complain about limited access to M.R.I.'s, difficulty in getting permission to use certain procedures, problems with patient caseloads, difficulty in finding hospital beds and, lately, the freezing out of new medical school graduates from being able to practice in certain localities.

It seems evident that all of the above problems will shortly exist in America. How can 37 million new uninsured be covered without causing even more problems? The money will come from either providing less service to those currently insured or by raising taxes.

Consider that 37 million uninsured translates to 15 percent of the American population. Why should 213 million people suffer a severe degradation in their care to help the 37 million uninsured? Americans, however, are not sympathetic to the notion that persons in America should unduly suffer because of their inability to afford medical care. I personally sympathize with this feeling. But the plan put forward by both parties will inevitably cause most of us to either lower our current health standard or pay considerably more in taxes.

An alternative does exist. Move America away from trying to control its citizens, especially in the area of chronic pain and anxiety related health issues. It costs two billion dollars alone just to prescribe Prozac. If we take steps to reduce health care costs significantly, we can add the uninsured without hurting the rest of us.

There are also major benefits to this change in thinking for all of us. Why should a person dying of cancer have to struggle with pain and plead for painkillers or tranquilizers? Why should the elderly have to be subjected to long waits in a doctor's office only to find little comfort being offered for chronic pain? And why should the doctor be placed in the middle between the patients in pain, the medical malpractice attorneys, and the state narcotics investigators who constantly monitor how much pain medication is prescribed?

Certainly people will hurt themselves, perhaps even die because they elect to misuse their access to pain controllers and mood modifiers. But, people are also killed because they elect to drive too fast, eat too much, work too hard, etc. The point is that most of us, if given the opportunity to select our own medication, would visit our doctor for consultation, create informal or formal support networks, and gain better, more effective control over our lives.

In my own practice, I often work with persons who suffer from the effect of acute and chronic painful conditions. One patient, J. S., is dying from bone cancer. As is typical in persons deteriorating from bone cancer, she has good days and bad days. On the bad days, she experiences considerable pain. But she has learned that if she hits the pain just as it begins, she does not have to use as much pain medication. If she waits, however, the pain becomes so bad that only an injection of morphine will stop it.

Recently, she was in the hospital and when she awoke, she felt a pain sequence starting to build. She asked the attending nurse for pain medication. The physician on call, who was not well experienced in managing pain, did not give her a sufficient dose to stop the sequence. She politely told him what she needed (J.S. prior to her illness was a respiratory therapist and thus knew a lot about medication). He responded by telling her that either she was a drug addict or would rapidly become one.

He refused to give her what she needed and she went into what she called "break out pain." Pain, which is unbearable and can only be stopped by large doses of injectable morphine. Four hours later her own doctor came in and ordered what she needed. J.S. for four hours lived in a hell created by her having to depend on physicians who knew less about controlling her pain level than she did. J.S.'s case is not unusual.

In fact, more unusual was the fact that she found a doctor who took the risk of trusting her judgement.

But should we blame the doctors for this problem? Many physicians report if they too readily prescribe painkillers, state investigator start breathing down their necks. The point here is that the middle class needs to re-think what we really expect from medicine and how much control we must relinquish in deference to other professional expertise. I believe the net effect of giving back control to Americans is a vast reduction in the cost of medical care.

Not all members of Congress have lost their senses on the Health Care issue. As Senator David Durenberger, a Minnesota Republican, stated, "The cost of not doing it right is greater than the cost of not getting it done."[56] The Middle Class can and must resolve the health care issue-but not so as to create a new fiefdom! Health care can and will evolve into a truly meaningful and beneficial service as the Middle Class exercises renewed

Resolve to take it away from the "elitists" and return it to the people.

We can return it to the people by respecting the integrity and rights of the elderly, cancer patients, chronic pain patients, traumatic injury patients who have been otherwise stabilized to manage and make their own decisions about what kind of pain medication and how much to use. We can move the federal bureaucrats out of the health care business and allow communities to make their own decisions on how to deliver health care. We can reduce significantly the amount of use Medicaid patients make of emergency rooms vs. Doctor's offices, etc. etc. As we change the focus on health care to respect the rights and privileges of each American, we can also add benefits which should be added such as allowing the elderly on Medicare to have the same benefits many of us have, i.e., having a small co-pay for the drugs their doctors prescribe. Much is possible, if we have the will to do it and don't allows special interests to stop us.

The Drug War—Vietnam Re-Visited

Ring out a slowly dying cause,
And ancient forms of party strife;
Ring in the nobler modes of life,
With sweeter manners, purer laws.
Ring out the thousand wars of old,
Ring in the thousand years of peace.
Alfred Tennyson, 1809–1892[57]

After obtaining my Ph. D. in Clinical Psychology my first "real job" was with the Central Intelligence Agency. Following graduation, I received a teaching offer in Colorado and mental health offers in Utah and Florida. But, I wanted to work on the East Coast (where I had not spent any adult years), so I accepted a staff position with the C.I.A.

The year was 1970 and protests against the Vietnam War were in full bloom. Of course, the government emphasized we had to take it slow and disengage with honor as well as contnue to protect the rest of Asia and Indonesia from Communist expansion. By then we had about fifty thousand dead and 250 thousand wounded, in addition to the millions of disillusioned and often drug addicted veterans.

My new position was quite different from life as a graduate student. Instead of the constant demands to write research papers, see clients, and study for exams, I evaluated only a few people each week and did limited consultation and research. I found the job boring and began to miss the challenge of a general clinical practice.

However, while with the Agency, I sometimes whittled my time away conversing after hours with other Agency employees. One of them, D. A. never discussed anything that hadn't already been printed in newspapers to avoid any accusations of divulging secrets. On the subject of Vietnam, D.A. noted with some cynicism and derision that Ho Chi Minh had been a pro-American rebel during the Japanese occupation of Vietnam. He added that the O.S.S. (the precursor of the C.I.A.) had been a strong supporter of Ho Chi Minh.

D.A. Indicated that if the United States had chosen to support Ho Chi Minh, Vietnam would have become another Yugoslavia, serving as a strong counter balance to China. Instead, President Eisenhower ignored the advice offered by Intelligence agencies and elected to follow State Department advice to support France and oppose Ho Chi Minh.

Another reason for Eisenhower's justification for Vietnam was that Republicans generally used Cold War rhetoric to make Democrats look soft on Communism. Republicans needed to have this tactic to counter "New Deal" liberalism, which had won the loyalty of the poor and the middle class since the Depression. By the time of the Vietnam War, however, the New Deal generation was dying out, and Democrats were forced to play the "Cold War" game with the Republicans.

Each president after Eisenhower, Democrat or Republican continued and enlarged the Vietnam War. They too feared being accused of "giving in" to the Communists. To protect their political position, they sacrificed the lives of tens of thousands of citizens.

When the middle class finally had enough and voted against Johnson in the primary elections, the Vietnam War began its agonizing demise. The public was no longer willing to continue the Vietnam War, and Johnson's "New Deal" rhetoric, (i.e., "The Great Society"), didn't seem all that appealing.

But after the demise of the Vietnam War, a new threat was needed. Who would be the new villain? I'd like to think the choice of a new villain was made by well-meaning idiots and not calculating psychopaths...but history will have to the final say. In any event, the new rhetoric became drug abuse and crime. With the new emphasis on the drug war, drug arrests increased from 559,900 in 1981 to 1,089,500 in 1990 (and still mounting).[58]

Originally and long before the Vietnam War, Mr. Well-Meaning Idiot (my euphemistic term for scheming politicians), noted that millions of persons, particularly the rheumatic elderly, were addicted to laudanum (a morphine-based pain killer), available everywhere (even in a Sears Catalog). In fact, from 1784 when our government was formed until 1931 there was no long against raising our using opium in the United States. But then the bureaucrats in Washington advocated our participating in the International Opium Convention and then by treaty allow Congress to take away from each citizen their right to use opium for pain control.

Mr. Well-Meaning Idiot's idea was that we must not allow our population to become hooked on drugs. Further, to have painkillers available at all, they had to be controlled by physicians. When it was soon discovered that physicians couldn't be trusted either, Mr. Well Meaning Idiot employed *another layer of bureaucrats.*

Employed by most states, these bureaucrats had to make sure that doctors gave their patients only the bare minimum of pain killers and did not become prescription happy, or enrich themselves at the expense of poor, stupid, benighted citizens. The use of illegal drugs did not elicit much interest, (except in the ghetto) until Vietnam. Since so many veterans returned from Vietnam drug-addicted, a renewed emphasis on drugs began and continued long after our exit from Vietnam. President Nixon started the ball rolling, "The War on Drugs." As with the Vietnam War, the war was expanded by each succeeding president, resulting in increased drug arrests. U. S. District Court drug cases shot up from 4,000 in 1980 to 12,500 in 1990.[59]

In retrospect, we find the public, represented by their most able Congresspersons, voted to control drugs so that only properly licensed physicians should dispense them. Physicians had the mission to protect societies from the specter of a drug-addicted population. But physicians were immediately placed on the horns of a dilemma. What about those citizens already addicted to painkillers? Some doctors couldn't turn their back on the already addicted. Other doctors and zealous bureaucrats felt mortally offended by the idea of *any* addiction; they were more than willing to allow patients to withdraw "cold turkey".

Two things happened. One, a doctor and pharmacist were arrested for dispensing drugs too freely. Two, pressure from various local legislatures increased, initiating a watch dog system to make sure that "evil" doctors didn't prescribe drugs to those unworthy to receive them.[60] To this day the watch-dog system survives constantly monitoring doctors to make sure no drugs are given to "undeserving patients."

As a result of drug laws, casualties have developed, some obvious and some known only to those who investigate further. Let's start with the obvious casualties. All wars, even wars against our own citizens, have a cost. Remember, the old cliché-, you can't make an omelet without breaking eggs? You also can't have a war without victims, intended or unintended. In this case, victims are those who are hurt, killed, wounded, or damaged in the process.

In the case of the drug war, casualties are enormous. I want to list a few.

1. The drug users who use illicit drugs and place themselves at risk by using dirty needles; spending all their resources, and engaging in illegal activities to support their habit.

2. Those who become victims of the drug user who search for resources to buy drugs. Those include the user's family, friends, acquaintances, and those recruited into using drugs to pay for the user's habit. Additionally, let's also include the victims of drug-related crimes.

3. Drug users eventually developed a multi-level marketing strategy. The principal of networking is that you first join the multi-level organization and then convince others to join. Each time someone joins under you and makes purchases you get a commission. Amway was not the first organization to develop multi-level marketing. To fund their own habit, users sold drugs to others at a marked up price, using the profit to buy their drugs. Drug dealers soon discovered users often recruited users.

4. Recruiting other users was usually confined to the ghetto neighborhoods where drug use was most common. But when the Vietnam War veterans returned home, a larger new networking market surfaced. The bridge between the ghetto and suburbia was breached. Now residents of urban, suburban and rural areas had to wonder if their sons and daughters would learn to "just say no."

5. According to the Department of Justice statistics[61], the majority of ordinary crime (burglary, theft, etc.) is associated with drugs: Specifically, thirteen percent of jail inmates committed offenses for money to obtain drugs; thirty-three percent of those who committed robbery and burglary did so to obtain drugs; forty-eight percent of property offenders reported daily use of drugs; thirty-nine percent of violent offenders reported daily use of drugs; and 60 percent of males arrested for larceny, burglary, and auto theft admitted being under the influence of drugs when they committed their crime.[62]

Given the huge number of burglaries, robberies and theft, it doesn't take much imagination to understand that all U.S. Citizens are rapidly becoming casualties of the drug war. In 1991, there were 13 million property crimes—an eleven percent increase from 1982. Citizens of the United States lost 16.1 billion dollars in property crimes in 1991. We all pay for these losses every time we buy auto insurance, homeowner's insurance, or renter's insurance.

But there is an even bigger loss. According to the U.S. Department of Justice there were 34.7 million victims of crime (violent and property) in 1991. **That means, on an average, you will be the victim of a property crime or violent crime every five years!**

6. Other casualties are less obvious. Michigan spent 803,399,600 dollars in 1990 for prisons. That figure is just the tip of the iceberg. What about the cost to hire police, administer courts, handle appeals, staff local jails, etc.? At the very time I am writing this chapter, several counties in Michigan are having to sue the state for more money to run their courts. Where does that money come from? It's taken from education, roads, health, social welfare, etc. These costs also increase the tax burden.

Each and every one of us pay dearly and directly through taxes to maintain prisons; and our children pay through reduced educational opportunities, and the general deterioration and greater risk of simply living in a drug-combat zone.

The money just doesn't stop with the costs of the criminal justice system. The Federal government must pay for the drug problem. Monies to assist state and local governments increased from 28 million in 1981 to 1.016 billion in 1991. Now that President Clinton wants to have a "War on Crime," how much more will we be spending? Consider these further costs: Prison costs grew from 88 million in 1981 to 1.265 billion in 1991. Drug law enforcement grew 6.3 billion from 1981 to 1991. State and local justice systems spent 5.2 billion in 1988.

Health care for rehabilitation and treatment of drug offenders cost 1.73 billion in 1989. In 1990 the proportion of drug offenders in the federal prison system was 50 percent and in state prisons 30 percent. That figure of course, has steadily risen.[63]

What about other costs not as easily obtained? What about the cost of investigating property and violent crimes? What about the cost of health care to victims of crimes and the family members of drug users?

What about lost productivity? What about loss of property values? And what about the stress of never knowing when **you are going to be next?**

7. Casualties don't stop with increased taxes and increased chances of being a victim of crime. What about the elderly? Those who live in the combat zone of poorer inner city neighborhoods live lives of desperate fear. They are afraid to walk to their local store, leave their doors unlocked, or answer their doors at night. The elderly in the suburbs and rural areas must also worry about burglaries, theft and violent crime.

A friend of mine, a circuit court judge, recently described a case in which a pair of young adults, high on drugs, invaded an elderly couple's home. After taking everything of immediate value, they insisted the couple have sex while they watched!

8. Among the black population, blacks have the highest rates of victimization in the United States. With respect to violent crime, blacks have 61 victims per one thousand persons while whites have 38 victims. Blacks have 208 property crimes per one thousand households while whites have 157.[64]

And there are the working poor, who each time they leave for work or a simple visit, wonder if their belongings will be there when they return. The poor in low-income neighborhoods are forced to send their children to schools, which are often inhabited by drug pushers. Every day events such as drive-by shootings, street violence, and turf wars are facts of life in the inner cities.

9. A less obvious casualty of the drug war is the value of inner-city property. Few people, given the choice, would opt to live in a combat zone. Those who can afford to leave the inner city do so. This leads to a dramatic drop in property values, abandoned homes and businesses and a downtown area, which becomes a tax eater rather than a tax producer.

If the inner cities were safe, they would become a natural haven for the elderly, who could use mass transportation to travel to nearby hospitals, museums, libraries, social support centers and churches. Another source of demand for inner city apartments would be students of nearby universities and young workers who do not earn enough to have cars or newer homes in the suburbs. Without crime and the drug war, the inner cities would again become thriving heterogeneous life-giving and life-producing centers.

In simple economic terms, consider the difference between an abandoned huge department store building which pays no taxes, and a thriving busy block in which the owner pays property taxes, the businesses employ workers (which reduces welfare costs). In the latter scenarios, residents would enjoy the *friendly* give and take of life in the urban city.

10. There are other victims of the drug war who are ignored. The sick and disabled. Persons afflicted with chronic or acute severe pain, or life threatening or debilitating illnesses. If given the opportunity to manage their own pain, they would be able to secure their painkillers in doses, which would provide relief.

Although the average citizen can not obtain prescription drugs without a doctor's help. Over the counter painkillers such as Tylenol, Advil, Excedrin, Bayer Asperin and Mylanta can be purchased. In 1992, over two billion dollars was spent on the ten top over the counter drugs.[65]

Instead of dispensing controlled drugs, doctors fearful of malpractice suits and state bureaucrats dole out painkillers in insufficient doses or prescribe non-addicting drugs such as anti-inflammatories. These alternative drugs often have severer consequences and side effects such as creating ulcers. But since no one gets "high" on anti-inflammatory drugs (they just get sick), no one seems to care. Possibly however, you care. At least you should care since two million persons a year are hospitalized and 140,000 die due to the side effects of prescription drugs.[66]

In effect, politicians in federal and state government as well as the media are feeding the body politic of the United States. The delusion is that doctors can find safe alternatives to painkillers and that doctors are free to dispense painkillers when needed. The illusion is that the system is working. If you are ever unfortunate enough to have to struggle with chronic pain, you will soon find out how miserable life can be.

11. Finally, there is the constant erosion of constitutional rights. As the drug war intensifies, police and allied law enforcement agencies become increasingly frustrated and dehumanized. As a result, more and more citizens are in jeopardy of having their home, property, or person invaded as the police pursue their endless quest for perpetrators.

Several of my clients recounted in great horror how their home had been invaded in the middle of the night. They were jerked (sometimes naked) from their bed, handcuffed and made to assume a prone or standing position with a loaded gun trained on them. When the police found no drugs and discovered they'd invaded the wrong home, they didn't even offer an apology.

12. The final problem with the drug war is the same one that President Eisenhower raised when he gave his farewell speech at the end of his presidential term. In that speech he warned of the growing power of the military/industrial complex and how that complex could become a self-feeding, self-indulgent monopoly. Cold war rhetoric sustained the military/industrial complex to the tune of hundreds of billions of dollars. To maintain its power and position however, there must be an enemy or potential enemies. Just as an army can not exist without a potential need for it, a prison can not exist without prisoners and a police force can not exist without real or potential felons.

As the police infrastructure becomes more and more powerful, what politician or politicians dare suggest that we are moving in the wrong direction?

With all these victims (intended and unintended) of the drug war, why haven't we either quit the war or won it? The answer is painfully obvious and relates to the earlier discussion on Vietnam. We continue the war because politicians are afraid to do otherwise. The "drug war" has become the new "cold war" rhetoric. Each politician who considers voting against the drug war imagines a hungry opponent screaming to the media (especially T.V.) **MY OPPONENTS VOTED TO GIVE DRUGS TO ADDICTS, VOTE FOR ME I'LL PUT THEM IN PRISON!** The only exception I can think of to the general deception engaged in by politicians is the recent campaign of Jesse Ventura for Governor of Minnesota in which he equated the Drug War to Prohibition and said it's time to end it.

Because tens of millions of persons each year are intended or unintended victims of the drug war, it's time to cease this war. I will offer an alternative to the drug war but first, I would like to offer five reasons why the war can never be won:

1. The length of borders of the United States. Our country is essentially an island country with millions of miles of coastland. Our border with Canada is essentially unguarded. And if we can't keep our border with Mexico secure from unsophisticated peasant crossings, how can we protect it from sophisticated drug dealers? Even employing the Army to stop unauthorized intrusions along our borders with Mexico produced few results.

2. Interdiction—stopping the drugs from being grown, has been tried for over thirty years with no hint of success. Once we convince one country to stop growing opium or cocaine, the drug dealers simply move to another country.

3. Punishment has only served to dramatically raise our taxes with no discernable effect on the number of persons using or selling drugs. Punishment has enabled politicians to expand the bureaucracy so that drug offenders could be prosecuted and incarcerated. But for each one imprisoned, others lie in wait, and willing to step up to the plate. Although Michigan already spends close to one billion dollars a year on prisons, Governor Engler wants to expand the system to accommodate five thousand more felons at the cost of two hundred million more dollars.

Many states are already at the point that they simply can't afford to continue the war on drugs.

4. Education. The "Just say no" campaign and other programs designed to educate our youth and adults has had an effect. But there will always be the ten-percent who can't be educated or choose not to listen.

5. Therapy. Even if we had and effective therapy program for all drug users, we don't have enough therapists to begin to touch the problem.

So what is the answer? Some advocate the legalization of drugs. Legalizing drugs has been tried in some countries and advocated in ours, but that's no solution either. Drug users are a thorn in society's side who inflict pain on others and themselves. Drugs often lessen the moral constraints and restraints of the user. Users are often a public nuisance or a social menace.

I propose several ways to deal with the drug problem, which protects society, eventually leading to a resolution. Consider the following:

1. License all drug users. Set aside reservations near centers of population where the user can use any and all drugs to his or her heart's content. I emphasize any and all drugs in unlimited doses. Some users will learn to control their drug-use through behavior a sense of wanting to stay alive, while others will simply overdose and kill themselves. Further there will be no illegal drug market because there will be no incentive to purchase drugs that are available for free.

2. Require a licensed drug user to be on verifiable birth control. Why allow drug users to produce addicted babies? Birth control pills should be administered not only to the women but also to the men.

3. Require all licensed drug users, who are arrested for breaking the law, to be confined for 72 hours in a holding area with no access to drugs. Many drug users are also addicted to crime. They get "high" from the excitement of breaking the law and are not afraid of jail, but they are very afraid of withdrawing cold turkey.

4. Once all current drug users are licensed, future drug users are given a license only if they name their supplier. Thus, the only crime related to drug use would be that of supplying drugs. Addicts have

little loyalty to themselves or others; they would turn in their own mother to have access to free drugs.

5. Since drug addicts have contributed much to the decay and degradation of inner cities, require them to donate 10 hours a week on urban renewal and infrastructure improvement in return for free drugs.

6. License patients with significant pain-related conditions to have free access to painkillers. Why should only addicts have access to drugs while denying victims of trauma and disease access as well? My personal experience as a medical psychologist shows that most patients are better at managing their pain than their doctors, who have to be cautious when writing prescription drugs manage.

The minority of patients who are unable to manage their own pain appropriately may need the help of support groups or therapists. But why must the majority be punished to save the few potential abusers?

Many might argue that the above recommendations are examples of right-wing fascist, addle-headed thinking. But they would be quite wrong. Admittedly, some of these suggestions could result in the premature deaths of up to five hundred thousand addicts a year (approximately ten percent of an estimated five million users). Some might argue that this approach resembles the thinking of the WWII Nazi's. Again, they would be wrong. The choice of death is coming not from the state, but from individuals who choose to place themselves at risk. What is recommended is a practical, effective way of winning the war on drugs—without destroying our society.

The number of possible self-inflicted overdoses sounds high, but how many persons die as a result of prolonged abuse of their bodies through poor diet, smoking, and alcoholism? The numbers of persons dying from legal self-abusive behaviors are actually far higher than the worst figures you can imagine from adopting my proposed plan. The benefits of my plan are 1) the light at the end of the tunnel; 2) we would not bankrupt our society. Remember, each new cell added to the prison system costs society one hundred thousand dollars! The total cost of the "drug war" at present is estimated to be in excess of 200 billion dollars per year.[67]

The new mayor of New York City is urging his police department to again get tough on drugs and arrest as many drug users as possible. Such efforts have been tried in other major cities. Other major cities found that their courts, jails, prisons and police soon became so overloaded that they could not function.

Politicians have has suggested that if the prisons are full, build more prisons. This is a stupid suggestion. They ignore the horrific cost of *maintaining* hundreds of thousands of prisoners in prison, plus the additional costs of prosecution and eventual release of these inmates. Michigan has taken the Limbaugh approach and built more prisons. As a result, Michigan is unable to properly maintain its schools, roads, welfare programs and other costs of government. Michigan is even unable to reimburse local counties for the costs of operating the court system.

The time is now to work smarter rather than harder! If there has to be a drug problem, it's time we stopped trying to cure and rescue the drug users. We must "bite the bullet" and allow the users to kill themselves. But we must make sure that innocent citizens are safely out of their way.

Remember the first step to curing the drug problem is to get rid of all political incumbents—local, state and federal. These are the politicians who convinced society of the need to have a war on drugs. The politicians and their continued support of the "drug war" have led to society's increasing decay. I'm sure that if a significant number of blacks, elderly, and the middle class (the current victims of the drug war) join forces to oust all incumbents, we will soon see more rational and practical approaches to the drug problem.

If you would like to study this problem further, I would suggest you read the book, *AMERICA'S LONGEST WAR* by Steven B. Duke and Albert C. Gross (see endnote).

Consider this quote from the jacket of their book; "The major accomplishments of our war on drugs has been to squander literally hundreds of billions of dollars, flood our streets with guns and gangsters…" Authors Duke and Gross demonstrate how the drug war has led to record levels of crime, corrupted the police, overloaded the courts, saturated prisons, and strained the health care system. Dropping the drug war would vastly reduce the cost of both Medicare and Medicaid? And what is equally appalling is regaining the lost rights of the majority of American Citizens in pursuit of the drug war.[68]

It appears to me that the cost of punishing and wreaking vengeance on drug users is not only unsuccessful but also counterproductive. Judge Lois G. Forer asserts that she and many other judges have seen the light.[69] She resigned her position as a judge rather than participates in "drug insanity." And she notes that many federal judges refuse to hear drug cases for the same reason. The time has come to stop the insanity!

N.A.F.T.A., International Trade and the Big Lie

Bob Herbert reported the story of Pearl Novak (61), Marie Whitt (56) and Jeanie Kowalewski (56) in *The New York Times*.[70] Jeanie stated, "We always felt like a family—Both sides, employers and employees, helped each other to grow together. But there's been a drastic change. They no longer think of us as people."

The C.E.O. of Leslie Fay Fashions, John Pomerantz, responded to Jeanie's union's complaint before Congress by stating in his letter to the subcommittee, "The movement of low skilled jobs out of the United States is what the NAFTA debate was all about and that debate is over."

It may be over in Mr. Pomerantz's mind and in the mind of his lackeys in Congress and the present Administration, but it is not over in Mexico and Guatemala. Dorka Nohemi Diaz Lopez (20) traveled to Washington to present her complaints. She works for Global Fashions, a company under contract to Leslie Fay Fashions. She and other employees, including some as young as 13, are locked in a factory for 12 hours a day, forced to work without food, water and breaks and paid 41 cents an hour. Dorka was fired because she tried to organize the workers to improve their conditions.

Meanwhile, Pearl Novak, Marie Whitt and Jeanie Kowalewski prepare to lose their $7.80 an hour job, as Leslie Fay Fashions like thousands of other companies closes down their operations in the United States and moves their factories to the semi-slave states of Guatemala, Honduras, Malaysia, Philippines and India as well as the prison labor colonies of China.

These three ladies try to accept their fate with reasonable good humor and logic. But how long will millions of others like them who are forced out of work in the United States continue to do so? And how long will the semi-slave states continue to be lackeys for the rich and the powerful?

Mexico is a country with a long history of revolution and they honor the idea of revolution—not apologize for it. Students, peasants and Indians are becoming increasingly restive and I don't think it will be too many years before their restiveness takes a more active form of rebellion and insurrection. And then workers like Pearl Novak, Marie Whitt and Jeanie Kowalewski will be hearing from management again. This time, thousands of C.E.O.'s will press their public relations people into action.

Leading newspapers and newsmagazines around the land will carry lead articles and pictures of "Communist insurgents in Mexico." Stories of "leftist guerilla leaders and horrible mutilations" will surface. *The New York Times, Los Angeles Times, San Francisco Chronicle, Chicago Tribune and Washington Post* will press for action. Then in their little town in Northeastern Pennsylvania, workers like Pearl Novak, Marie Whitt and Jennie Kowalewski will stand solemnly along the street waving a little U.S. flag as their local V.F.W. band plays a stirring martial tune and their children or grandchildren will march off to "save Mexico from the Communists."

Hopefully, Pearl Novak, Marie Whitt and Jennie Kowalewski will not be asked to pay the ultimate sacrifice of numbly watching their tear-stained hands blindly stroking a plastic-wood coffin which may or may not contain the partial or complete remains of a beloved child or grandchild.

Perhaps the following Sunday, she and close friends and family will pray in a simple little church in hopes of the resurrection of their loved ones as C.E.O.'s are shuttled in their limousines to their churches and then to a quiet luncheon at their country club to discuss with some satisfaction the demise of the "Communists" in Mexico.

Perhaps their conversation will drift to their children or grandchildren who are attending private Ivy League schools or on how they made a tidy little profit by switching some of their investments into stocks in defense-related corporations.

No, I don't think workers like Pearl Novak, Marie Whitt and Jeanie Kowalewski have heard the last of management.

Although I expected the C.E.O.'s of the country to push for using the youth of America to protect their investments in Mexico, it never occurred to me that a president of the United States would have the chutzpa to ask Congress to guarantee 40 billion dollars in Mexican bonds. His public reasoning was that we have already gained one hundred thousand jobs from N.A.F.T.A. and we don't want to lose them.

Apparently Clinton never heard of Leslie Fay Fashions and all of the other businesses that have exported jobs to Mexico. Nor did he attempt to explain how we continue to pile up one huge trade deficit after another. But he need not have worried, no one in the national media will call his dissembling to the public's attention.

If governments and government leaders learned anything from World War II, they certainly learned the value of the "big lie."

International competitiveness to maintain our place in the global market place is nothing more than a huge artifice. Few economists, and *no Western political leaders*, had the courage to disagree with the bald-faced distortions, which surround the illusion of international competitiveness.

One exception to this general rule of presenting blatant falsehoods as truths is Dr. Paul Krugman, a professor of economics at the Massachusetts Institute of Technology. Dr. Krugman in an article entitled "Competitiveness: A Dangerous Obsession" (March/April 1994 , *FOREIGN AFFAIRS*) outlines the blatant distortions made by leaders of both political parties in America and political leaders in Europe and Japan. The first falsehood that a President Clinton state (which is endorsed by his senior advisors and leaders in Europe and Japan) is that each nation "is like a big corporation competing in the global market place." If you believe this it follows that the economic progress of America rest or fall on how well America does competing in world markets.

Because President Clinton and the Washington Beltway crowd believe, or pretend to believe, this dictum, a whole industry says Dr. Krugman, "of councils on competitiveness, geo-economists and managed trade theorists has sprung up." As Dr. Krugman points out, this diagnosis is flatly wrong!

Dr. Krugman makes three points in his article, which will be commented upon in this chapter. First, he demonstrates how concerns about competitiveness are almost completely unfounded relative to the economic health of the United States. Secondly, he explains why politicians continue to state the "big lie," even though they know it's not true. Thirdly, he suggests that believing the fallacy of the importance of international trade leads to distortions in government and economic policies.

First, let's discuss the issue of competitiveness and economic growth. The fact is that Europe's, and Japan's, economic growth has stagnated in the last 17 years. But how could this be, if all a country needs to be rich is to have a *positive* balance of trade? Fact, Japan has a huge positive balance of trade, (144.9 billion dollars) and the United States has a huge *negative* balance of trade, (146.5 billion).[71] Yet in the year 1994, Japan's unemployment rate increased while the United States unemployment rate decreased.[72] Curiously, the United States performance in output, demand and jobs is four times better than Japan's.[73]

The truth is that nations primarily produce and consume their own goods. Citizens of the United States, as is true in Europe and Japan consume Ninety percent of the products of the United States. The real reason why the United States, Europe, and Japan have done poorly is not the success or lack thereof in the international market place. The culprit is closer and much more obvious. Richard Rothstein in the

American Prospect, (Winter, 1993)[74] notes the real reason for our problems. The truth is that hundreds of thousands of high paying American jobs have been exported to low wage countries. The reduced buying power of the middle class has hurt both our country and Japan (which has done the same thing by transferring factories to other countries).

Why then do politicians spout the religion of international competitiveness even though they know it is irrelevant? The real reason that citizens of the major economies of Western Europe, Japan and the United States are doing poorly is due to the political/economic policies of their decision-makers. Employers and businesses are reluctant to hire more workers because they simply can't afford to generate more expensive jobs when their own country supports exporting these jobs to other lands. And many workers are not willing to work for "peanuts" if they can live on welfare.

Politicians get elected when they stress "economic justice." Remember the 1992 presidential campaign. President Bush tried with little success to use the "character" issue, while Clinton successfully countered with, "It's the economy, stupid." Political fortunes rise and fall based on the *perception* of how the economy is doing.

But how many politicians are willing to stand before the public and flatly state, "Well we have a slowing and increasingly poorer economy because the bureaucrats we have employed are making so many regulations that businesses are fleeing our lands." And they wouldn't even dare mention the financial contributions that international corporations donate to their campaigns. Obviously they are unwilling to point out the economy is not generating jobs for high school graduates because the taxes and regulations they implemented help to destroy jobs and productivity. Instead, Western Europe, Japan, and the United States all play the "blame game" to avoid having its citizens ask the wrong question, i.e., why are you creating taxes and regulations that destroy jobs and reduce productivity?

Finally, the third problem with emphasizing international trade as the standard by which countries measure their health is that it leads to gross distortions in government policy and decision making. Instead of considering the impact on the economy of regulations and taxes which hurt small to medium-size businesses, many newspapers carry stories about how President Clinton forced Japan to use more Motorola's cellular phones!

President Clinton and his host of economic advisors (Council of Economics Advisor's Chairperson Laura D'Andrea Tyson, Ira Magaziner, and Robert Reich concentrate on economic justice at home but never close the barn door, which swings wide open to fleeing corporate jobs. But think for a moment. At present, the American economy is fueled by 100 million jobs, and as Dr. Krugman points out, only ten million of these jobs are involved in international trade. If the government takes an action, which adversely affects ninety million jobholders and only benefits ten million jobholders, what happens to the economy?

The answer, of course, is obvious. And that is why our economy has steadily deteriorated for high school graduates since 1973. We simply have to remove our incumbent politicians and take serious steps toward reducing the bureaucracy and their maze of regulations which has served to hold back productivity in this country!

Productivity is not the only problem that faces our economy. Consider this front-page *New York Times* article, "Canada's U.S. Trade Experience Fuels Opposition to the New Pact" The writer, Clyde H. Farnsworth notes increasing opposition within Canada to both the new N.A.F.T.A. pact and to the previous free trade agreement between the United States and Canada. Opposition is coming from the middle class, which has lost tens of thousands of jobs. These jobs have gone to the United States and are in process of going to Mexico.

Yet President Clinton engineered N.A.F.T.A.'s approval by the United States Congress. Farnsworth points out that unemployment doubled in Canada following approval of a free trade pact with the United States.

While total dollar trade is currently improving in Canada, it is not producing nearly as many jobs because the industries, which are in process of developing, use low-wage labor.

The same date, another article in *The New York Times* by David E. Rosenbaum, "Clinton's Policy on Jobs Holds Trade Pact's Fate," indicates that in every year of the 90's decade *TWO MILLION SOLIDLY MIDDLE CLASS JOBS WILL BE LOST.* According to Rosenbaum only a quarter of the Democrats in Congress supported N.A.F.T.A. (If you really believe that you ought to be a good target for the next pyramid scheme).

The real problem is that the special interest groups that pay for each Congressperson to be elected (with the exception of labor) support N.A.F.T.A. Congress wants to approve N.A.F.T.A. The basic question is how to approve it and get re-elected.

One way to do so is to promise that N.A.F.T.A. will produce more jobs than are lost. Canada's experience shows that the argument is a lie and will come back to haunt the politicians who utter it. Although Vice President Gore presented the big lie in his debates with Perot and seems to have gotten away with it.

Another way to push the "big lie" is to say that special training programs will be established to train displaced workers in new occupations. This is an even bigger lie. When Massey, the biggest industrial producer in Canada, closed its doors to Canadian labor, where were the industries for which the displaced workers could be trained? They didn't exist. Nevertheless, key members of the Canadian government continued to sponsor a training program, which had few or no consumers.

In his article Mr. Rosenbaum further states, as a given, that politicians, "cannot vote against competition from Europe and Japan, against American plants moving overseas in search of cheaper labor, against companies at home cutting their work force or against the lower military budgets that are costing so many jobs in the defense industries. But they can vote against NAFTA." What drivel! Of course, politicians can vote against competition from Europe and Japan and against American plants moving overseas in search of cheaper labor.

Of course, they can't vote against it if they want to have their campaign contributions from Europe, Japan, Asia and the money people who own the moving factories. Of course, we the middle class voters who stand in jeopardy of losing our jobs can also vote. *WE CAN CHOOSE TO VOTE AGAINST EACH AND EVERY INCUMBENT, LOCAL AND NATIONAL, WHITE AND BLACK, MALE AND FEMALE UNTIL SUCH TIME AS THE POLITICIANS SUDDENLY DISCOVER THAT THEY CAN DO SOMETHING ABOUT TRADE WHICH WILL PROTECT AND ENHANCE MIDDLE CLASS JOBS!*

And we also have to consider what is right, just and fair about losing high-paid jobs to slave labor countries. Harry Wu wrote about his imprisonment with millions of other Chinese in China's Gulag. Prisoners there, are given a simple choice: work or starve. Conform or be beaten and tortured. The Gulag produces products that used to be made by middle-class Americans, such as shoes, textiles, and toys.[75]

An independent international money manager Chih Kwan Chen writes elsewhere that China is increasing trade with the United States by ten percent per year.[76] Last year China exported to the United States 27 billion dollars worth of goods and imported four billion dollars. Where did the balance go? It went to Japan to buy materials there. In other words, China through cheap labor and slave labor was able to destroy over 600,000 middle-class American forty thousand dollar-a-year jobs and a 250,000 ancillary middle-class jobs.

Interestingly, Mr. Chih Kwan Chen argues that we should not try to force Japan (and other Asian Nations, i.e., China) to make specific changes to help correct this imbalance. Mickey Kantor, the U.S. Financial Trade Representative has made remarkably little success in changing the balance of trade.

Why not? Why should *The New York Times,* a supposedly liberal newspaper, side with other nations against the middle class of America?

And why should Congress not intervene to rescue and protect middle class American jobs? Certainly, Japan and Europe do not allow China to destroy their labor force with China's cheap labor and slave labor camps. Why do we? The answer is painfully obvious and incredibly sad.

Firstly, the State Department so anxious to have influence abroad, it will gladly sacrifice middle-class American jobs so that other countries, (Japan, China, Korea, Latin American, etc.) will defer to us in international relations. Secondly, business interests have steadily been raping middle-class American jobs since 1974. Special interest groups in combination with the American State Department have basically sold out middle-class American jobs in order to pursue their own agendas.

Included in the special interest groups that sponsor raping the middle class is *The Washington Post* and *The Atlantic Constitution*. Phyllis Schlafly recently wrote an article entitled "The Secret Media Subsidies in WTO/GATT."[77] Schlafly notes within the provisions of the new WTO/GATT agreement is a secret addendum to the treaty, which will allow the owners of the both major papers to have a subsidy of at least 65 million dollars and possibly several hundred million dollars in cellular phone licenses. Could it be that major newspapers are in reality the willing servants of the rich and powerful? Could it be that major newspapers are slavish followers of Clinton and Congress because they too, are dipping in the wells of greed that accompany the destruction of the middle class? Is it possible that California's loss of 400,000 jobs due to foreign trade inequities and New York's loss of 260,000 jobs has not been trumpeted in the major newspapers because money talks and the middle class walks?

When Ross Perot debated Vice President Al Gore on NAFTA, he made (according to the national media), the mistake of calling the Vice President a liar. Mr. Perot pointed out that the NAFTA agreement was deeply flawed and that once it was in place, Mexico could easily turn the tables on us by devaluing the Peso. Vice President Gore pooh poohed his response and instead diverted the audience by making glowing statements about the hundreds of thousands of jobs that would be created in the United States by NAFTA.

Three things can be learned now that time has passed. The first is that Perot is not a politician. Politicians speak the language of Machiavellian deceit. They call black white, bad good and make promises they have no intention of keeping. Perot called a spade a spade; in this case a liar a liar and proved to the world that he was not a politician. On the other hand, we now find that just as Perot predicted, Mexico devalued the peso in January of 1995 by thirty percent. This devaluation had the effect—as Perot predicted, of increasing jobs in Mexico and destroy jobs in the United States.

The situation in Mexico is now so bad that Clinton wants to use forty billion of our dollars to prop up the Mexican economy.[78] The purpose of this aid is to cover Clinton's mistake. Instead of producing a greater market for the United States, we now find that U. S. Products are 33% higher and Mexican products are 33% cheaper. Clinton intervened to support the peso to protect not us, the middle class but his own reputation and the investment of big money banks like City Bank of New York that purchased Mexican bonds. As *The Economist foreign banks own (<biblio>) 70% of Mexico's bonds.*

You might ask yourself another question, if Clinton is willing to take forty billion of our dollars to rescue Mexico's falling economy, would your flesh and bones of your sons and daughters be far behind if civil disorder breaks out in Mexico?

The second thing we find out is that Gore's solemn predictions and comments about NAFTA were all lies. He is truly a politician and a master of Machiavellian deceit.

The third thing we find is that not one major publication in the national media apologized to Perot and said something like "Oops you were right about NAFTA and Gore." Perhaps not only the politicians are masters of Machiavellian deceit, possibly the national media has also become practitioners of the big lie?

Pat Buchanan believes America is becoming two countries.[79] While new partners at Goldman Sachs celebrated Christmas with bonuses of $5,000,000. each, one million more Americans fell into the poverty range. While middle-class income in real dollars fell twenty percent in twenty years, where are the politicians and media to speak for the middle class? Instead, we hear a deafening silence while *The Washington Post* slavishly laps at Clinton's and Congress's feet and solemnly reports the profound sayings of former Labor Secretary Robert Reich that free trade has had nothing to do with the attrition of good manufacturing jobs.

And the fall of the middle class has been exceedingly great. Rosenbaum quotes Calvin Johnson, a lobbyist for the A.F.L.—C.I.O., who said "the problem is what to do with a 40 year old auto worker who's used to making $45,000 to $50,000 a year. No one has ever figured out how do we retrain the middle class." Rosenbaum further cites Anthony Carnivale, the chief economist for the American Society for Training and Development who reported studies which show that 60 percent of displaced middle-class workers are back to work within one year *at jobs which are ten percent lower for service workers and twenty percent lower for manufacturing workers.*

What is not emphasized is that 35 to 40 percent of the middle class never again earn the monies made in their original jobs. Think about that! Two million jobs a year throughout the 90's are being lost. And 800,000 middle-class workers never again able to earn what they do now.

A friend of mine who is a managing engineer at G.M., reports that one of their new employees was forced to sell his $400,000 home in California for $250,000. In a very real sense, his whole life savings were wiped out in one year. When he came to Michigan, he had barely enough funds to rent an apartment, let alone buy a new house.

Former U.S. Labor Secretary Robert B. Reich, is supposedly an expert in training and retraining workers. He hopes to overcome the hostility of the middle class by again proposing vague and extended training programs. This of course, is another exercise in the big lie! What value are extensive training programs if there are no new developing industries to employ them?

Let's consider the whole issue of international trade from the perspective of the middle class who suffers the most. Imagine that we are laborers living in Southern Italy. We need an income to support our family. The Mafia barons, who control everything, drive up in their luxury vehicles and ask each of us to stand on a tree stump and state how much a day we are willing to work for. Then they take the laborers who ask for the least.

The first thing to go is social security, followed by Worker's Compensation, than Unemployment Compensation. Health insurance is not even mentioned, child labor laws are ignored, and the mere mention of a union is enough to land you in a cement box. Pollution controls are a figment of one's imagination and a minimum wage is nonsense. Would you stand for that? Would you allow that to happen in the United States? Guess what? You already are and the politicians (who are owned by special interests) have so far successfully hidden it from you.

The two million middle-class jobs lost each year are going to countries where labor costs the least. They go to countries such as China (who often have *SLAVE LABORERS ASSEMBLE TOYS IN LABOR CAMPS TO BE SOLD BY TOY STORES IN THE UNITED STATES*), Asia and Third World countries. Do you seriously believe that these countries have a social security system, worker's compensation, unemployment insurance, health care, child labor laws or pollution controls? They do not. And as Ernest F. Hollings states what they do have is easily circumvented.[80]

How can the Democratic Party seriously propose increased social security taxes, health insurance, and other social programs, yet wring its hands and say we can't protect American jobs in the "global economy." Nonsense. These jobs can be protected. They choose not to protect middle-class jobs simply because they don't care, and because the middle class does not fund their campaigns.

Think about this for a moment. If social security is a good idea (which it is), why punish American workers by requiring employers to cover their employees? If the Democratic Party *really cared about the middle class they would simply make sure the playing field is equal!!* How to do this? Nothing could be simpler. If you tax American employers 7 percent of wages to pay for social security, then each country that does not have social security has a tax of 7 percent levied on the proportion of their product produced by labor.

If Japan does not have a social security plan and ships a $25,000 car to the United States and $19,000 of the car's cost is labor, then a tax of 7 percent would be added to the $19,000 to make the playing field equal. And tax monies from this equalization tax would be assigned to the Social Security Fund. Of course, if this were actually implemented, you'd hear howls of pain and anguish from the rich and monied interests who pay the election costs of Republicans and Democrats.

We would also hear dark words about trade wars, depression, and other nonsense. The point is simple. If politicians want to impose a certain basic minimum of economic justice for workers based on principals of common decency, they also have an obligation to prevent Americans from losing jobs to countries which lack these same standards.

But, they choose to ignore this contradiction. Why? Because of the implied non-verbal contract between Democrats and Republicans. The Democrats purport to be known as the "party that cares;" in return, the Republicans, allegedly conservatives who represent business, are allowed to transcend all the liberal programs by moving their plants *out of the country!*

This same agreement occurs throughout the industrial world and affects Canada, Germany, France, Italy, Sweden, etc. But this doesn't have to be. If the middle class were to *INSIST THAT IN A GLOBAL ECONOMY THEY HAVE A RIGHT TO AN EQUAL PLAYING FIELD,*

*YOU WOULD NOT SEE THE UNITED STATES LOSING TWO MIL-
LION JOBS A YEAR.*

Consider Japan again. Government leaders tell us we must stay competitive with Japan. But is Japan competitive? Are we allowed to sell our
rice in Japan? Of course not. Japan claims a right to protect their three
hundred thousand rice farmers. But government leaders say nothing
about the millions of autoworkers, electronic workers, steelworkers, and
glass workers who have lost their jobs. Why? Because the Democrats
don't care about middle-class jobs, and the Republicans have figured
out a way to get around the problem of economic justice by moving
plants overseas.

The Republicans watch the Japanese shaft the United States middle
class and basically copy their methods, while the Democrats pretend
none of this is happening. The question has to arise: Why would the
Democrats choose to ignore this gross injustice to the middle class?

The answer is much simpler than it looks. Middle class workers tend
to be conservative, and if they anticipate a rosy future will vote
Republican. Only when faced with the danger of losing their job or
anticipate a problematic future will they vote Democrat. George Bush
and Dole was defeated because he chose to ignore middle-class hopes
and aspirations. Now, Bill Clinton and the Democratic Party are deafening in their silence about middle-class jobs and aspirations. Why?
Simple, they don't stand to benefit by helping the middle class.

A middle class that is fat, happy, and optimistic vote's conservative.
So the trick is make sure things get worse while giving the appearance
of doing something for the middle class.

National health care is a typical smoke screen behind the Democrats
is hiding behind. They wring their hands and acknowledge that middle-
class workers are losing their jobs and benefits and risk everything by
not having health care. Their solution? A compulsory labor tax, which
will cause a torrent of jobs to leave the United States. If they really cared,
they would simply tax every product that comes from countries, which

do not provide health care to the same rate it, costs employers in the United States.

Have you heard President Clinton or his First Lady suggest an equal playing field? Of course you haven't. Why not? Simple! *IT'S NOT THE ECONOMY, STUPID! IT'S WHO PAYS FOR PRESIDENTIAL ELECTION CAMPAIGNS!!!*

Remember this fact, however. You don't have to allow the destruction of the middle class. You can do something! If only a small minority of the middle class votes against each and every incumbent in each and every local and national election, you will be literally amazed at how quickly new elected leaders suddenly discover ways to help the middle class improve their life.

Do you really want to protect your job? Then talk to your spouse, your voting-age children, your friends, your co-workers, and despite all the lies you hear in each and every campaign, vote against the incumbent. No matter how much you hear the incumbent talk about jobs, don't believe them. Remember that each and every T.V. commercial, each and every radio blurb, each and every newspaper advertisement, and each and every poster was paid for by someone who either wants to raise your taxes or move your job overseas!

Of course you may argue, that's also true of the challenger who wants to unseat the incumbent? You're right. But if the American middle class continues to vote incumbents out, regardless of political affiliation, race, sex, or education, we *eventually* will get incumbents who want to keep their job enough to turn on the special interests which paid for their campaign.

My own estimate is that within six years, in three national elections, we would see a dramatic turn around. Unfortunately, most people prefer the devil they know as opposed to the devil they don't know. Thus, the natural tendency of the middle class is to stick to the known. Remember, though, that in this case the known means losing at least two million jobs a year.

I humbly submit that a dose of the unknown in the form of consistently kicking out all incumbents is preferable. If you would seriously like to study this issue more, please obtain a copy of the following four books: Paul Krugman, *PEDDLING PROSPERITY: ECONOMIC SENSE AND NONSENSE IN THE AGE OF DIMINISHED EXPECTATIONS;* Wallace C. Peterson, *SILENT DEPRESSION;* Dr. Ravi Batra, *THE MYTH OF FREE TRADE;* and Ross Perot, *SAVE YOUR JOB, SAVE YOUR COUNTRY.* The first three are economists.

Mr. Perot has successfully been smeared and labeled as a mental case, a paranoid megalomaniac with poor judgement and hostile, grandiose intentions. When my patients ask me if they are paranoid. I tell them this: *If they really are out to get you, it's not paranoia.* Despite his well-known and well-publicized limitations, Perot touched a nerve. He pointed out the perfidy of our politicians and state department. Now, we have to take the next step and remove them all from office!

In his televised debate with Vice President Gore, Perot suggested the need for a social tax. What he meant by that was the need to protect the gains that Americans have made in economic justice, i.e., unemployment compensation, worker's compensation, health insurance, vacation time, forty hour work week, over-time compensation, safety standards in the work place, etc.

Vice President Gore chose to ignore Perot's point and instead changed the subject. Gore chose to praise the virtues of having a huge trading block consisting of Mexico, the United States and Canada. He proclaimed the stability and bright prospects of Mexico. Gore believed that Mexico could spend the United States and Canada into prosperity. Let's leave Vice President Gore and Mr. Perot in Washington in the throes of their debate.

The issue as C.E.O. John Pomerantz of Leslie Fay Fashions wrote to Congress has already been settled, NAFTA is a reality. So instead of belaboring NAFTA, I would like to praise the virtues on a person who only had a sixth grade education. A man who never in his whole life earned more than $132.43 a week. My father married my mother in 1933 in the midst of the Great Depression. To him, the cause of the Great Depression was simple. The great robber barons of industry had successfully co-opted the American Labor Force and forced the average working man to work for 25 cents an hour (which in real wages far exceeds the 41 cents an hour the Guatemalans are currently being paid).

So, the robber barons of industry produced goods that Americans couldn't buy! It wasn't tariffs that produced the "Great Depression" it was good old-fashioned greed. Henry Ford recognized this problem when he defended the higher wages he paid his employees by saying that he had to at least pay his employees enough to purchase one of the cars they made!

So as fewer and fewer Americans earn wages sufficient to participate in the "American Dream", politicians distract us by extolling the virtues of having this huge trading block of Mexico, the United States and Canada. The stability and bright prospects of Mexico are proclaimed while others such as Hugh Dellios present a touch of "cold water" (*Chicago Tribune*, March 27, 1994).

Mr. Dellios pointed out that even before the assassination of Luis Donaldo Colosio (the presidential candidate of the dominant P.R.I. party) there were signs that "Mexican society was more troubled than supporters of NAFTA would admit." Rebels of the Zapatista National Liberation Army were attacking outposts, seizing land, taking over town halls, and killing political leaders. Seeing their livelihood threatened and their hopes of having their own land dashed, Zapatistas reacted with violence.

The fact is that Mexico is not the democracy that Vice President Gore portrayed it to be. The dominant P.R.I. party has been in power since 1929. Given 65 years of continuous one party rule, can it be anything other than authoritarian and corrupt?

What then is the attraction to Mexico, China, and other cheap labor countries? The answer is all too simple. Politicians in this country have made conditions so difficult for employers, they feel compelled to move their factories out of this country and our same politicians have done and are doing nothing to protect the just gains of American workers.

Politicians hide behind the facade of trade war and the implied threat of another worldwide Great Depression. Am I suggesting that we close our borders to international trade? No. But I again state emphatically that we need a social tax, and we need to hold our politicians more accountable for their actions.

Each time there's a regulation or tax on goods made in this country, we should tax goods coming into this country who do not have the regulation or tax in their country at the same rate. Such actions make it immediately obvious to all consumers what the politicians and bureaucrats in Washington are doing.

Forcing politicians and bureaucrats to come out of the closet and present their actions in the broad light of total disclosure will go a long way toward increasing productivity, thus improving the real economic growth of every American.

I started this chapter with a true story and I want to end it the same way. This story is one, which is taking place this moment. Jim, Bill, and Walter have been picketing an engineering firm all day in 90-degree heat and 100 percent humidity. They have worked for this firm for over 25 years. Each earns the top union wage of $14.56 an hour. Jim, Bill, and Walter have not received a wage increase in ten years. During the ten years their wages have increased and then have been cut as they struggled to keep their plant open in the face of "international competition."

The "final straw" came last week. The 110 employees were told that the company wanted to stop paying insurance for its retired employees. They were also told if the employees didn't agree, the company would move its factory to Mexico within two years. Backs against the wall; Jim, Bill, and Walter voted with their union to strike. As Jim told me, "If you don't have your integrity, you don't have nothing anyway. How can I turn my back on these guys (retirees)? Some of them can't even afford to pay the co-pay on our miserable insurance plan, what are they going to do? If we have to lose our jobs anyway, to *hell with it and them, I'm going down fighting!"*

NOTE

Common Cause reports that since the 1992 Presidential Election, Democrats have collected $40.5 million dollars in "soft money".[81] And once the master of deceit, President Clinton entered office, the forty million dollars became a drop in the bucket. Soft money is money that does not have to be officially accounted for as to source and purpose. President Clinton dined with 1,800 prosperous contributors who paid $2 million dollars for the privilege June 22, 1994. Common Cause now labels the Clinton Administration the "king of the corrupt soft-money system."

Common Cause is further bothered by the fact that many of the same contributors who provided hundreds of millions of dollars in "soft-money" to Presidents Reagan and Bush are now attending the same soft-money events that produce dollars for the "New-Democrats". Perhaps Pearl Novak, Marie Whitt, Jeanie Kowalewski, Jim, Bill and Walter need to ask themselves and their friends a simple question, *if the same monied interests that supported Presidents Bush are now supporting President Clinton, is it possible that these Administrations aren't really that different?*

Reducing the Cost of Government

"What is your mission? Is it still the right mission? Is it still worth doing? If we were not already doing this, would we now go into it?"[82]

How many times have you heard politicians promise to "bring back dollars from Washington?" When they say that, they are in reality promising to support, continue and expand government waste.

Peter Drucker, the father of corporate restructuring, notes that if were really serious about reinventing government, we could eliminate the deficit within a few years and that would mean we could cut interest in half and substantially cut your taxes. But he also notes that the bureaucracy, federal employee's unions and Congress would not stand for *real restructuring!*

Although we are now in 1999 told that there is a surplus, what do we hear? We read in newspapers and see on television that the importance is not the surplus but how we now must spend it. Do we use it for shoring up Social Security or do we cut taxes or do we add new government programs or increase the size of existing ones? Notice no one says, leave it alone, let it build.

There are three approaches to restructuring: 1)-making government more efficient. When politicians talk making things more efficient they are really saying keep on doing the same thing but make it cost less. In other words don't take services away—just pay less for them. Advocating this approach pushes for savings that results in small savings if any, but doesn't cost votes; 2) meat axing government which produces yells and pain and which the bureaucracy usually turns to its advantage. Clinton sandbagged (Newt Gingrich and the new Republican Congress when he refused to sign the budget. President Clinton conveniently forgot about reinventing government.[83] Instead, he smiled as Republicans were stupid enough to cut popular programs. This was the same strategy that the socialist party used in Sweden to regain political control. They allowed the Conservative Party to cut so many programs they alienated Swedish citizens); and 3) rethinking your mission. Rethinking usually results in improvement of services and a cost reduction of about 40%.

But to rethink there has to be enough pain and pressure to cause the "rascals in control" to change their mode of operation. Our particular rascals are well adapted to stealing our hard earned tax dollars. As an example, do you know the tremendous burden increasingly shouldered by the middle class to pay for government pensions? (See *Wall Street Journal*, 6-1-94). In 1970 Federal retirement programs cost the taxpayers $5.3 billion; in 1993, taxpayers paid out $65 billion. A retired Congressman who contributed a total of $50,000 from his salary now receives $9,410 a month, or over $100,000 a year. Half of his monies come from cost of living adjustments that Congress awarded federal retirees at our expense. This Congressman expects to receive over **ONE MILLION DOLLARS IN THE NEXT TEN YEARS!** That million dollars comes directly out of our taxes. Is this an exception or the rule?

Congress evidently thought it to be the rule. As a cost cutting device, they once passed a law which would have frozen cost of living increases for governmental employees over five years as part of the

Gramm-Rudman-Hollings Law for a savings to the taxpayer of over $130 billion dollars. Congress quickly rescinded their law after one year when the National Association of Retired Federal Employees delivered a threat to key Congresspersons to go after them in the next election.

Let's consider several basic truths. Firstly, Congress can be influenced by dedicated dissatisfaction of even a minority of voters (such as retired governmental employees) and secondly, once they start a program in motion, they create a constituency of beneficiaries who begin to depend on the program (such as cost of living adjustments) who become furious with Congress when it changes directions and tries to stop the program. Thirdly, Congress has learned to start spending programs but is deathly afraid to stop them! The only answer for Congress is to hide the fact that they play fast and loose with our monies. Instead, they talk as if they are going to do something when they know that the only real thing they are willing to do is take even more of our monies to feed their pet constituencies.

In true Machiavellian form, "they must promise us everything and provide us nothing." Consider Vice President Al Gore's 1,100 page book on "Re-inventing Government," a ponderous pontification of ways to cut or control government costs. Shakespeare's Macbeth could truly have described it as "a tale told by an idiot, full of sound and fury, signifying nothing." If you were a "true believer" and supported Vice President Gore's quest, I suggest your write your Congressperson and ask for a copy of "Re-inventing Government." On the other hand if you are a realist, I suggest you read Martin Gross's book, *A CALL FOR REVOLUTION,* or the February, 1995 article in *The Atlantic Monthly* by Peter Drucker.

Rather than bother with the "big lie," this chapter will be the shortest one in the book—and probably the most effective, if the principles stated herein are followed.

First, a few personal stories. For seven years, I worked for the State of California as a psychiatric technician. Following that period, I worked for the Utah State Training School as a behavior modification technician. Later, I worked for the Utah State Hospital as a clinical psychology intern. After receiving my doctorate, I worked for the Central Intelligence Agency, then became an administrator of a mental health clinic in Michigan. Before finally entering private practice, I was an associate professor in psychology at Saginaw Valley State University.

Since I have had several years of experience working as a government employee, a story told by one of my clients did not surprise me. Jim, an administrator for one of the local social service agencies, came into my office one day quite disgruntled. "I just don't understand people," he said, shaking his head.

"What do you mean?" I asked.

"In our lunch room, I overheard two social service workers bragging about all the free services and money they were getting for their clients. Boasting, they said they were counseling welfare recipients not get a job and instead to get as much as they could from the government. I don't understand it. Don't they realize that money is *our* money?"

Jim is an unusual administrator. Most of the administrators I have encountered would have patted the two workers on the back and not thought once about the cost to the middle class. In my experience, bureaucrats seek security by continually justifying their positions. They protect their jobs by creating needs. Either they encourage recipients to ask for more and more services, or they create more and more regulations.

Why? For the singular purpose of building their nest, i.e., hiring more employees, having a bigger budget, a more spacious office, greater influence, etc. Then they reward the major politicians who help them by spending a portion of their budget in the politician's district. Thus, the politician can brag how he is furthering his district's economic growth. One wonders why newspaper editors congratulate politicians for "bringing dollars back home?"

Why do they ignore the real fact that they only way politicians can "bring dollars back home" is by sending our dollars to many other homes!

As each presidential candidate campaigns for office, everyone vows to reduce government waste and corruption. What nonsense! They have no intention of doing so, for one simple practical reason. By the time they have enough stature to run for office, they have learned a sad lesson: bureaucrats are expert at padding and protecting their nests. When the budget fails to cover government expenses, rarely if ever do the politicians try to reduce costs. Instead, they reach for the taxing manual.

One of my first experiences with governmental budgeting occurred when I was a psychiatric technician in a large California mental hospital. Due to my indecision about my college major, I had taken a few years off to work before returning to school. When I did return I was married, so I needed income enough for both living and educational expenses. I worked my way through school by working in a mental hospital.

One day while on an errand for a RN, I heard loud arguing. To my surprise, I saw the director of the hospital listening to a shouting match between the director of food services and the Business Manager. As a lowly peon, I did not want to stare or appear to be listening to their conversation. So I turned the corner and remained out of sight. But I heard every word.

The gist of the argument was simple. The director of food services had economized during her first year at the hospital, saving the hospital over $250,000. This was 1963, a quarter of a million dollars was not chicken feed. The business manager was incensed. Because of the peculiarities of budgeting in California, if she turned the money back to the state, the hospital's food budget would be reduced by that very amount the following year. The business manager argued that if their population expanded or food costs increased, they would lack the extra money to cover expenses. It was one month before the budget year ended and he wanted her to spend every penny.

The director of food services, however, believed she had a responsibility to do her job as economically as possible. This argument continued for several minutes until both fell silent and turned to the hospital director. After a long pregnant silence, he uttered only two words, "Spend it."

For the next month, 4,200 patients and 1,200 employees ate like kings!

If you are have any experience in civil service—municipal, city, county, state, or federal—I'm sure you know similar horror stories. How do the bureaucrats get away with such an amazing record of waste? The problem is relatively simple. Bureaucrats are limited in how much money they earn, so instead, they look for other sources for their strokes, i.e., power, plush offices, big desks, bigger budgets, etc. They also understand that the more people that they hire, the more padding they have before they can be laid off. They also become expert at creating a demand for their services by manufacturing regulations or needs which increase their budgets. If politicians threaten their turf, they squeeze the politician where the squeezing is easiest.

As a simple example, take your local school district. What is the first thing to go when the school declares it lacks the funds for their program? Bussing and athletics are the first programs to get the axe. Why? Because they are the most popular. Who ever heard of a School Board threatening to lay off the assistant superintendent, vice principal, or curriculum director?

Bureaucrats have learned that if you want to protect your budget, you develop popular programs. If your budget is threatened, the most popular program gets the axe first. This generates tremendous pressure from the public to give more money to the program. Politicians are not fools. They know that if they urge bureaucrats to cut the budget, the voters in their district will protest. So the politicians say the right thing (reduce expenses and waste) but have no intention of actually following through.

In a photo opportunity session in 1993, Vice President Gore presented President Clinton with his 1100 page book on how they would re-invent government and reduce costs. Have we yet seen any confirmation this will really occur? Or, for every dollar they save re-inventing government, will they find five dollars to spend on new programs? This seems just another example of the big lie, in which government and politicians specialize.

In addition to the normal waste and ever-increasing budgets, which plague our country across all levels of government, there is another disturbing and popular source of legalized robbery. That is, "bringing back our tax dollars." This comment is frequently heard from politicians who run for office. This phrase is another way to say that our politician will exert as much pressure as they can to create government *spending* in their district. What they fail to add is the only way they can accomplish their proposed task "to bring back tax dollars," is to get other politicians to agree to *spend* the tax dollars.

We know that the "old boy network" lives and dies on the premise of "if you scratch my back, I'll scratch yours." Each time your elected representative "brings back tax dollars," rest assured the representative also agreed to spend your tax dollars on projects in the other politician's districts. For each dollar sent to your district, the fact is that many more were sent elsewhere.

Although I have dwelled for the most part on problems at the federal level, be aware that the federal government is the model for the state, county, city and municipal governments. If the federal government rarely if ever tries to cut spending and focuses on increasing income (taking your money in various disguised forms), you can be sure other taxing districts will follow the same pattern.

In 1999, the effect of E-mail on the post office produced a proposal from the post office that each mail sent should be taxed 5 cents. Their explanation was that they had lost several hundred million dollars in unsent mail because of the inter net. Notice that they choose to expand their income not cut their services.

If we are finally to get control of our money and improve our lives, we must shock the whole system, not just the President and Congress, but the whole system. This is why I continue to stress that to regain control of our lives and improve the lot of the middle class, we must conscientiously vote against each incumbent at every level of government. We need to do this until one of the major parties decides to represent the middle class, or a new independent American party is formed which owes its allegiance to the middle class.

You might ask at this point, how can the middle class hope to control the growth of bureaucracies if they are so adept at padding their nest, hiding their skeletons, and generating public support by slashing popular programs? The answer is absurdly simple. In my long years of professional practice I have learned that there are simple answers to complex questions. In real life there are usually only simple answers and simple questions, providing you have the courage to ask the question and listen to the answer.

How to gain control of and reduce, even downsize, the bureaucracies? The question is do we really want to downsize government? Remember, bureaucracies do not generate money or goods, they simply take your money, and in order to justify their existence, try to restrict your life "in your best interest." Is a significant number of the middle class prepared to risk downsizing government? I believe they are.

Downsizing government can be accomplished relatively easily. We simply bonus each mid-level and above bureaucrat a sum of money equal to 15 percent of annual pay when the bureaucrat has succeeded in reducing the department's budget by two percent. During the next ten years, if we targeted those offices which we did not want to grow and offered these bonuses, you would be amazed at how easily the bureaucrats would suddenly economize and gradually cut their budgets,—and do so without generating popular anger and pressure on incumbent politicians.

Reducing the administrative budgets of each department at all levels of government by two percent a year would, in and of itself, save hundreds of billions of dollars. Inflation would cease, the budget deficit would disappear, interest rates would go down, and your taxes would be reduced.

Another important benefit arising from a reduced government would be that our life and the lives of our business concerns (which create the jobs that support the middle class) would be freer. Bureaucracies have to justify their existence by creating regulations, which then require them to hire more bureaucrats. If we now reward the bureaucrats for downsizing rather than increasing their budgets, I believe we will see them re-examine the necessity and importance of their many regulations.

A key factor is to make sure the bureaucrats don't collect their bonus without really downsizing. This means we need new bosses who have a real awareness that their jobs depend on making sure that the bureaucrats do not play number games. Who are the bureaucrat's bosses? The politicians *you* elect. A new crop of politicians will be very aware of the fragility of their positions if they fail to keep a cold, stern eye on bureaucrats at all levels of government.

I'd like to close this chapter by discussing an experience of one of my clients. A systems analyst, Jan was employed by a city near Detroit to improve the efficiency of their services. Soon she had all of their basic systems on computer, which allowed them to cut in half clerical support. But Jan, who now monitored payrolls, noticed how many of the police officers made sixty to eighty thousand dollars a year working overtime. She offered a plan to reduce payroll, which would have affected many police officers. Shortly, thereafter she was fired.

She moved to Ohio and became a city manager of a mid-sized municipality. Again, she controlled costs, but then made the mistake of trying to improve the efficiency of the parks department (which had entered into a "sweetheart" deal with a contractor who was the brother-in-law of one of the elected politicians). Again, she found herself out of a job. Not surprisingly, Jan any longer works for government. She owns and operates her own small business.

As citizens we can not look over the shoulder of every politician in every level of government, but we can provide a powerful stimulus to get them to police themselves.

Several years ago, James Blanchard ran for governor of Michigan on a campaign of "Jobs, Jobs, Jobs." But after his election, in consort with a Democrat-controlled House and Senate, he passed "taxes, taxes and taxes." Citizens of Michigan, incensed by this betrayal, recalled some members of the state legislature. The politicians in Michigan have never forgotten what happened. Prior to the recall, they had believed the people to be so stupid that a tax increase could be passed early in the Administration and then forgotten by the time new elections happened.

Citizens of Michigan, and now the Citizens of New Jersey, have proved otherwise. But the lesson has still not been learned. In typical deceitful form, soon after President Clinton was in office another tax increase was passed. This package was supposed to eliminate the deficit. Now we read in the *New York Times*[84] that Clinton has decided not to reduce the deficit. But as fate would have it, the decrease in interest rates allowed the deficit to be eliminated. Were it not for reduced interest and an improved economy, your taxes would have gone to a politician who decided to bring the money back home. If we are really serious about improving our lives, isn't it time we sent a message to politicians at all levels of government?

You might wonder why I have so easily dismissed the efforts of our Vice President and his "Re-inventing Government Committee." In that regard, I agree with Sir Thomas More (1478-1535) whose view of Utopia was that in an equitable society, the vast majority of laws are not necessary as each person could be relied upon to do the right thing. Conversely, he said laws were simply vehicles for wicked and dishonest people to hide behind. The "Re-inventing Government Committee" developed is an open invitation for calculating bureaucrats to practice subversion of the public's needs.

A simple example: One year President Clinton tells us we must tax ourselves to reduce the deficit and the next year he is spending billions of dollars to try to get Christians and Muslims to love each other. One could understand his intent if there was some creative effort to reduce the cost of other programs or increase their efficiency. Neither option appears to exist in his proposals in their present form. For instance, consider the crime proposal of "three strikes and you're out." How many more prison cells (at $300,000 a cell) will need to be built? How many young offenders will spend the next fifty years in prison (at $30,000 dollars a year maintenance)? The one simple way to reduce government costs? Take the same self-serving people who *expanded* government and now make it worth there while to *contract* government. Every other approach is simply so much whitewash or garbage.

To contract government, to eliminate the deficit, to reduce interest (cutting your house payment in half), and to cut your taxes in half, these simple questions have to be asked of each and every government program at every level of government. What is your mission? Is it still the right mission? Is it still worth doing? If we, were not already doing this, would we now go into it? These questions are what Peter F. Drucker calls rethinking government.[85]

As a simple example, only three percent of the population of the United States is still engaged in agriculture and only family farms represent half of the three percent. Yet we are spending 70 billion dollars of your money, providing a cabinet level position and tens of thousands of workers for what? The same question has to be asked at every city, county, state and local level. You have a right to keep your money in your pocket and you have a right to be as free as possible. Some government is necessary, but let's only keep the amount of government that makes sense. Going forward in the direction of challenging and rethinking government is neither Democratic nor Republican. And probably the only way we will succeed is to form a third party.

TAXES—The Argument for a flat tax

One chapter cannot cover all the myriad ways the middle class is abused in the taxing process. If you wish to pursue this topic further, I suggest you read the book, *AMERICA, WHO REALLY PAYS THE TAXES?* by Donald L. Bartlett and James B. Steele. Here, however are the basic highlights along with some of my own ideas.

Taxes are often portrayed as an incredibly complex maze of regulations, rules and exemptions. When Jesse Ventura was elected governor of Minnesota he was amazed to find that there were several thousand taxing districts within the state of Minnesota. Undaunted he has put together a focus group composed of representative citizens of Minnesota in hopes that common ground can be reached in finding ways to reduce taxes.

Actually, the issue of taxes can be extremely simple. But it is the nature of humans to make things complex-particularly when we are afraid to hear the answer. If we have the courage to ask the right question and are willing to listen to the solution, the complex often becomes simple.

Let's first ask the correct question and then listen to what answers we can obtain. Principally, we must consider the real issues. The economy is the engine of our nation, which provides the resources needed to live, and the means by which to obtain a living.

Economies have two general aspects, 1) a zero-sum game or 2) a zero-plus game. In a managed government, bureaucrats think of economies as a zero-sum game, but in a free market government, the people consider their land a zero-plus game.

Zero-sum basically means there is a fixed bowl of soup, and when one takes a cup of soup from the pot, they take away the opportunity for someone else to have a cup of soup. In a zero sum game, anything that helps one person has the potential of depriving another. In a zero-plus game, each transaction has the potential to benefit both parties. For example the post office bureaucrat who advocates taxing E mail is saying that each internet transaction takes away from potential income thus there are only so many possible letters and so much possible income. Each Internet message hurts the post office's budget. Classic zero sum thinking.

Zero-sum games exist in managed economies such as in the former Soviet Republics and in Cuba. They are rarely, if ever, successful. While the goal of managed economies is basically a noble one—to make sure everyone has a piece of the pie—, they often fail. Why? Inevitably, citizens in managed economies take the position, "if it helps you, it hurts me." This produces a self-centered, cynical view of life with little desire to be productive or cooperative.

The more an economy moves in the direction of being a zero plus game, the more likely the economy will be dynamic and powerful. Americans historically have had a zero plus game economy. Unfortunately, America is now moving toward a zero sum game.

Taxes and politicians in Washington are responsible for the dramatic change in our economic climate. Deficits and an ever-increasing tax burden are pushing us more and more into a zero-sum game, in which few do well and the economy continually worsens.

As an example, consider Joe Lunchbucket and Mary Hairspray. Joe earns $20,000 a year working for Ames Discount Tire; his wife Mary earns $10,000 a year working part-time in a nursing home. If she increases her hours to forty hours per week, they believe they'll have enough more money to buy the four-wheel drive truck they want. Not true! For every extra dollar they earn over $30,000 a year, they will have to pay 30 cents to the government.

This problem also affects Jim Teacher and Jane Secretary. Together, they earn $55,000 a year. Jim and Jane want to buy a cabin up North. Jim decides that part-time teaching position will earn him earn enough to begin payments on the cabin. Not true! For every dollar extra he earns for teaching a class, he will have to pay 43 cents to the government. The $6,000 extra he earns will amount to $3,420 after taxes.

But what about Frank Executive and Marilyn Business-owner? Their combined income is $300,000 a year. Marilyn wants to remodel her kitchen at a cost of $40,000. By extending her store hours, she estimates earning another $20,000 a year. Her added income will be taxed at the same rate of 43 cents a dollar. In 1965, it was taxed at 50 cents a dollar.

Well, you may say, at least things won't get worse. Not true! Social Security is expected to go bankrupt in 2029, Medicare will run dry in sooner, and the Social Security Disability Fund will run out of funds before that. As funds are added to these programs, added taxes will be proposed.

The basic fact of life in America at present is that politicians in Washington have raised the basic cost of hiring people while lowering employee's income earned. The result is a contracting economy with higher deficits, fewer job opportunities, and declining expectations. This fact of life is not peculiar to America. A study of 17 countries shows conclusively that big increases in payroll and personal income tax have resulted in massive job loss.[86] To further substantiate this fact, in the 1960's, payroll taxes were less than half of what they are now and unemployment averaged 4.6 percent. Increased taxes and declining job opportunities are responsible, I believe, for the ever-increasing dissatisfaction that most Americans have with politicians in Washington.

When President Clinton campaigned against Bush, he aptly responded to Bush's attacks against his character by saying "It's the economy, stupid!" However, as soon as he got into office, he immediately created the potential for worsening the economy by increasing taxes.

In the game of taxes for entitlements, a curious standoff has occurred in Washington. The Democrats have rather successfully portrayed Republicans as "nattaring nabobs of negativism." Thus, rather than say no to programs which inevitably move us toward a zero-sum economy, Republicans try as best as they can to reduce the pain to their primary constituents, instead of challenging unwise decisions. If there is any reason for an independent third party in America, it certainly manifests itself in the area of taxes. A third party could continue to characterize the Republicans as "nattering nabobs of negativism," while accusing the Democrats of being "whining whimps of waffledom."

It has become increasingly popular for the Democrats to insist that everyone pay their fair share. Another example of the big lie. The Democrats have absolutely no intention of having everyone pay their fair share. Only a year ago, the Democrats convinced us that they wanted to enact their 1993-tax increase in order to reduce the deficit. Many of us were skeptical about their so-called intention to reduce the deficit. The deficit actually was reduced but probably only because he refused to approve Republican programs and they barely cooperated with his proposals. LET'S HEAR IT FOR DIVIDED GOVERNMENT!

Will proposed tax increases reduce the deficit? Not if they continue to add more entitlement programs. Politicians in Washington want "voting clients" whom are convinced that the only way to survive is to "feed off" of the government. Feeders range from defense to agriculture, to law enforcement to prison administrations, to welfare. Their ability to graze at the government trough relates directly to how much *you* have to pay to support the government's programs. Remember, the politician's main interest is to please "voting clients" not improve the status of the middle class. To do this they want to exempt tens of millions of citizens who are too poor to pay. In fact, President Clinton's promise to "reform welfare as we know it" is not a program to reduce welfare costs. Although the details of the Administration's plan are yet to be approved, it is estimated that enacting welfare reform will cost at least an additional ten billion dollars a year. It is, in reality, a program to put more people on welfare and thus develop more "voting clients".

I have to give the politicians in Washington credit for their tremendous ability to lie with comfort. For instance, consider the term, "federal rebate?" In what sense is it a rebate? Did the low-income family pay money to the treasury, which is now being rebated? No! From whom is the money being rebated? From the taxpayers. It should really be called "a mandated income transfer from the middle class," which is money taken from you and given to "voting clients" of the incumbent politicians!

Is it only the Democrats who are playing games with your money! No, but the Democrats are less able to hide their actions, while the Republicans constantly seek for tax breaks for the rich. Consider all the monies paid to huge corporate farms for not producing anything, tax-free municipal bonds, building weapon systems we don't need, and transfers of hundreds of millions of dollars to newly defined personal charities. This clearly indicates how many politicians arrange to serve their "special clients."

According to *Newsweek* magazine (June 13, 1994), the estate of Jacqueline Kennedy Onassis is estimated to be approximately $200 million dollars. Over 90 percent of this will go to establish a charitable foundation to be managed by her two children, Caroline and John Jr. Not one penny of her vast estate will be paid in taxes! But this situation is not special or unique. Billionaire J. Paul Getty did the same thing! It's not new for billionaires not to pay taxes, Howard Hughes managed to pay no taxes while he was living in Las Vegas. Contrast the ability of billionaires and multi-millionaires to avoid paying any inheritance tax to the story of one of my clients whom inherited a machine shop from his father. The tax assessor estimated that he had one million dollars in equipment and buildings and issued a tax bill far beyond his means to pay. His company was actually just breaking even, as we were in the midst of an automotive downturn. He was soon forced into bankruptcy, and the entire contents of his business and equipment sold for less than his tax bill!

Isn't it time to stop this nonsense? Taxes should exist only to support the absolute minimum government expenses needed to further the interests of American society! Since the middle class comprises 80 percent of American society, tax laws should primarily benefit them and not hurt them, as is currently the case. Instead, both parties pretend to protect our back pockets by talking about tax incentives, economic enterprise zones, and "Federal rebates." Their *real* aim? Again, to create more "voting clients." The Democrats specialize in proclaiming how special efforts should "help the poor and those below the poverty line." But the specific things "done for the poor" usually creates more poor people.

In *The Economist,* an article entitled "Asian Values" (May 28-June 3, 1994) points out that ascribing the economic success of Asian countries to some secret and wonderful value system is ridiculous. There is a huge diversity in values among the countries of Japan, China, Singapore, India, and Malaysia. The Asian economies that have been brilliantly successful have in common three basic facts: low marginal tax rates, low welfare costs, and high investments in education!

It is time to drop the misconceptions that both Democrats and Republicans are foisting on the middle class. Poor people are not any more "noble" than others, and the rich are not inherently evil or despicable. Neither group should have a free ride. The poor pay through flat-rate social security taxes. The rich do not pay, as the Democrats and Republicans saw to it that the rich paid next to nothing to support the social security system. If we, as a society, endorse the idea that each of us should pay our fair share, then let's actually do so!

If the middle class intends to regain control of America, one of the first things that needs to be done is to prevent Washington politicians from being able to "feed their special interests." It's time to do away with tax shelters, tax loopholes, and special considerations. I propose the following changes to directly benefit and expand the middle class:

1) a ten-percent income tax with no deductions for individuals with deductions for businesses and corporations limited to the actual cost of doing business or producing goods,

2) a five percent national sales t ax ,

3) a five percent social security tax which only taxes the employee's income and not the employer, 4) a five percent wage tax to cover the cost of unemployment and worker's compensation,

5) a five-percent import tax on goods coming from countries, which do not have unemployment compensations, and worker's compensation.

If these taxes were implemented, you would soon see dramatic increases in real income and employment plus dramatic reductions in the cost of welfare! Each individual would pay a15% tax—10 income and 5% social security. Contrast that to now when if a person works overtime, as much as 40% of the added income could be taken in taxes. Also, every income—no matter how big or small would pay the same proportion. The billionaire who has an income of one hundred million dollars would pay ten million in income tax and five million in social security tax while the person who makes ten thousand a year would pay one thousand in income tax and five hundred in social security tax.

Consider the first proposal, a straight ten percent income tax with no deductions for individuals and only limited deductions for businesses and corporations. The first major cost advantage? We would drastically reduce the number of employees in the I.R.S.! Salaried employees would not have to file a complicated income tax form at the end of the year. Their tax would already have been collected and sent to the I.R.S. Only businesses and corporations would be audited to make sure they reported their earnings correctly and sent in the appropriate deductions on their employees.

Another major savings for the middle class would be in the area of accountants, business consultants, and attorneys. All these people have made their living by steering their clients through a maze of tax loopholes to protect the clients's income from taxes. No more of this garbage should be allowed. No tax loopholes and no excess taxes. Everyone can and should pay their fare share. A share of ten percent, regardless of income changes.

One of the loudest opponents of this idea would be Congress who would be advocating for their "special interest support groups." They would direly warn that municipal expenses would be higher because they wouldn't be able to sell tax-free municipal bonds. This is a plus not a minus. Millionaires would not be able to have hundreds of millions of dollars in tax-free municipal bonds and escape paying income tax or social security tax. And municipalities would find it more difficult to issue bonds except in the case where the public believes it is truly needed.

Conversely some in Congress would argue that the "truly poor" should be exempted from paying their fair share. While this may sound Christian and noble, the idea on examination, reeks of stupidity and deception. A graduated income tax serves as an escape clause for Congress. They can then go to you and say, I can provide this service and *someone else will have to pay for it!* Everyone in our society should pay an equal percentage so that no Congressperson can ever come to us and say you can have something for nothing! That kind of deceit has led to our present problems!

The next point to consider is the national sales tax. We all know an underground economy exists. Money that comes from crime, selling drugs, unofficial employment, etc. goes somewhere. Where? It ends up in products, real estate, or stocks and bonds. All of these should be taxed on sale at five percent. One client of mine was a gifted computer expert who regularly took money under the table for his special expertise. Officially, he earned so little his family qualified for food stamps! Of course, special interest groups will scream at the idea of a five-percent sales tax. They want their special exemptions. And if any of these are exempted, it will be at the cost of quality of life for the middle class.

Stockbrokers will argue that foreign investors will not want to invest in the United States. Hogwash! What else can they do with the money they make from selling products to Americans?

Mutual funds will argue they will not be able to sell their investments whenever stocks rise fifty cents or decrease fifty cents. Good! The purpose of stocks is to provide corporations with liquid funds to build their businesses and invest in the future. Mutual funds are now geared to day-to-day changes in the financial markets. A five-percent sales tax will force them to reorient their outlook to the long-term as opposed to the short term. This will force a sense of stability and moderation in a market, which has become too dominated by program buyers and computer experts. *IT IS TO THE ADVANTAGE OF THE MIDDLE CLASS TO HAVE LONG TERM STABILITY AND PREDICTABILITY IN THEIR FINANCIAL MARKETS!!!*

The imposition of a universal five percent sales tax will go a long way toward tapping the underground economy and, simultaneously, allowing the middle class to share their tax burden with everyone.

Let's consider the third point: The five-percent social security taxes which only the employee would pay. One of my ex-clients whom I call a "practicing psychopath," had a favorite comment: "Convince the man that you are protecting his back pocket while you take all you can from his front pocket." He said he found it surprisingly easy to show his new client how he saved them client five or ten dollars while he "took" the client for one hundred or two hundred dollars!

The Democrats have been particularly adept in engaging in class warfare. They pretend to be the protectors of the poor and lower classes, but in fact they rob American citizens of their wealth and hopes for the future by strangling our economy with increasing taxes and regulations. Republicans, on the other hand, are so busy protecting their wealth from the Democrats that they have little time for the middle class. The social security tax is an excellent example of how the Democrats and

Republicans combine to steal from our front pockets while pretending concern for our back pockets.

In 1968, President Johnson struggled to present a budget package, which would have monies for "guns and butter." As a result, an accommodation occurred in Congress. Democrats supported the proposition of a "unified budget" so they could continue developing "voting clients" through the "Great Society," and Republicans obtained their funds to feed the "Military-Industrial Complex" to further America's defending the world from Communism.[87] By having a unified budget, Washington was able to take in all monies from all funds and then write I.O.U.'s to the Social Security Trust Fund, while they spent its monies on welfare and war. To make matters worse, they tapped the poor and middle class for most of the monies while the wealthy got off scot-free!

The way the Social Security Tax has been massacred is an excellent example. The Democrats insist they are protecting the working individual by making sure the Social Security System is safe and well funded. Of course, this means increasing the taxes that we all pay. So they are protecting our back pockets while stealing from our front pockets. In point of fact, our government *owes* the Social Security Trust Fund *one trillion dollars!* If it had to pay interest on the debt, it would be paying the elderly 70 billion dollars a year—more than enough to pay for Medicare or for increased benefits to the elderly. But the government merely writes an I.O.U. instead of paying the elderly, telling us the Social Security Trust Fund is in danger of running dry and we need to increase payroll taxes!

The government has quietly and psychopathically convinced us that politicians in Washington are concerned about Social Security and are doing everything possible to protect us. What nonsense! If your salary amounts to less than $60,000 a year, you pay a social security tax every week, while the wealthy who earn ten times more pay social security for only the first five weeks of the year. And if all of your income comes from investments, property, stock, bonds, etc., *you pay nothing!* Notice the tricky accommodation, which exists in Congress. Democrats get to rape the Social Security Fund to pay welfare costs, and Republicans agree to it as long as their wealthy patrons don't have to pay into the fund!

The other major problem of social security as it is presently constituted is that by taxing both the individual and the employee, it becomes a major block to hiring new workers or increase wages. Small business, which hires most American middle-class workers, has to pay a 7.5 percent payroll tax on each of their employees and the small business owner has to pay a 15 percent social security tax on his salary. How does he do it? Three ways: 1) He gets by with the fewest workers possible. 2) He pays the least amount he can to his employees. 3) If he can, he hires "contract" employees on which he does not have to pay a social security tax. Or he does as much of his own work as he can.

The social security tax acts as a major drag on our economy. One could tolerate this , if it were fair and really helped the elderly. But how can it be fair when many of the wealthy don't pay one dime for social security? How can it be fair when the elderly are taxed out of their benefits if they choose to work past retirement age? And how can it be fair when a monstrous bureaucracy is employed to manage the fund?

Then the scoundrels turn around and create S.S.I. a system by which those who have never worked or worked too few years to qualify for social security and are thus unable to compete in the market place of competitively employed are able to collect social security benefits including Medicare.

Consider for a moment this simple but startling example. If you are middle aged and middle class and earn an average of $30,000 a year and your wife earns $30,000 a year. You are contributing $4,500 a year into the system. Your employer(s) also contributing $4,500 a year into the system. If you work from the time you are 22 till you are 62 that would mean you would have contributed in your name an average of $9,000 a year for forty years. This would amount to direct contributions of $360,000. If you even received simple interest of 5% a year compounded on your contributions your income at retirement should be close to $100,000 a year. If you really want to make yourself sick, call up your local insurance agent and ask him for the exact figures you could expect to receive from a policy which is funded for forty years at $9,000 a year vs. what the Social Security Fund will give you. *Then you will really know what the politicians in Washington have done to you rather than for you!*

Once the middle class gains control of government, social security needs to be re-evaluated so that the elderly get a fair life-sustaining share while wage earners contribute a reasonable proportion of their wages. My own belief is that once we straighten out government, a five-percent contribution will be more than enough to generate a comfortable retirement income.

We also have to consider the amount business contributes. Each time a small business has to contribute more in taxes, it responds by hiring fewer people or running closer to the edge of bankruptcy. Does it really make sense to tax wages? I think not. It is to the benefit of the middle class to make it possible for as many small to medium-size businesses to become as successful as possible.

Once the middle class gets the attention of incumbent politicians, a task force needs to be formed to really evaluate if it is in the best interest of the middle class to tax wages and if it is, how much should be taxed. By not taxing wages and by drastically reducing the social security bureaucracy, our nation could probably pay each of our elderly citizens at least fifty-percent more than they currently receive and the drag on the economy of taxing wages would be eliminated. This would mean that millions of more jobs would become available to the middle class with a resultant inevitable increase in wages. Remember the law of supply and demand. As demand for a product increases (in this case, wage earners), the cost usually also rises.

Instead of the middle class continuing to see their real wages decline as they have since 1973, they would experience real gains in income. Not just because they are paying less taxes but also because there would be more incentive for employers to pay them more. Having a set limit on income for the government will create subtle and continual pressure to reduce government expenses. (See Chapter 8 on reducing the cost of government.)

Consider a article in the Chicago Tribune (April 10, 1994) entitled "For some federal employees, work but a minor diversion." The article points out that the chaplain of the U.S. Senate receives $100,000 a year to open the Senate with prayer three days a week. He works at most 156 days a year from 9 A.M. to 3 P.M. Another wonderful job is that of Consul General to Bermuda., a job usually given to a high contributor to the party in power. A former owner of the job was Kellog heir L. Ebersole Gains. In return for contributing to the Republican Party , he was awarded a hilltop mansion, $100,000 a year in salary, tax-paid assistants and membership in a golf club. (When politicians sell influence to special interests, it is usually a great buy! For every dollar the special interest pays they usually can expect to receive at least a hundred of *your* dollars back! Of course, the politicians don't care, it's your money not theirs). Once we enact some simple cost saving incentives (described in detail in Chapter 7), and we maintain strict limitations on the taxes we pay, these nonessential non-jobs will disappear.

Another source of destruction of middle-class jobs is unemployment compensation and Workman's Compensation. Middle class jobs are particularly at risk when states play the game of cheaper worker benefits. Corporations move from state to state as states struggle to compete, by reducing unemployment compensation and worker's compensation. Big business moves plants to states that allow them to subvert the intent of worker's compensation.

First, we need to stop states from being forced to bid against each other. Then, we need to establish a standard benefit and standard tax to pay for unemployment compensation and worker's compensation. If we set the benefit for unemployment compensation at six months, period and we limit it to 80% of wages, we will stop states from bidding against each other at the expense of middle-class jobs. This will create long-term stability in the workplace.

Worker's compensation is supposed to protect workers from economic harm if they're injured at work. In reality Worker's compensation has developed into a system that protects big business, insurance companies and legions of attorneys, benefiting wage earners next to nothing. Worker's compensation, in effect, has destroyed more jobs for Americans than it has ever enhanced, seldom providing the protection for which it was initially designed.

Many factories have to pay anywhere from eleven cents for every dollar earned to a dollar for every dollar earned by their employees. My brother-in-law owned a sawmill. For every one hundred dollars he paid his employees in wages, he had to pay fifty dollars in Worker's Compensation taxes. In addition, since his line of work was seasonal, he also had to pay ten dollars for every hundred he paid in wages up to the first $9,000 earned plus seven dollars and fifty cents in social security taxes. Sawmills in Illinois only pay eleven cents an hour in Worker's Compensation for every dollar earned. As a result, he could not compete with sawmills from Illinois. As he fought to stay in business, his profit continually reduced to the point, he finally gave up in disgust. Needless to say, he didn't stay in business very long. Were it not for the onerous taxes he had to pay, he could have continued to employ almost twenty employees.

One could almost justify the high cost of Worker's Compensation if it really helped the worker. Not only do corporations close or move from to another state, they also leave the United States for countries in which there is no Worker's Compensation. Further, since Worker's Compensation is a direct tax on wages, business and corporations strive to keep wages as low as possible.

In addition, there is the personal element of Worker's Compensation. I'd like to share with you a typical case often seen in my practice. I emphasize typical, (meaning frequent, the norm, or business as usual). This case has happened so many times I've lost count of the number.

Jill injured at work, filed for Worker's Compensation, which is designed for two things: (1) Have Jill receive some form of compensation until she is able to return to work; (2) Pay all necessary medical expenses that are necessary to heal her injury. In return for these two benefits, Jill surrenders her right to sue her employer for the damages sustained on the job.

However, Jill's particular injuries did not heal quickly. After two months, her insurer, frustrated by her lack of progress in recovery, filed a Notice of Dispute. This action resulted in her insurer no longer paying for lost wages or reimbursing her for medical expenses. Now on her own, in desperation, she visited a Worker's Compensation attorney.

Doctors however, refused to see her when they weren't paid and others provided grudgingly minimal service. The same attorneys who represented Jill also lobbied successfully in the state legislature to pass a rule that allows those receiving worker's compensation to avoid payment of medical bills when the worker's dispute is resolved. This meant fewer doctors would risk treating patients, and more patients would settle for less than they were entitled because of their precarious financial situation. Her expenses mounted. It was then obvious to Jill how important savings are or other means of support , without resources, she could wind up homeless, or become an increasing burden on those whom she depends. As savings decrease, anxiety increases. An increased stress level interferes with the healing process. What does she do? If she is like ninety percent of the patients I have seen, she calls her attorney with mounting desperation and frequency. He apologizes and says he is waiting for a hearing date, which are few and far between. When they do come, there may be as many as fifteen cases scheduled on the same day. A case could also be scheduled five or six times over a period of two to three years before one is finally heard.

Jill is unaware that her attorney has several other cases scheduled for the same hearing date. In fact, with the opposing attorney , he discusses what cases they are willing to make an offer on and which clients are desperate enough to accept a "reasonable" settlement. When her attorney feels Jill is desperate enough, he reports he has an offer from the opposing side, also informing Jill that her case has "some problems." He might be able to get her wages re-instated (she earns $30,000 a year). She could collect her last eighteen months back pay plus medical expenses. But there is a catch. Jill's employer could file another Letter of Dispute, and they'd have to go back to court. However, if she is willing to sign off her case, the company would pay her $110,000, minus attorney's fees.

A desperate Jill accepts gratefully and thanks her "wonderful" attorney. But what's happened here? She has signed off on twenty years of income at $30,000 a year ($600,000); hoping her sudden fortune will pay off her current bills and help her find another job suited to her weakened condition. Who really benefited from this sick system? Certainly not Jill! She was given the royal shaft. Who benefited? The winners were her employer whom Jill could not sue because she was "covered" by Worker's Compensation, the insurance company which paid one sixth of its potential liability, both attorneys and the State of Michigan (which by keeping Worker's Compensation awards low maintains their competitive basis against other states).

Many politicians are also attorneys. Obviously, Worker's Compensation was designed by and for attorneys. If the injured worker is actually helped, it's usually by *accident* (no pun intended).

When Hilary Rodham Clinton proposed combining health insurance with Worker's Compensation and No-fault auto accident benefits, she no doubt did so with persons like Jill in mind. The problem is: how can we trust the same psychopaths who designed a system which "shafts" the average middle-class worker to now design one that will help them?

A new crew of politicians, with a new mandate to serve and protect the middle class, might well design a much-improved and fairer system. One, which does not discourage small business from hiring workers and also helps the worker injured during the course of employment.

Finally, we need to consider an import tax on products that enter the United States from countries who do not provide benefits such as unemployment compensation and worker's compensation to their workers. Let's simply tax products entering the United States from these countries with no benefits and apply the proceed s to the funds which pay for unemployment compensation and worker's compensation, social security and Medicare.

I would like to offer a challenge for you to consider: Inheritance tax and charitable exemptions. Why should a multimillionaire or billionaire be able to protect all of his inheritance from taxes at their death by establishing a charity or trust? I strongly doubt that the founding fathers ever considered that there would be multimillionaires and billionaires who would mask their inheritances by creating charities. Why should billionaire J. Paul Getty, for instance, be able to leave his money to an art museum and avoid taxes in the process. In reality, you and I paid for the J. Paul Getty Art Museum. We had to compensate for the taxes that J. Paul Getty's estate did not pay.

It seems only fair that all estates should be taxed at ten percent to those who inherit the money or property. Of course when a husband or wife dies, the surviving partner already entitled to half of the spouse's goods, would only have to pay a five-percent tax. Children or other beneficiary would have to pay ten percent on the balance. Thus, living trusts and other vehicles that avoid taxes would be eliminated.

Charities should also be considered. In the 1993-1994 *AMERICAN ALMANAC*, figures for 1991, charities received deductible contributions of $124 billion dollars! The assets of charities are over $2,000,000,000,000 (two trillion dollars). The founding fathers would have fainted in disbelief at how their conception of the separation of church and state has been perverted by special interests and politicians.

As of this moment, charities own property and monies equal to $100,000 for every man, woman and child in the United States. At the time America was originally populated, many of its citizens came from countries, which terrorized the common person to benefit the official "state-religion." Many countries had official state churches, which had the power to legally tax their citizens. As a result, great churches were built, land was taken, and the working class became increasingly poor and landless. Many starved to death or became homeless while the state religions hoarded their wealth. The reason the Communist Party of Russia was able to attack the Russian Orthodox Church when it came to power was the huge wealth the former acquired vis a vis the ordinary peasant.

Our founding fathers came to America determined not to establish a specific church or give churches the power to tax the citizens of the several states. Tax exemptions were viewed as a way to avoid double-taxing church members. Why for instance should the parishioners of a local simple church have to pay a tax and then again share in the burden of supporting government by having their church tithes taxed? This simple concept has been grossly perverted! Now we have a situation in which great wealth is protected and hidden under the guise of charity!

This needs to be radically changed! The middle class can not afford to fund the enormous amount of charities that now exist for the sole purpose of not paying their fair share. The middle class needs to exempt only places of worship and the direct cost of maintaining places of worship. All other aspects of charities should be taxed at the same ten percent rate that all of us have to pay. No exceptions!

Anyone working as a minister or employee of a church that receives more than twice the annual average wage (78k) should have his wages taxed at ten percent also. For example, suppose the Church of the Winding Gate has an income of four million dollars a year in donations (which is tax-free). The Church of the Winding Gate pays its preacher one million dollars a year in wage and benefits and its administrative director five hundred thousand dollars a year (Don't laugh: if you consider the income that some T.V. evangelists receive, my figures are underestimated). The Church of the Winding Gate pays no tax at present on these wages to the preacher or administrative director. Under the new law I propose, the Church would have to pay a ten percent income tax on the one-and-a half million dollars it is paying in excess wages and benefits.

A commission appointed by newly elected politicians could also design other fair and reasonable ways to reduce the cost of taxes to the middle class and eliminate the monstrous inequities that now exist.

To do this, the middle class needs to act now. We can cut taxes to a reasonable level, reduce the cost of government, and eliminate many inequities that now exist. But to do so, we have to terminate the careers of our current representatives. Are you ready? Are you game? Are you willing to take a chance? I am! Taking a chance, at first, will mean voting out all current incumbents and voting in new faces whose only hope for re-election will be to support middle class interests. Persons such as Richard W. Fisher in Texas (*NEW YORK TIMES,* "Texan Tries for Victory as New Sort of Democrat", April 6, 1994 will have to be elected and then booted out if they don't perform.

If you are willing to do this however, do not look for support in the national news media or major publications such as *TIME; U.S. NEWS AND WORLD REPORT, NEWSWEEK etc.* All of the major news sources are controlled or heavily influenced by special interests. Consider for instance *TIME,* magazine essay (April 11, 1994) by James R. Gaines. He suggests that America should not only continue to give China most favored nation status despite it's dismal human rights record but also give most favored nation status to Vietnam as well. Most favored nation status is another word for cutting tariffs so that middle class American jobs can be transferred to China and now to Vietnam.

As a middle-class person, can you think of even one reason why an American president or Congress should be allowed to trade your job to another nation so that nation will be kinder to its citizens. The very concept is typical of how Democrats think (who want to influence the world and, in the process, maintain a significantly large poor class: their "voting clients"), and how Republicans think, who want to take advantage of workers in countries which grant workers no rights at all. The national news media and both political parties are more than willing to trade your job and your taxes for influence in other countries. Can you change matters? Yes. Simply terminate the positions of *all current incumbents.*

WELFARE—Empowering the Poor—Abolishing Welfare Slavery

"Alcoholics and addicts crouching in tenements. Children without parent roaming the streets. Homeless men lining up at free soup kitchens. Abandoned women struggling to keep hope alive."[88] The year 1870.

"If I could offer a single prescription for the survival of America, and particularly Black America, it would be: Restore the Family." William Rasberry[89]

My office is in a town with an inner city. The city is small enough and I have lived there long enough to know "everyone that is anyone." I do not mean to sound snobbish. The simple fact is that in my line of work, you get to know the persons who run the infrastructure. J.K. is a clerk in the county courthouse, which puts her in contact with all requests which need an "official stamp of authenticity" (paternity acknowledgments, custody changes, birth records, etc.).

After a particularly nasty child custody dispute, I was loafing in the basement cafeteria, J.K. discussed with me the current state of affairs in Saginaw. "It's a real shame that over 75 percent of the births in this county are in single parent households. And now I see a new twist, these young girls are giving their babies to their mothers, aunts, or anyone else who needs them so they can go on welfare. They're nothing more than baby factories!"

R.S., who worked for protective services nodded, adding, "Their boyfriends whomp on them too if they don't give them some of their A.D.C. check, since they feel they wouldn't be getting A.D.C. if it wasn't for them!"

I thought of one of the allegations in the custody dispute. I had been asked by the court to evaluate both parents. The father was a convicted felon, the mother, a dancer in a topless bar. As each accused the other of criminal activity, the circuit judge felt ready to throw up his hands and place their two children in foster care. Mother, stated indignantly that she was not "dealing drugs."

During my interview, I asked her how she could afford her new Cadillac, her obviously expensive clothes, and a brand new trailer house. She replied defensively that she made $1000 a week in tips and could easily afford to maintain her standard of living. Why was she on A.D.C., I asked, if she was doing so well. The question floored her. Stumbling for an answer, she finally admitted, "Well the money is cash. It's under the table."

Smiling suggestively, she added, "Actually, it's in my panties. Anyway, the money is cash, you don't have to declare it. Besides, all the girls are on A.D.C." In other words, the middle class is paying $25,000 per year in welfare costs to several young ladies who earn more than many middle-class wage earners. Not a good idea!

Alternative Possibilities

There are two general approaches to dealing with welfare, both of which I believe, are wrong. One approach is Social Darwinism. "survival of the fittest.". Darwin's theory of the struggle for survival, which was one of the basic tenets of the Nazi era in Germany. Those with positive traits and are able adapt to changing conditions pass on these survival characteristics. The others die before they can breed. The frontier term "Root hog or die," recognized this principal in its basic form. Either you "sucked it up and kept on trucking" or you died.

The second approach to welfare is based on humanitarian principles, which include compassion for those unfortunates unable to partake of the "American Dream." The problem with this second approach is it's failure to distinguish between false benevolence and true benevolence. Its limitations are revealed in the trite phrase, "Give a man a fish and you've fed him for a day, teach him to fish and you've fed him for a lifetime."

You might ask yourself this simple question, if the solution to reducing welfare costs is so obvious, why hasn't it happened. The answer to that is relatively simple. Just as you can't have a prison system without prisoners, you also can't have a police force without criminals and you can't have a huge welfare bureaucracy without the poor. The welfare bureaucracy does its part by continually expanding the number of persons on welfare (and making sure they stay on welfare) and the poor do their part by staying dependent and needy.

I'd like to share a simple true story with you. In Saginaw, during the Christmas holidays, they have a program called Santa's Helpers. This is a program that is designed to help struggling poor people. But to qualify for the program, the poor people must be welfare recipients, not working people who are temporarily in dire straits.

The difference will become clear as you read further. One of my clients learned about a family in the program that needed a washer and dryer. He wanted to get them one. He contacted the program and found out that they had electrical hookups. So he took a re-conditioned washer and dryer to their home. The woman became irate when she saw the washer and dryer (it was the wrong color). My client was so distraught, he stated he would never volunteer to help the needy again. I had to explain to him that there is a difference between the temporarily hurting needy and the trained, professional poor whom social service agencies literally worship.

In 1960, 5.3 percent of All-American children were born to unwed mothers; now 28 percent of All-American children are born to unwed mothers.[90] In many cities such as my own, the percentage of unwed mothers and single family households is much higher.

Governor Engler with the support of the Michigan Legislature passed a law two years ago which denied aid to single persons who could work. His intent was to get them off the welfare rolls and on to the workfare rolls. The actual result? A dramatic increase in the number of children born to unwed mothers. Single women obtain support by having a baby, and single men roam the streets feeding off the single women.

It's time we 'bite the bullet" and dropped both approaches. They simply are not working. If you doubt my conclusions, I suggest you read the books, *THE TRAGEDY OF AMERICAN COMPASSION*[91] and *LOSING GROUND*[92] what then is the answer? The response is in two parts. In this chapter, we'll discuss welfare. In the next chapter, we'll deal with the homeless issue.

The major and growing welfare problem arises from four sources: 1) unwed mothers who receive help for themselves and their children, 2) persons with some disability which prevents them from working competitively in the workplace 3) legal and illegal aliens who are unable to find work, and 4) indexed increases in entitlement programs.

U. S. News and World Report (January 16, 1995) notes several related issues which makes efforts of Republicans and Democrats dubious. The related issues are 1) two thirds of A.F.D.C. recipients have not graduated high school and has less than eighth grade reading and math skills; 2) many of the welfare recipients are second or third generation recipients that is, they not only have never worked but neither have their parents—they simply have not a clue of how to act to obtain and keep a job; 3) many of the welfare recipients are depressed and disabled; 4) many women are welfare are abused, threatened and beaten if they go off welfare by their boyfriends; 5) many welfare recipients are alcoholics or drug addicts; 6) a high proportion of the welfare recipients are unwed teenage mothers; and 7) the jobs programs that have been designed to replace welfare are inadequate in size or scope.

All of these problems have increased dramatically since the

inception of the Great Society. The middle class has participated heavily in an income transfer of $5,000,000,000,000 (five trillion dollars) in a humanitarian effort to help the poor. Our country is rapidly becoming impoverished in programs, which not only don't work but also in effect, make things worse. If we hadn't spent five trillion dollars, we would not have a national debt, and *your* taxes could easily be cut by two thirds.

Let's deal with the first issue. Our society has spent billions of dollars over the years trying to make up for an absent father.[93] Each ten billion dollars spent costs you and every member of your family, $42 a year in taxes. We have spent tens of billions of dollars trying to take care of the single unwed mother. For our efforts, we have increased crime, community de-stabilization, inner-city decay, and a cancerous and ever-expanding problem. WE CAN AND MUST STOP THE CYCLE OF SINGLE PARENTING!

Remember this simple basic principle of human behavior: Humans naturally seek pleasure and avoid pain. This law is called the "pleasure-pain principle." We simply need to find creative ways to apply this problem of single PARENTING. As a first step, I suggest the following. We need to discriminate between situations in which a woman who chooses to have a child, and those in which a woman has a child with no visible means of support.

Whenever a woman applies for welfare to support herself and her child, two things must immediately happen. First, both her and the father should be subject to a court hearing. Secondly, if convicted of irresponsible and negligent behavior, (See my chapter on crime), the judge would have the authority to place them on probation and order them to enroll in programs designed to help them and society. Further, as a society we need to communicate the fact that a couple who have no means of support choose to have a child, it shows a serious lack of judgement and contempt for society which they believe is obligated to support the mother (overtly) and the father (covertly). (Recently, a new client, bragged he had four young woman with children and three of them supported him and his alcohol dependency). This contempt of society would justify the court in sending the man to prison and the women to a work-training center. They would work on infrastructure projects for two years (see chapter on building the Infrastructure).

With respect to the man that impregnated her, I believe we have to give serious consideration to forced celibacy or a vasectomy. Possibly even a new slogan, "Strike two and you lose your dick!" If we can send a felon to prison for life for committing three felonies, why can't we order a man who irresponsibly impregnates woman to be sterilized through chemical or surgical means? Then place him under court injunction to maintain his sterilized condition until he's able to demonstrate to the court's satisfaction his willingness to accept the responsibility of PARENTING and rearing children?

Having such strict laws will result in a drastic reduction in A.D.C. and welfare costs, as well as crime, inner-city decay, and the continual decline in the standard of living of the poor. Those persons who receive A.D.C. and also money from the underground economy, would immediately drop off the rolls to avoid being drafted into the infrastructure workforce. And those men who impregnate woman to live off of them, will immediately stop because firstly, the women won't be there; and secondly, the consequences of indiscriminate, irresponsible PARENTING will be severe. Thirdly, many women and men will think twice about going on welfare. Instead, they will turn to extended families, and hopefully work together to maintain themselves without relying on welfare. Eventually, they'll become wage earners rather than wage eaters.

We need to take a serious look at reducing welfare costs, which the following story illustrates vividly. Although I am primarily a medical psychologist, one fourth of the patients I see are the more traditional clients of general clinical psychology. A woman referred by her family physician, came into my office and tearfully said: "Doctor, I think I am going to have divorce my husband".

I learned she had married her truck-driver husband, because she admired his optimism, self-confidence and independence. Although relatively young, he had an entrepreneurial spirit, which she also admired. How many men in their late 20's own their own eighty thousand-dollar rig? They had been married for three years. And now at age 25, she wanted to have a child.

Lately, however, he's become increasingly depressed. And, she's worried. As she explained, "He just sits there and listens to Rush Limbaugh. He says that people on welfare should be killed. No matter what he does he can't get ahead. Muttering about liberals, he doesn't want me to quit work and have a baby because we can't afford it."

As we talked, she began to understand how her husband had become a victim of middle-class stress. He feels burdened by an unending string of taxes he has to pay. But due to increased competition he can't raise his rates. Thus, he's become progressively discouraged and depressed. His depression has a realistic foundation, but the solution is not to hate the "liberals." The solution is to join with other middle-class workers and demand a change in how we spend our tax dollars. He needs to fight for reduced government spending so small business owners like himself won't be forced to lower their standard of living more than it is.

A *New York Times* editorial (1/31/94), criticized President Clinton's proposal to move people off welfare and talked about the failure of the C.E.T.A. (Comprehensive employment and training act) program, which pressured welfare recipients into jobs in the community. The problem, it said, was if the welfare recipients were given real jobs, organized labor complained, if they were given jobs in social service or state agencies, the local social service agencies or state agencies said it took too much effort to supervise them.

Here, both the Democrats and Republicans join forces. The Democrats do not want to alienate either organized labor, or the bureaucrats who "serve the welfare recipients". These two groups represent a solid block of voters that keep the Democrats in power in Congress. Republicans are unwilling to support job programs because they don't want to spend anything on welfare related programs. So the welfare programs are fashioned to make sure that teenage mothers don't work, and the number of welfare recipients and government workers keep growing. This growing pool of teenage mothers and bureaucrats can be depended upon to vote and keep the Democrats in power.

Meanwhile the pressure on middle class citizens such as the truck-driver continues. The truck-driver can't afford to have children; and young, uneducated, husbandless women can't afford *not* to have children. Taxes (gas, highway, social security, and state income, federal) and costs go up. Both the middle-class husband and wife are forced to work, the number of children, except for welfare children (now one in three births) go down, and feelings of desperation rise.

St. Mary's Medical Center, basically is a trauma and high-tech hospital, and is located within the inner city of Saginaw. Because of its location, a substantial number of the patients from the surrounding area are either on welfare or living off of someone who's on welfare. Life for them is a boring, deadening process of either participating in underground operations to get money, (drugs or petty crime), or running a scam. Not surprisingly, many of them become depressed and, in their desperation, attempt suicide.

About twice a month, I was called into consult on these cases. I had to decide whether they should be discharged, referred to outpatient services, transferred to an inpatient psychiatric facility, etc.). Based on my experience over the last twenty years, 80% of these patients are young, black, and depressed.

Jane S., age 15, is a typical case. She has a one-year-old child and is expecting another. She was supporting a boyfriend (not the father of her first child), who used her welfare money for drugs and alcohol. He wanted her to "turn a few tricks" for more money. When she refused, he beat her, took her T.V., and split.

Jane had quit school when she was 14 ("It just didn't mean nothing to me"), had never had a job and was reared by a mother who never had a job. When we talked about finding meaning in life, it was *totally out of her awareness that she could make a different future for herself.*

All Jane looked forward to was the next day, talking with her friends, partying a little, putting up with the kid, fending off her mother who was trying to help her (mother had recently been set on fire by her alcoholic boy friend), and dealing with constant, low-level depression. "If this is all there is, why continue?" she moaned.

Welfare, as presently conducted, is the worst travesty ever to be perpetuated on the middle class and the poor. It has contributed to the progressive deterioration and destruction of life in the inner city. Why? Because people on welfare have few resources and little motivation to improve their environment. A teen-age mother's major contribution to society is to produce more unwed daughters and sons, and more crimeprone children.

The average working middle-class citizen is frozen out of welfare, which has been carefully constructed by Washington bureaucrats to be *primarily available to young unwed teenage mothers with few resources.* Money is stolen from the middle class and given to the poor, but the result has been ever more increasing welfare, disruption, falling property values and crime.

An excellent book on this subject is *A Call for Revolution* by Martin L. Gross. He points out that at present we are spending over 300 billion dollars a year on 78 uncoordinated welfare programs, $126. for you and every member of your family. And another 300 billion dollars a year is given by the government to charitable organizations to help the poor. Your money does little more than rob from the middle class and give to the poor. He argues convincingly these programs have resulted in more and more poor, and 30 years of Johnsonian programs has hurt both the middle class and the poor. If this is true, who has been helped? The answer is obvious: big government, welfare agencies who feed off of the poor, and the Democrats who depend on a 90 plus percent vote by the poor who vote.

Gross further states if we were to take the five million families on A.F.D.C. (aid to families with dependent children), cut off all welfare benefits and put them to work on a variety of infrastructure tasks (see chapter on Building the Infrastructure), we would save one hundred billion dollars a year—even if we paid each head of family a minimum wage of $14k a year. In my chapter on Building the Infrastructure, I propose ways to not only employ welfare recipients on infrastructure tasks and also get them off welfare.

Many sources claim forcing people off welfare will require the government to create two million new jobs. The White House denied it and stated only five hundred thousand new jobs would have to be created and that these jobs would be at minimum wage levels. But we have five and possibly ten million families on welfare.

Why, is there a difference of such major proportions in these numbers? More importantly, why would the government lie ? The answer is simple. The White House has no real intention of abolishing welfare. The ox that would be gored would be the seventy-eight welfare bureaucracies at a federal level who live off the poor, plus the numerous bureaucracies at state or local levels, who take the remaining crumbs.

It costs over fifty thousand dollars a year to care for the average welfare recipient. It doesn't take a great deal of imagination to realize that there are hundreds of thousands of bureaucrats who feed off of the poor, and most of them vote Democrat. There is no way in the world that President Clinton would try to eliminate welfare, as we know it because the democrats in Congress would scream for his hide. Rather than eliminate welfare, they would do their best to impeach Clinton.

Do we just give up, and keep on paying billions of dollars a year in dysfunctional programs? If we weren't paying these hundred billions of dollars in "do nothing make things worse" programs, your taxes could be cut in half! And we still could reduce the deficit!). *OR, DO WE REALIZE THAT CONGRESS IS THE ENEMY?!?*

Before I describe a psychologically sound proposal to reduce welfare to very manageable proportions, you must realize that with Congress as presently constituted (Democrats who stay in power by causing welfare-slavery and bureaucrat-dependence, and Republicans who do little or next to nothing because of inherent selfishness, greed, and short sightedness), the first step to solving the welfare problem is to get rid of its root cause—which is *CONGRESS AND STATE LEGISLATURES!!!*

If you really want to reduce your tax burden and truly help the poor, then you must vote every present incumbent in office out at each and every election, until federal and state legislators enact *meaningful* substantial programs.

I propose a program which, I believe, would not only break the welfare cycle, but also help cut the huge federal deficit without taxing us one penny. In fact, tax cuts could and would commence. My program is simply based on history.

Let's consider the Great Depression. My father was fortunate enough to have a job from 1927 to 1933; he was in the Army. He had hoped to make the Army a lifetime career. But while in the mountain infantry, he was stationed in Panama and caught yellow fever.

After his discharge, he worked as Borden's Milk Company earning twenty-five dollars a week. When World War II began, he worked as a security guard at a nearby defense plant.

His oldest brother Joe had a different story. During the depression, he received 15 dollars a week so that he wouldn't starve. Then Congress decided that "free" checks could destroy the moral fiber of America. So the W.P.A. was created. Joe went to work for twenty-one dollars a week and spent some years building libraries, bridges and roads. When the war came, he joined as an officer and, built bridges and roads for the Army.

What can we learn from this? First of all, Roosevelt's heart and the heart of most Democrats were in the right place. They didn't want to see millions of Americans starve or become homeless. Republicans viewed the situation as temporary, basically taking the position that you can't make an omelet without breaking a few eggs, i.e., nothing special should be done for the "unfortunates." When the W.P.A. was created, the Republicans did all they did all they could to ridicule the W.P.A. program.

A popular joke at the time was the image of a laborer leaning on a shovel by the side of a road he was supposed to be working on. The W.P.A. worker noticed a rattlesnake curled up near him and said, "You S.O.B., if I had another shovel, I'd cut your head off!"

When the war started, everyone was needed. The labor force contracted. The W.P.A. was no longer needed and was disbanded.

The history of the W.P.A. points to a basic tenet of successful PARENTING. The job of a good parent (biological or governmental) is to work himself/herself out of a job. The W.P.A. passed this test, and because of it, was an excellent program.

In this conflict, we see the seeds of the basic problem with both political parties. The Democrats want to feel good; they make a religion out of government by sponsoring dependency at our expense and stay in power. The Republicans want to rely on market forces, and the devil takes the hindmost. Neither position helps the middle class or increases our basic feeling of safety. Those of us who are older, know that life is like a dewdrop on the tip of a blade of grass and can fall that quickly! The middle class, and most Americans, wants a safety nets but not one that entraps us in its strings.

While I was writing this book, my oldest daughter called and said her best friend was utterly distraught. Her husband had just been told he would lose his job because Word Perfect was going through a reduction in force. He'd have two months pay and severance pay. I referred my daughter to my brother Danny, who owns a small computer company. I know my daughter's friend's family doesn't qualify for assistance that is available for the poor. Why should he? He's an unfortunate victim of downsizing. Besides, he voted Republican, and the Democrats could care less what happens to the middle-class worker temporarily out of a job and the Republicans of course, don't care about anyone.

So what to do? Remember, if all of us had our taxes cut in half, there would be such a large amount of money freed up that corporate down-sizing would be minimal, and a massive amount of new jobs would be created. But what do we do now?

We have to recognize that people, even poor people, are controlled by a simple motivational system common to us all. To seek pleasure and avoid pain. As long as the government makes it pleasurable to be on welfare, more and more citizens will go on welfare. But when it becomes painful to go on welfare, fewer and fewer citizens will do so.

As Gross suggested, place all 78 federal welfare programs under one head. Combine them all into one agency for the purpose of downsizing, eliminating as many of the programs as possible. Secondly, re-establish the W.P.A. and start building the infrastructure of the United States to Mid Twenty-First Century levels. Thirdly, (and this is where I differ from Mr. Gross), only pay the families who enlist in the W.P.A. a mini-mal amount, enough to cover personal needs. They would have to live in barracks as families, eat in large cafeterias, serve in massive work crews that build the infrastructure, or work in service areas such as watching the children of other workers, cooking, cleaning, etc. Number four, once they have worked for two years and, hopefully, have devel-oped work skills, they would be discharged and given a bonus of several thousand dollars.

Congress would choke on this part, the Democrats would fear that they would become independent or Republican and disappear from the welfare bureaucracy; the Republicans, in their idiotic self-seeking think-ing, would resent giving them *anything*. Nevertheless, the W.P.A. would graduate each worker with a discharge bonus of several thousand dollars.

Each discharged worker would have enough money to return home, seek an apartment or rent a house, and find employment.

Should they be unsuccessful in their attempts and return to the welfare roles, they again would be drafted, this time within three months, into the W.P.A. The only choice they would have would be to work, avoid taking welfare, or be drafted. In this kind of system, I doubt that welfare which is presently costing us over three hundred billion dollars a year would cost more than fifty billion, five years from now.

Finally, in most states, welfare recipients receive more money each time they have another child. This practice must immediately cease and instead, if a woman has a child while on welfare, *both her and the father of her child would be considered to have committed a felony and it would be up to a jury to decide what to do with her* (see my chapter on crime).

Let's leave the subject of A.D.C. and deal with the second major problem of welfare, the disabled, those who fall between the cracks, the mentally retarded, mentally ill, blind, deaf, disabled, etc. When I worked in a mental hospital, I was initially surprised to observe that the therapy , which helped the patients the most, was *industrial* therapy. Patients would be assigned tasks such as ground maintenance, painting, plumbing, food care, cleaning, etc.

After a few weeks of successful working, they would be granted privileges such as ground parole, smoking, going to local in hospital activities (movies, shows, etc), and in general treated as a contributing member of the mentally ill society. Many of the patients flourished under this regime.

The point is, regardless of the ability or inability of a person, it is in their best interest to find a way in which they can contribute. Consider Stephen Hawkins, one of the world's leading theoretical physicists. He contracted Lou Gerigh's Disease in his early 20's. He could have applied for S.S.I. in the U.S. and quietly died of what the English call "Motor Neuron Disease." Instead, he finished his degree at Oxford and obtained an advanced degree at Cambridge. He not only contributed mightily to the world of physics, but also to the general level of popular knowledge by his books on science.

Unfortunately, I at the time had little understanding of this concept that working is good for the soul. When I was teaching at Brigham Young University, a student in one of my classes was severely disabled and wheelchair bound. I taught statistics, which had an accompanying lab. Given his massive disabilities, I was surprised to find him in my first lab, and thoughtlessly told him that I would accept his class work and that he did not have to come for lab. I will never forget the pain in his face when I said this. He took my misguided support for rejection and contempt.

But, I felt only the highest respect for him and his determination to continue in school despite his deficits. To him, I had struck a grievous blow to his feeling of self-worth. The young man died a few months later. I never had a chance to say how sorry I was for unthinkingly offering to excuse him from an activity in which he hoped to participate.

When we simply give something to one who has a disability, without first learning what they can contribute, we do that person a tremendous disservice. S.S.I. and S.S.D., although well meaning, probably have done more harm than good. It has stolen from the elderly their rightful earnings, and given to the disabled solely because they can not compete equally in the *competitive market place*. While this may be true of many of the disabled, there is absolutely no justification for just handing them money!

Many jobs could be created to improve our infra structure, continuously making our cities safe, improving our transportation, and developing ways to cope with massive catastrophes. I can not believe that there is no place to employ the disabled. Work would build their self-esteem, reduce indolence and, in the end, cost *less* than we are currently paying for S.S.I. and S.S.D.

Remember, welfare can be solved! If you have the courage to make the simple but painful decisions necessary to do it. And *if you vote out of office every incumbent!*

The Homeless—Dealing Appropriately with the Mentally Ill

There are many ways to start a chapter—particularly a chapter on the homeless. One could be theoretical and quote many of the books and studies that have been written. Or one could quote case histories. I've decided to do neither. Instead, I would like to share with you my personal experience with the homeless. But first, I have to share something of myself.

As I've noted in other chapters, my father was brain injured and my mother suffered from numerous health problems during the course of my childhood. And, I was not an easy child to rear. It was as if I had been personally delivered by the American anarchist, Emma Goldman who as a midwife had dreamed of whispering in each baby's ear as it entered this world, "Rebel, Rebel!"[100] I don't know if any special angel whispered rebellion into my ears, but certainly my behavior would suggest that it was an early and constant companion of my childhood, youth and adult years.

I was so rebellious that I was either fired or invited to leave the first nine jobs that I held. By being constantly at war with others, and myself anxiety and confusion dogged my steps. Eventually, after being pressured out of a Treasury Department job, I decided to return to school and discover more about me (it's called majoring in psychology). But, I was married to my first wife and didn't have the funds to both go to school and maintain a small apartment. So my first wife's uncle, who was a chief resident psychiatrist at Metropolitan State Hospital stepped in and suggested that I apply for a position as a psychiatric technician.

State mental hospitals were trying to change their image and so they had done away with the old fierce image of the hulking attendant and were trying to encourage college students to work with their patients. Reluctantly, I agreed to try working at the hospital. My self-concept was low and although I couldn't admit it to myself yet, I wasn't sure if I should work at the mental hospital or be treated there. In any event, my first day on the psychiatric ward was fraught with anxiety. I had no idea what to expect nor was I sure that I could cope with the challenges that would be offered.

The ward (one I would be in charge of two years latter as the night shift supervisor) held one hundred and four patients. One supervisor, three assistants and four students staffed it. I was one of the students. As the locked door was opened (I was not trusted with keys yet), I had my first glimpse of insanity. The ward was a warehouse of living beings that had been hospitalized for at least fifteen years and at most fifty years. It was surprisingly quiet. Some patients walked the long hall, which led from the door to the nurse's station. They wore faded blue pants and worn shirts. Neither their shirts nor pants were ironed. Most were disheveled, as if they had slept in them. None were clean—(they were shaved every third day). Many had numerous stains on their shirts from eating carelessly or drooling tobacco juice.

As I walked down the hall, past the "quiet" rooms, one of the patients approached me and said mechanically, "Got a light? Got a light?" As he asked, he made no eye contact. There was no tone to his voice and he treated me as if I was a "coke machine" which might or might not accommodate him. Mechanically, I lit up his "roll your own" cigarette and observed blackened, cracked fingers which were obviously the result of smoking too many "roll your owns" to the very last quarter inch. inhaling deeply, the patient turned and walked away. There was no thank you, no expression of gratitude, I was just another machine which this time had paid off.

Mr. Borello, the ward charge, liked to test new students by assigning them roles in the daily morning cleanup. I was assigned the task of cleaning the bathroom. This meant that I had to find four or five patients to supervise (I was not allowed to do the work myself). Given a population of 104, finding four or five patients did not seem such a difficult task until I really looked at the patients.

The patients had been wakened at 6 A.M. Most simply moved from their Army surplus cot beds to the front room where they sat in plastic covered large chairs (too large and too heavy to throw). There they stared off into space, often mumbling to themselves, seeing things, or simply remaining passive and unfocused. A T.V. was on but none of them were watching it. The T.V. they were watching was in their head and only they had access to the program. It took me half an hour to find four patients who were willing to clean the large patient bathroom under my supervision.

Supervision had to be constant because if I left their presence or turned my back, they would instantly leave and go back to their chair or start pacing and listen to voices that I could only guess at.

One day rolled into another. Each day followed the same set routine. Patients were awakened at 6 A.M. Food was served at 6:30 A.M. The ward was cleaned from 7 A.M. to 8 A.M. Lunch was served at 11:30 A.M. Patients were taken outside (if it wasn't raining) from 1:30 P.M. to 2:15 P.M. Patients ate supper at 5 P.M. Patients went to bed at 8:30 P.M. None of the patients had ground parole. None were allowed to work outside of the ward. All were chronic, "burned-out" schizophrenics. They ate, they slept, they sat, they paced, they went to the bathroom, they hallucinated and they talked to voices or back at voices or mumbled in a strange chaotic language.

Despite the bizarre appearance of the patients and the surroundings in which I worked, I felt strangely at home. My anxiety and confusion left. I felt a kinship with humans, a bond that I still feel whenever, I encounter the "truly mentally ill." Perhaps it is because I understood how they responded to this warehouse from hell. To the normal human being that roves this country, this ward would frighten, confuse, terrify or revolt them, but to the patients, **it was home!**

Some of the staff, psychiatrists, psychologists, social workers, nurses and attendants intuitively understood the importance of the hospital both to the patients and to many of the staff. It was a refuge from a world, which could be terribly frightening and confusing. One of the first sayings I learned as a "new student" was the only difference between the patients and the staff was one of them had keys.

Many staff members laughed and thought the saying trite and cute, I didn't, because I believed it contained a strong kernel of truth.

The year was 1962 and vast changes were occurring in mental health. A curious combination or accommodation was beginning to form between "liberals" and "conservatives."

Liberal writers such as R. D. Laing and Thomas Szasz opposed mental hospitals as instruments of societal repression and degradation. They were able to convince many that the "mentally ill were just like us, only more so (a favorite saying of the Meninger Clinic)." Conservatives on the other hand, looked at the tremendous cost of mental hospitals and the thousands of patients that were being warehoused in them and felt that society wasn't getting much of a bang for its buck.

As the federal government developed programs such as Medicaid, Medicare and S.S.I., financial vehicles were in place to transition mental patients from mental hospitals into group homes, nursing homes, flop houses and hostels. In 1975 the Supreme Court ruled in O'Connor vs. Donaldson that mental illness in and of itself did not justify involuntary hospitalization. This last ruling paved the way for emptying the ward I had long supervised. Of course, I had already left years before in my pursuit of "higher" education. But the patients had stayed until this last ruling. These patients whom I had worked with for a little over six years were mentally ill but they were not dangerous to others or themselves. They were neither homicidal nor suicidal.

They just didn't have any sense of time, or of money, or of cleanliness, or of paper work, or of following regulations or of manners or of location. These patients were simply dumped on convenient corners, sort of like a person would do with unwanted kittens or an old lame dog. It was to become an exercise in Social Darwinism. If they lived, they obviously should not have been hospitalized and if they didn't— "Oh well, there was no family, friends, priest, pastor or significant other to care or worry. They would just end up a nameless corpse and begin a new venture as a teaching instrument for medical students to hack to cut to pry and eventually to incinerate.

One third of all the homeless are patients such as the ones I have described. Victims of disordered biochemistry or structural insufficiencies in their brains, each day is one they barely cope with. Living in trash bins, parks, caves, under the streets in discarded tunnels, in nicks and crevices and sometimes if it gets cold enough to get their disordered attention, in shelters. Scavenging garbage cans, picking up discarded cigarettes and cigars, drinking from cast off pop and beer cans, each day is like every other day. Only this time, there is no set time to get up, to eat, to lay down, to sleep or to bathe.

It is up to them to be "responsible for themselves." Liberal politicians mouth platitudes about community mental health centers and foster care homes or low cost hotels. Conservatives politicians, glad to close expensive state hospital after state hospital, only complain that the state is still paying more than it should. Both continue to support the idea of de-institutionalization while the "truly mentally ill don't even know that they were institutionalized and that now **they are free!**

Of course the "truly mentally ill" are not only the victims of political deceit and deception, they are also inadvertently the persecutors of the middle class and the elderly. They make it impossible for the young mother to let her children play in the park. One or two encounters with the debris (including human feces) of the "truly mentally ill" as well as the strange sights, sounds and smells of persons who haven't bathed in months or years does not a pleasant outing make. Not only have our parks become off limits to many members of the middle class but also our great libraries have become day hospitals for the "truly mentally ill" as they seek refuge from the cold and the rain.

It is somewhat difficult for students, the elderly and young mothers to make use of facilities which are occupied by burned out reeking hulks of humanity who aren't even aware of themselves let alone their impression on others.

As politicians congratulate themselves on their "new programs for the homeless" in Washington and in state capitols, the homeless are not amused. Most don't even know that there is a Washington or a state capitol. They never read about programs and the closest they get to information about new mental health programs or new hostelries is when the drape the paper that contains the stories over or under themselves as they prepare to rest or sleep.

The "truly mentally ill" homeless only make up one third of the homeless.[101] The other two thirds consist of alcoholics and drug abusers. The "truly mentally ill" homeless is a relatively recent phenomena. Most of the "truly mentally ill" were confined to institutions prior to

1950. At that time, the homeless consisted for the most part of adventurers and substance abusers. Studies at this time reflect that about two thirds of the homeless are frequent users of cocaine—probably in the form of crack.[102] This group of homeless are scavengers who prowl from shelter to the streets to crash pads and back in their everlasting pursuit of "temporary highs" and sustenance. Some work, some dress normally, most use and abuse drugs. Some prowl the streets in search of victims to provide the cash they need for their next high.

The elderly in particular, are marks for the drug addicted homeless. Being often weak, frail, unable to fight back, having poor vision and memories, they are a safer target for the drug addicted homeless. Many of my elderly clients lead lives of quiet desperation as they lock and bolt their doors at night. Some even fear to leave their homes in broad daylight to shop or visit a friend. Too often they hear tales of relatives or friends who have been accosted at home or away.

One of my clients, Leon 67, told me his story. His neurologist had referred him. Leon had left his home at 8 A.M. to walk one block to the local 7-Eleven. Halfway down the block, a homeless person leapt out from behind a bush in front of an empty lot. Leon was struck by a thick tree branch and fell to the ground. His wallet was taken and he was left bleeding on the sidewalk. Several moments later, he dazedly struggled to the porch of the nearest house. The occupant, and elderly woman wouldn't answer the door or respond to his repeated pleas.

Eventually Leon, feeling increasingly weak and numb, stumbled into the 7 Eleven parking lot where he fainted and was taken unconscious to the hospital. A retired schoolteacher, Leon had hoped to travel and write short articles about his adventures. Following his head injury, he could neither write nor read (both activities he had looked forward to with joyful anticipation when he retired).

Leon was not angry with the elderly woman who wouldn't open her door or help him. He stated, "I can understand why she did it. Maybe I would have done the same thing. You never know what is going to happen if you open your door nowadays!"

Frank stated this same thought. Frank, 37, was referred by his neurologist. He had been jogging in the park at night. While jogging, a man grabbed him from behind, held a knife to his throat and said, "Wallet, Wallet."

Frank was too slow in producing his wallet and the man cut his throat and then kicked him in the head. Luckily, an artery was not cut. But he bled profusely and no one would stop to help him. It was not until he collapsed in the middle of the street that someone called 911 on their cellular phone. Frank, recently returned from South Africa lamented. "You know, we ban products from South Africa and lament their violence. Yet, I'm home one week and I have my throat cut and my head bashed in. I jogged in South Africa for over a year and never felt one worry. As soon as I get better, I'm getting the hell out of this hell hole."

According to the best estimates available, there are between three and four hundred thousand homeless.[103] One third of them are the "truly mentally ill and two thirds are substance abusers. Each is both a victim and a persecutor. They are victims in the sense that society has made an attempt to deal with them, albeit stupidly.[104]es Politicians rarely seem to get it right. They so often forget that for each action there is usually a reaction. For each "savings" there is a cost. For each effort to control there is a rebellion.

The issue of the homeless can not be solved by building more shelters or by building more low cost homes. Certainly low cost housing can help persons on the lower end of the income scale. But the homeless who have become both the scourged and the scourge are not the ones who will benefit from platitudes or elegant well meaning but in the end, idiotic programs.

If the middle class is to take back its streets, its parks, its libraries, its sense of safety and sanity, two simple but controversial programs are needed. The first, having to do with the "truly mentally ill" homeless, will take a constitutional amendment and the second having to do with substance abusing homeless may also.

First, we need to straighten out the Supreme Court decision which basically said, just because you are mentally ill, is no reason to hospitalize you against your will. This is like saying to a five year old, well you know best what is good for you, so if you don't want to take a bath, go to school, stay in the house at night or eat a balanced meal, its perfectly all right. What nonsense! The United States is the only industrial nation, which has turned its back on the "truly mentally ill." We have basically returned to the middle ages where the mentally ill were left to roam the streets, alleys and forests, scavenging for food like stray dogs or cats.

This does not mean that we have to or should resurrect the great warehouses of the past, which entombed tens of thousands of mental patients in wards. It does mean that we need to have defined areas of residence where the mentally ill are kept until they demonstrate that they can perform minimal activities congruent with living in society without becoming a scourge of society.

We have several abandoned military bases, which could house tens of thousands of the "truly mentally ill" both helpfully to them and with reasonable cost to the middle class. These locations should be governed not by physicians but by educators who can use physicians and other professionals to help the "truly mentally ill" and also develop means by which the "truly mentally ill" can receive whatever training they are capable of so as to evaluate their ability to re-integrate into society.

Based on my own experiences however, I suspect that the vast majority of the "truly mentally ill" will end their days in these camps. Their end however will be far more peaceful both to them and to society.

The substance abusing homeless however, need a different approach. These members of the Homeless population are ever on the lookout for money to fuel their habits. It is not particularly important to them how they get their money. They just want it as they endlessly pursue their "highs" and avoid their "lows". The elderly, the young and the middle class have a right to a "safe" society. They have a right to live free from "fear". They have a right to rock on their porch. To open their door at night when it is knocked. To visit a friend. To walk to their local party store. To enjoy the night's soft breezes.

While one can sympathize with the plight of the addicted, it is no reason to turn the life of millions of elderly and middle class citizens into nightmares of fear and anxiety.

The answer to the drug addicted homeless is explained in detail in my chapter on the Drug War. But to reiterate. The best approach to dealing with the drug-addicted homeless is to establish drug-using reservations. Each major center of population should have several drug reservations where drug users can enter and use drugs to their heart's content. In return, they will have to "use birth control" and "volunteer" for community building projects such as tearing down abandoned building, repairing, painting and refurbishing other buildings, streets, bridges, parking lots, etc.

In addition, the drug addicted homeless who break the law should be cast into temporary holding pens where they are forced to undergo involuntary drug withdrawal. Drug addicts are not frightened or deterred from crime by the thought or jail or prison. But they are terrified of involuntary withdrawal. That threat, the threat of involuntary withdrawal may be enough to protect many innocent citizens from the depredations of the drug addicted homeless.

Currently, the fear of involuntary withdrawal drives the drug addicted homeless to attack innocent citizens in their search for monies to feed their drug habit. Let's change the rules and now have the drug addicted homeless flee in fear of breaking the law by knowing the consequences will be certain, unassisted withdrawal.

With both the "truly mentally ill" and the "drug addicted" homeless off the streets, there will be few homeless left. If the group that is left is large enough to create problems for the middle class, (which I strongly doubt), other simple answers can be applied.

Should those remaining homeless constitute a threat to the normal course of civilized society and should they be unwilling to participate in using appropriate shelters or housing, there is always the alternative of 90 days of forced labor to encourage them to reconsider their ways. I doubt that it would take too many 90-day "excursions" to convince them that living on the streets is not the best alternative.

Building the Infrastructure

"With the exception of a few of the largest metropolitan centers, American cities no longer truly exist.... One sees office buildings, hotels and government buildings...a closer look and the buildings reveal themselves as individual fortresses and the downtown mall is certain to be accessible for but a few hours each day."[105]

Peter Shaw, *"Let a Hundred Cities Bloom."*

American cities were once thriving centers of commerce, cultural transfusion, education, communication, finance, recreation and medical care. Both formal centers of life and also informal centers. Strange foods, unusual smells, a polyglot of language, and the eternal excitement of living always present. One could see every age and every race going about their lives, and adding to the *energy* of the living city.

Now the cities, for the most part, are dead. The great department stores have fled to the surrounding malls. The little boutiques, sidewalk restaurants, and cafes have closed and not been replaced. Instead, we find convenience stores, sex shops, massage parlors, gas stations and bars. *No one except the Homeless, Predators, and Victims Walk the Streets!*

Politicians and their policies have allowed and encouraged making the cities repositories for the homeless, predators, welfare recipients, as well as the underclass of immigrants, marginal workers, and elderly who can't afford to live anywhere else. Most live in fear. A simple drive through the cities at night reveals virtually no one on the streets.

It both amazes and depresses me when I compare Detroit, Michigan to Windsor, Ontario, Canada. Detroit is on one side of the river, Windsor on the other. On any given day or night, you can drive through Detroit and see deserted streets, boarded-up buildings, and a few guarded fortresses of hotels and office buildings. And just across the river is Windsor, boasting a thriving downtown busy both day and night. Citizens casually walk the streets, shop, sit and converse in outdoor cafes, laugh and enjoy the life that rightfully belongs to every American City.

Contrast Windsor to any American city near you. Which is more likely for you to find, a Windsor or Detroit environment? The answer is obvious. In America, Detroit rules!

But we can change this, and in the process add a new vision, a new life, and hundreds of billions of dollars to our economy. Consider for a moment the economic consequences of having an abandoned, boarded up building which pays no taxes and serves as a haven to drug dealers, drug users, and the homeless, to the same building now valued at several million dollars and occupied by offices and stores, which produce jobs, and pay sales taxes and property taxes. The one vacant building consistently uses up the city's resources and pays nothing for its upkeep, while the second generates hundreds of thousands of dollars in income to the city, and also helps keep people off welfare. Now multiply the one building by tens of thousands of buildings, and you begin to see the incredible waste occurring in the centers of American Cities.

To change each city from a Detroit to a Windsor is incredibly easy and simple. But we need politicians with the will and willingness to do so. It means cleaning up crime, abolishing welfare as it is currently practiced, and removing the homeless. By allowing drug users to use drugs in unlimited doses in special enclaves (see chapter on Drugs), putting those who commit crimes under the complete authority of jurors (see chapter on Crime), and by resolving the problem of the homeless (see chapter on Homeless), the city now becomes a viable possibility. What else is needed? Sweeping a place clean does not necessarily mean that it will be replaced with something vital.

We must provide services unique to the city that makes city life "special." The first step is abandoned building, tear them down or renovate them. Secondly, transportation has to be frequent and absolutely safe. Subways, trolley cars, monorails, and buses have to be able to move every fifteen minutes, day and night, and be absolutely clean and safe. Little boutiques of all types have to throng the street level of buildings, along with bookshops, cafes, and stores of all types. You say it can not be done, visit Toronto, Canada! Or that is, visit it before Canadian politicians destroy it by following the American model.

As the city comes to life, it will become a haven for everyone, a melting pot of race, color, religion, and culture. Which is exactly what it should be! The great resources of each city will also thrive: museums, libraries, hospitals, etc. will also spring new life as the pressure of population creates demands for their services.

But *how* can we create this haven? The answer is simple. Abolish welfare. Only short term (three or six months), will be permissible. After that, each person on welfare will be drafted into a workforce for 18 months to two years. One of their jobs will be to renew and invigorate the city. Tear down buildings, repair buildings, repair streets, build subways, monorails, trolley car lines, etc.

The second source of labor to build the infrastructure will come from *legal* aliens. If we are willing to make the effort to build an America for the twenty-first century, there is absolutely no reason why immigrants to America should get a free ride. One of the conditions for admittance for citizenship should require the immigrants to work to build or re-build the infrastructure of America for two years.

The third source of labor to build the infrastructure should be American youth. Each youth who reaches the age of 19 should be drafted into a workforce to build the infrastructure. In return for contributing one year of labor, each youth will be allowed two years of scholarship to attend higher learning or technical schools.

In addition to building the cities of America, other major tasks need to be done to build the American infrastructure. Before discussing them, let's consider the ideas of former Labor Secretary, Robert B. Reich. Reich , former director of policy planning for the Federal Trade Commission, and former economics professor at Harvard University, has written several important books which include: *MINDING AMERICA'S BUSINESS, THE NEXT AMERICAN FRONTIER,* and *THE WORK OF NATIONS.*

Reich divided work into three categories, 1) routine production services, 2) in-person services and 3) symbolic-analytic services. He recognizes that the middle class is shrinking, and there are more poor, more rich, and fewer middle-class citizens. He believes the reason for the diminishing middle-class is that routine production services move to countries, which can perform the work more economically.[106] He believes this country can not stop the hemorrhaging of routine production jobs. According to Bob Woodward,[107] President Clinton invited Mr. Reich into his cabinet because of his great respect for Reich's ideas. Obviously, President Clinton must agree with Reich's assessment that routine production jobs are increasingly doomed in the United States.

According to Reich, jobs, which involve in-person services, are also on the way out. As companies move labor and supervisory positions to foreign lands, they find ways to also reduce service work. Thus the middle class has the luxury of knowing that our former Secretary of Labor believes that skilled trade jobs, supervisory jobs, and high-paying factory jobs will be a thing of the past, along with many service jobs such as banking, insurance, administration, etc.

I find it amazing that a President of the United States and our former Secretary of Labor can stand before the American people and apparently condone other countries who use slave labor, employ children, shoot labor organizers, eliminate unemployment compensation, occupational safety rules and regulation, environmental regulations, and worker's compensation.

Reich, in his rush to avoid offending countries, which unfairly trade with the United States, suggests instead building the infrastructure simply consists of building better or more effective higher centers of learning. He recognizes that a people which are "propelled solely by greed and fear is crippling the United States economy."[108] Then he utters meaningless platitudes, which involve basically more taxes and more welfare.

Building the infrastructure of America takes tough, hard political decisions. We need to not only use the workforce I've identified to rebuild the cities, free the inner cities of persons who have no business being there, but also have to rebuild our basic industries.

There is absolutely no reason why we can't modernize our steel, glass, electronic, and chemical industries, and direct part of our infrastructure labor force to build giant new industries that can compete with any country on earth. However, at the same time we direct our infrastructure workforce into rebuilding our basic industries, we need to create an equal playing field. How? By taxing products produced in other nations that do not have the same regulations as the United States. Basically, this means that Congress and the Administration cannot "show boat" new industry regulations without also applying them to products imported into the United States.

Senator Kennedy spoke on C-Span about economic justice during a health care debate. He mentioned United States factory shoe workers who labored under abysmal work rules and conditions. He spoke with pride how he and other members of Congress had forced factory owners to improve their worker conditions. What he carefully avoided saying, however, was the fact that the jobs he strove to improve no longer exist in the United States. Slave laborers in China, and children in Asia and Guatemala are now performing them. The American middle class does not need this kind of hypocrisy.

In addition to rebuilding America's basic industries, we also need to consider another fact of life. A comet broke apart and struck Jupiter. A simple look at our moon through a telescope will reveal other meteor strikes. It seems fairly certain similar impacts have occurred on this planet. Some scientists posit the destruction of the dinosaurs was caused by a huge meteor impact.

Earthquakes, wildfire, floods, droughts, hurricanes,, tidal waves, wind storms, extreme cold, extreme heat, volcanic eruptions, etc. are not "disasters" and should not be considered as such. Disaster implies an unexpected horrible event, a cataclysm, catastrophe or dire emergency. On a changing, living planet, change is inevitable, change is life. Even abrupt change should be expected rather than treated as an unusual event. If you live in an earthquake zone, you should expect to experience an earthquake. If you live near an active volcano, you should expect some greater or lesser eruptions. If you live near a huge river, such as the Mississippi, you should expect it to change its course or overcome its boundaries.

At one time in human history, these events were regarded as mysterious, a sign of anger from the Gods, a catastrophe. But in an advanced, civilized society these events must be considered the normal cost of living on a changing planet. There is no reason why we should not be prepared to deal with any and all events of change on the earth. This does not imply an arrogance or haughtiness, that there is nothing God can throw at us we can't solve. However, if we show good judgement and make adequate preparations, the normal course of things that we label "disasters" should be considered incidents to be managed.

If disaster management teams were now in place, an emergency force of several hundred thousand citizens would be immediately available to confront any and all natural events such as earthquake, flood, hurricanes, firestorm, etc., and repair any damages. Government would just need to prepare in central staging areas the necessary implements to immediately start the process of recovery. And a nuclear workforce of already trained leaders would have been prepared to put the CCC workers and draftees to the task of recovery.

One of the essential points of maintaining an efficient infrastructure is the ability to always have the means to overcome what we now call disasters.

Another essential part of an efficient infrastructure is to have the means to deal with disasters of civil order, such as riots, rebellion, racial and/or ethnic conflict, prison riots, invasion by individuals or organized parties of our borders, etc.

There seems to be no reason why another task of the expanded CCC and draftees could not function under Armed Service supervision. They would form a nucleus to deal with civil disorders, which have outgrown the ability of local law enforcement to handle.

Having a mobile pool of workers comprised of American youth and persons formerly on welfare, creates the opportunity to deal creatively with the demands of "disasters." Disasters, now will be called predictably unpredictable events, should be viewed as causing a necessary diversion of the workers, who would have been otherwise employed on normal infrastructure tasks.

President U. S. Grant before he died, shared his vision of America in his memoirs. His vision was of a vast country which connected East and West and North and South by railroads. His vision started to come true before Americans caught a new vision: highways and airways. The car, truck, bus and plane replaced railroads. As we approach the twenty-first century, it's time we turn again to Grant's dream.

President Clinton should be credited with mentioning as fuel becomes more expensive and the cost of transportation rises, the country with the most improved, efficient and least expensive transportation system will have a huge advantage in the international marketplace.

One major change in our infrastructure, which would benefit our society well into the next century, would be installing high-speed bullet trains and freight trains every three hundred miles, North and South, East and West. The ideal would be to enable any of our citizens to take a train in the East, for example, Boston, and arrive in Los Angeles, safely and inexpensively, within a day. Increasing the mobility of our population, while decreasing the cost of migrating, would enable the rapid movement of resources and people whenever necessary. Regardless of the location within the country of a "predictably unpredictable event," tens of thousands of workers plus the necessary equipment could be shuttled to the area within days while persons rendered homeless by the event could be moved to new shelters.

Another advantage of high-speed economical trains is the ability to move products and people throughout the country, thus the size of the country shrinks as the time from production site to consuming site contracts. Japan has already learned this lesson. The rest of Asia is planning to come on board with this concept. Should we allow ourselves to be left in the lurch? One of the arguments that capitalists use in locating factories outside of this country is the cost of labor. Low-cost efficient transportation, however, enables the middle class to have higher wages and still compete with third-world countries with inferior infrastructures. Building and maintaining the high-speed railways will invigorate the presently closed steel mills and factories of our industrial heartland.

Along with constructing high-speed railways, alternate energy sources would be another source of employment for the CCC and the drafted youth. Imagines thousands of square miles of vacant desert covered by solar collectors. Imagine thousands of square miles of vacant mountains covered with windmills which covert wind to electricity. Imagine vast tunnels that tap the inner heat of the earth to collect energy, which is transformed into electricity. Consider the erection of huge tunnels that tap the outflow of rivers, such as the Columbia, and pump fresh water to arid areas of the United States. Their contribution of fresh water would accompany the construction of huge desalination plants.

Picture uniform efficient nuclear reactors, along with rocket-launching platforms, which efficiently use the height of mountains to launch small, well-protected capsules containing nuclear waste into parking orbits in space.

Visualize an inner city, which is now a tax eater transformed into a taxpayer, as the inner city is repaired and we install trolley cars, subways and monorails connecting all parts of the city. After abandoned homes and businesses are torn down, or re-vitalized, picture the whole area well maintained, policed and safe.

Envision an inner city where the elderly, young workers, and current residents all interact in peace and harmony, as the problems of crime and welfare are eliminated.

In the past, politicians have avoided making the decisions necessary to maintain and improve our infra structure. Instead of repairing roads, bridges, the inner city, improving transportation, and maintaining the quality of life—where the great universities, libraries, museums and population centers are located—they have encouraged programs which have generated white flight and urban decay.

Employing vast armies of formerly indolent welfare recipients and the youth in the never-ending and ever-improving task of maintaining our infrastructure will create a new twenty-first century, which will ensure the continued quality of life of our country and the safety and future of the middle class.

Starting this process, however, will require us to *shock* the entire system. How? Again, by voting against each and every incumbent. These incumbents, Democrat and Republican, have participated in wasting our resources, as the infrastructure of the United States declined. It is not too late to start re-building America. But we need a new crop of dedicated leaders more interested in work than in give-a-way programs, more interested in investment in the future, than paying off segments of the population.

The major residents of the inner cities, Blacks and Latinos, are often portrayed as welfare bums or crime generators. Welfare hasn't helped them. Instead, it has served to keep them in an emotional bondage. The inner city population will initially have the honor of having more of its population drafted into the CCC, and segmented into drug-using reservations with concomitant high rates of self-induced suicide. But it will also benefit more quickly by a newfound peace, quiet and safety as the level of crime drops dramatically and new sources of income replace the old industries of drug distribution and accompanying illegal enterprises.

Imagine an inner city where the elderly, black and white, can roam the streets at 1, 2 or 3 A.M., walk to an all-night grocer or coffee shop, kibitz with neighbors on a hot night at a sidewalk cafe, or watch the youth walk safely hand and hand down the street.

Is this an unattainable dream? I don't believe it is. It already exists in some cities in other countries. It is time this became the rule rather than the exception in our country.

The supreme accomplishment of a true infrastructure revolution would be to have every inner city from New York to New Orleans, from Los Angeles to San Francisco, become crime free, care free, and industrious. Citizens could rest easy at night, knowing that civil disorders and geological catastrophes will inevitably occur, but that hundreds of thousands of their fellow citizens will always be available to rush to their aide .

The 82nd Airborne is always on eleven-hour notice. They can be dressed, equipped and in the air within eleven hours to defend the United States. With the installation of high-speed railways, we can also have an infrastructure workforce on the way within eleven hours.

Crime—Casting Politicians Aside and Returning

Power to the Judges and the People

"Mandatory sentencing laws...vest the sentencing power in the prosecutor not the judge...abolish individualized sentencing...violate the principle of proportionality...punishment should not exceed the gravity of the offense...crimes were...arbitrarily selected and bore no relationship to public safety, dangerousness, culpability, law enforcement or deterrence..."
Lois G. Forer, Trial Judge[109]

As a medical psychologist, I've discovered a simple truth: *the nature of humans is to be unable to change their nature!* Humans are the same today as they were yesterday. Two thousand years ago, individuals struggled with the same basic problems and the same emotions of joy, anger, fear and love. As they responded to basic feelings, they engaged in societal-condemned behaviors of aggression, thievery, murder, fraud, non-conformity, suicide, etc.

Although our physical environment has changed from two thousand years ago, our internal environment has not. People have not changed.

How do we explain our society? How is it that we have imprisoned 1,300,000 persons and are less safe today than when only 400,000 were in prison? How is it that the formerly racist nation of South Africa at its worst never had as many black males in prison as there are in the United States? South Africa at its zenith of white supremacy imprisoned 681 blacks per one hundred thousand, while the United States imprisoned 3,370 blacks per one hundred thousand. In other words, America's environment for blacks is *five times worse than South Africa's ever was!*

And what about the United States middle class? Does having so many hundreds of thousands of Americans in prison make us any safer? Can we walk the streets of our cities at night (or even in the daytime)? Can we leave our cars unlocked? Do we comfortably leave our homes unattended? As we drive through impoverished parts of the city, do we silently pray that we won't have a flat tire or run out of gas? Or do we entirely avoid certain areas of the city and go miles out of our way out of fear for our safety?

The answer to these questions is yes. But why are other societies in other countries and cities safer than ours? Why are the same people we are fearful of in this country not feared in other countries?

Why can I walk on Jonge Street in Toronto, Canada at one a.m. in safety along with thousands of other Canadians and Americans, yet I can find neither company nor solace in the cities of Chicago, Detroit, New York, Los Angeles, San Francisco, or any of the other major population centers of the United States? Why do politicians of all stripes continually campaign for office by advertising that they are tough on crime, while our crime problem continually worsens?

Do we fear only criminals and the inner cities? Don't we also fear the police. How many of us realize that the police any time they wish can take our property and sell it and keep the profits by asserting we are involved in the rackets or drugs?[110] America has become a country in which agencies have tremendous power to arbitrarily take our property, restrict our use of property, and destroy our ability to work.

"Neither the legislators nor the bureaucrats have any sense of the sanctity of law," said James Bovard.[111] Laws are simply an arbitrary convenience to help politicians get elected, stay in office or serve the bureaucrats, which support it. "Nowadays laws increasingly exist to bind citizens and not government," Bovard added.[112]

The middle-class American increasingly has to dance a country Western tune of despair, as both safety from criminals and protection from arbitrary actions of government both lessen at an alarming rate. The middle class not only has to pay higher taxes for prisons which don't work, but also has to endure regulations and decisions which jeopardize property and vocations.

Some of the more obvious sources of crime and insecurity can be solved, as suggested in the chapters on Drugs, Welfare, and Building the Infrastructure. These suggestions however, only scratch the surface. We also have to consider changing the structure our country uses to deal with crime.

Crime was to have been vastly reduced when prohibition was abolished.[113] Americans were told that organized crime and bootleggers had to get honest work once the illegal market for alcohol was abolished. Not true, Criminals, Law Enforcement Workers, and politicians simply found new areas in which to operate. If we legalize drugs, abolish institutionalized welfare, reduce the incidence of teenage mothers and improve the infrastructure, (as I have recommended), I am not so naive as to believe that there will be a sudden miraculous end to crime. What is the answer? We must *ALSO CHANGE THE CRIMINAL JUSTICE SYSTEM ITSELF!*

Unfortunately, it is a simple fact of life that the bureaucrats who manage the many various law enforcement agencies have to justify their existence. They do this by arresting criminals. If there is not enough criminals, they find ways to create more by writing new laws and regulations.

Right now, bureaucrats are in the process of considering how to make tobacco first a drug, then an illegal drug. This will produces hundreds of thousands of new criminals for the bureaucrats who manage law enforcement agencies and prisons, to feast upon. Politicians will also feed at the trough of regulation and criminalization, as they have in the past. How else do you explain the fact that since 1970 Congress has enacted more than sixty laws which mandate long prison sentences?

In fact, politicians have discovered that they can increase their chances for election by beating their breasts about crime and claiming to solve the problem by increasing the length of sentences and reducing the possibility of parole. Bush won millions of votes for his first election by distorting and displaying the "Willie Horton" ads. How do politicians justify their approach? They claim that criminals will commit less crime when they know their punishment will be more severe.

Although the general public believes this myth, many of the politicians who run for office, and law enforcement officers who support increased punitive laws, know that increasing punishment does not stop crime. A simple review of history shows, in fact, quite the opposite. In the days of the celebrated author Charles Dickens, highwaymen and pickpockets were hanged in public executions. Politicians voted to have public hangings of those that robbed English citizens on the roads or picked their pockets in hopes that would deter crime.

In fact just the opposite happened. Since highwaymen knew that they would be hanged for robbing innocent travelers, they killed their victims so they couldn't testify against them! The highwaymen sensibly reasoned that if they'd be hanged anyway, they might as well kill their potential witnesses. At the same time, pickpockets found that the huge, jostling crowds who packed together to watch the spectacle of public hangings was also a great place to pick pockets!

In today's American society, politicians have saddled the middle class with three things that not only do not work, but also make things much worse for everyone. They are: mandatory sentences; sentencing guidelines, and capitol punishment.

Let's take a simple example that Judge Forer discusses in her book[114] *A RAGE TO PUNISH*. A young black man with no prior record, who had been employed for a year, lost his job. Temporarily out of work and desperate for money, he held up a taxi with a toy pistol and stole $50.

He was arrested and a year later convicted of armed robbery. The sentencing investigation found that he was married, had one child, had not committed any other crimes and was now working.

Judge Forer decided to give him a short sentence, a long period of probation, and require him to repay the stolen money. The prosecutor, however, insisted that the sentencing guidelines in the man's case called for a minimum of five years in prison.

Judge Forer refused. The Pennsylvania Supreme Court ordered her to sentence him to five years in prison. While the dispute raged, the man continued to work and support his family. This made no difference to the prosecutor. So Judge Forer resigned her position, rather than participate in a system which was manifestly so unfair.

Consider for a moment the gross unfairness to the middle class. Instead of M. working and supporting his family, he was sentenced to five years of prison. This cost the middle class $125,000. And his wife and family had to go on A.D.C.. This cost the middle class another $125,000. Did the prosecutor care that sentencing guidelines in this case were unfair, unjust, and a burden to the middle class? Of course not! Politicians don't care about justice, they care about getting elected or re-elected!

If we really cared about justice, we would consider the following three factors when a person commits a crime.: 1) the seriousness of the crime; 2) the character, history, and propensities of the offender; 3) the condition of the victim or victims.

THE SERIOUSNESS OF A CRIME

In a changing, vibrant and evolving society, the seriousness of crimes is constantly in flux. Consider the crime of taking the Lord's name in vain. In ancient Israel, a person could and would be stoned to death for doing so. In modern Iraq or Saudi Arabia, the same punishment still occurs for crimes of irreverence. In seventeenth-century America, having intercourse with animals resulted in hanging the person engaged in bestiality and killing the animal. Today, the latter would result in referral to a local psychiatrist and possibly a few months in jail if it was a repeat offense.

Thirty years ago, dumping a vat of chemicals in your own back yard was not a crime. Today, you could be sent to prison and have your property confiscated for dumping hazardous chemicals on your own property.

In many cases, the seriousness of crime amounts to what is popular or convenient to local politicians and law enforcement officials. Twenty years ago homosexuals were constantly harassed by police officers. Today, politicians avoid alienating the gay community. Unfortunately, as society ebbs and flows in what it considers serious crimes, hundreds of thousands of Americans are caught in the jaws of lawbreakers or lawmakers.

We need to modernize our criminal justice system to deal with conditions in the twenty-first century. But before we can consider the twenty-first century, we have to look at where we are now. Between 1966 and 1990, reported crimes tripled.[115] At present, one homicide is committed every 42 seconds, one burglary every 11 seconds, one car theft every 20 seconds, one robbery every 40 seconds, and one rape every five minutes. Compounding the problem is that crime is becoming a low risk venture. If we consider the probability of being caught and punished, the risk of jail time for each criminal act breaks down as follows: six months per burglary, two years per murder, six months per rape, two months per robbery, 8 to 9 days per aggravated assault, and 2 to 3 days per car theft.[116]

Van Den Haag in his reissued book, *PUNISHING CRIMINALS,* states "that with the risk of punishment so low, the surprising thing is not that we have so much crime but that we don't have a lot more."

His solution to the problem, however, is no more likely to be successful than the current smoke screen called the crime bill that both parties have passed in Congress. Van Den Haag rightly points out that the deficits of the crime bill are so numerous as to make its failure certain at the outset. Instead, he suggests we modify our laws to allow for the following: 1) have prisoners work in real jobs for real money, 2) build more prisons and increase the number and efficiency of the courts, 3) deny bail in many cases, 4) allow random frisking of citizens on the streets, 5) go from unanimous verdicts by juries to three quarters agreement, 6) allow juries to consider past behavior, 7) allow in evidence that has been obtained under "clouded circumstances" (in effect, allow the police to beat a confession out of a criminal), and 7) have age based punishment (keep the prisoner in jail until he is of an age where he is unlikely to commit further crimes).

In contrast to Mr. Van Den Haag's suggestions, the crime bill establishes the following: 1) racial quotas (if a black person kills another black or Caucasian, he can't be executed because too many blacks are being sent to death row), 2) encourages employment, 3) includes the three strikes and you're out provision and 4) encourages counseling.

Neither the sop to the public called the "crime bill" nor Van Den Haag deal effectively with the issue of the seriousness of a crime. Let's consider the case of Richard Davis,[117] the murderer of Polly Klaas, as discussed by Oliver Starr in *National Review* He walked into her home, kidnapped her at knife point, raped and strangled her, then buried her in a wooded area twenty miles from her Petaluma, California home. Davis is a career criminal. Prior to murdering Polly, he had committed kidnapping, assault, and robbery in California on several occasions, yet was continually released from prison after serving minimal time. Although both judges and court workers recognized Davis's increasing danger to society, the prison system was constrained by the California Legislature to release him back into society.

In contrast to Mr. Davis, consider Polly S. Polly is in her early twenties. Her mother asked her if she would be willing to deliver a package containing cocaine to a "friend." The "friend" turned out to be an undercover police officer. Polly S. was sentenced under mandatory sentencing guidelines to twenty years in prison. Polly S. had no prior record, not even a traffic citation, and will be in prison long after Mr. Davis is back on the streets of California searching for new victims.

The middle class of America simply has to do something to make our streets safe, our homes a peaceful refuge and our schools, places of worship and employment free of fear. Just recently, a friend of mine was in church when a homeless person came in and accosted one of the parishioners in the bathroom with a knife. He roughly fondled her breasts, almost bit off her nipple, stole her money and forever branded her church as a place of fear rather than refuge.

There is an answer to our ever spiraling decent into barbarity or fascism. There is a choice that exists which does not allow chaos to continue or require us to become a police state.

The answer is simple. Remember the truism that you have read throughout this book. When it comes to the really important things in this world, there are only simple answers and simple questions—providing you have the courage to ask and the ears to listen.

In asking myself about the crime I both see and read about, I asked myself what really protects us from total chaos? Fortunately, I have had the opportunity to work in an area where I have been able to develop friends who were judges, attorneys, and police officers and also I have seen in my practice victims of crime and perpetrators of crime.

I am convinced that the answer to solving the problem of crime does not rest in the state legislature or Congress. If anything, politicians usually make things worse. They are so intent on giving us what they want us to hear in hopes we will reward them by electing or re-electing them to office that they frequently propose foolish laws and terrible solutions.

The answer to our problem I believe is much simpler. We need to develop a safer society and also protect ourselves from self-serving politicians. I believe we can do so by doing the following:

We must initiate a constitutional amendment, which takes away from Congress and state legislatures their ability to affix specific penalties to specific acts. Instead, the constitutional amendment would prohibit Congress and state legislatures from doing anything other than making an act a felony or a misdemeanor.

Instead of resting our fate in capricious politicians, I propose we rest our fate and confidence in seasoned judges and juries. We need to change our approach to crime by having a two-part trial. The first part of the trial would be to consider if the defendant is guilty or innocent.

In this first part of the trial, the normal laws of evidence would apply. The function of the judge would be the same as it is now, to preside over the court and to be sure that actions of both the prosecution and the defense proceed on defined, accepted grounds.

Once the case goes to the jury to decide, a defendant would be convicted if three fourths of the jurors agreed that the defendant was guilty.

The second phase of the trial would then begin. The jury would be allowed to then establish the consequences or punishment of the defendant. Their consideration could include any and all information about the defendant including his past history, other crimes, the seriousness of the crime of which the defendant was convicted, the state of the victim, and the potential for further actions harmful to society. In this second phase, issues such as mental illness could be raised along with issues of potential for further anti-societal acts.

The jury would have five options. Convicting the defendant of a felony would lead automatically to the first option, 1) No prison and referral to the judge who would sent terms of probation and repayment of society for deeds that were committed. If the defendant chose to defy the judge's probationary conditions, the defendant could be remanded to prison for up to five years. 2) The second level of punishment would be prison up to five years and referral to the judge for exact sentencing of length of prison (no more than five years) and terms of probation. 3) The third level of punishment would be five to ten years of prison and whatever other probationary conditions the presiding judge thought appropriate. 4) The fourth level of punishment would be age related. The jury might feel that the act committed was onerous enough to warrant keeping the felon in prison until he reached an age in which further criminal acts were unlikely. Thus a twenty-year-old who committed a particularly vicious crime could be sentenced to stay in prison until he is over the age of acting out. The jury would simply sentence the person to category four and the judge would then decide in consultation with whatever experts the judge felt necessary what the appropriate age of parole would be. 5) Category five would require a unanimous decision by the jury. The jury as persons who have lost all right to live in a civilized society would define category five felons. Instead of pretending to believe we have capitol punishment (as of now only 32 persons were executed in the last year although several thousand citizens were murdered), category five would be reserved for persons the jurors believed have lost all right to not only remain in society but to ever return to society.

Category five felons would be transported to a secure area (possibly an island). They would be sterilized, tattooed, fingerprinted, voice printed and have a transmitter implanted in their body. They would then be released in the secure area and left to their own devices. Their only restriction would be instant death if they left the area. Other than that, they would have to live with their fellow category five felons. Food would be parachuted into the area once a week. No communication into the area or out of the area would be allowed. No contact with civilized society would be allowed. It would be as if they stepped into a black hole.

To make our society safer and more manageable, the constitutional amendment would also require anyone convicted of killing a police officer, court official or prison employee, automatically assigned to category five.

Basically, what I am proposing is that we make our society safer by returning the issue of crime and law enforcement to jurors and judges. I am convinced that the safety of society and the fairness and justice of our land would be much improved by trusting our society to CITIZENS and SEASONED JUDGES.

Case 1

Let's consider five actual cases and compare what really happened vs. what could have happened under a new system. Because Saginaw is one of the port cities on the Great Lakes, it is a receiving point of drugs. It is not unusual for the crime families that handle drugs to occasionally fight with each other. A few years ago, a leader of one of the crime families was shot in the head and then dumped on the street near St. Mary's Medical Center.

Curiously, he lived. When the family that arranged the hit heard that the was still alive, they sent a "hit man" to finish the job. When a man dressed as a priest showed up at the hospital asking for the wounded patient, security became suspicious and had the police detain and frisk the "priest". He was carrying a concealed weapon and a I.D. check revealed that he was a convicted felon with a long history of arrests for suspected murders.

The "hit man" was jailed. The next day an expensive attorney from Detroit came to Saginaw, bailed the "hit man" out and he was never heard from again.

Under our current system of law, the judge had no power to keep him in jail. Here was a man who obviously intended to commit murder and had committed many murders in the past. His penalty for attempted murder was one night in jail.

Under the constitutional change in the law I propose, two things would happen, first, the judge would have power to deny bail to persons who have been arrested and convicted of crimes in the past. Second, carrying a concealed weapon would still be a felony. After spending several months in jail waiting for trial, the "hit man" would be tried. If convicted, the jury would then decide what his penalty would be. They would have access to information about his past. And it is entirely possible that they might decide he should spend the remainder of his active life in prison (level four) or even be exiled from human society (level five).

Case 2

Case 2 was a young man who broke up a relationship he was having with his girl friend. He believed she had cheated on him. His girlfriend tearfully told her best friend. The best friend asked her boyfriend to "talk" to the young man. When the story reached the young man he understood that the "talk to" was in reality an excuse to have him beaten up for breaking up with his girl friend.

The young man, fearful for his safety, pocketed a pistol and under the heat of argument shot the other youth several times. When the case came up for trial, the jury rejected the defendant's plea that it was manslaughter and convicted him of second degree murder. They couldn't see how shooting a victim several times qualified for manslaughter. He is now serving an extended sentence in prison.

Under the new amendment, the jury would first decide if he was guilty of committing a felony. Assuming that they would have found him guilty, they could then consider other factors such as 1) he had no prior history of committing crimes, 2) he had been in a sense "set up" by the girls who were playing the game of "let's you and him fight," 3) had been told by a close friend that if you have to shoot in self defense, shoot several times to make sure the other person stays down. The jury might also consider that in cases such as these there is only a two-percent chance of recidivism.

Taking all those factors into consideration, the jury might decide that prison was still necessary but might limit his sentence to a level two (up to five years in prison, the exact length depending upon the judge's discretion) or a level three (five to ten years in prison, the exact length depending upon the judge's decision).

Case 3

Case 3 is a young woman who was asked by her mother to deliver a package. The package contained cocaine and she was sentenced to 20 years in prison. The prison sentence was a given, once the jury convicted her of possession with intent to deliver. Under the new amendment, once the jury convicted her, they could take into account that she had no prior convictions, that a psychopathic mother unduly influenced her, and that she was naive and immature. The jury would be free to assign her a level 1 (probation with no prison).

Case 4

Case 4 was a young man who invaded an elderly couple's house with a friend. After terrorizing the couple and taking their valuable possessions, the young man demanded that the elderly couple have sex while he watched to provide him some "entertainment". The associate who was with him was so shocked by his perverted thinking that he stopped the action right then and insisted that they both leave.

In this case, the judge let the man who protected the elderly couple off with probation while he sent the other young man to prison for fifteen to thirty years. Under the new law, the jury would again have an opportunity to convict both men and could also choose the same sentences that the judge chose in this case, letting the person who protected the couple off with a level 1 sentence (no prison) and giving the other felon a level 3, 4 or 5 sentence. In this case they might well have chosen a level 4 (remainder to prison until he is of such an age or disposition as to present no danger to society) or a level 5 (remainder to a reservation for the rest of his life with no opportunity to contact anyone in this society or to be contacted by anyone in this society).

Case 5

I took a personal interest in Case 5. He was a well known to the police, killer whom they believed had murdered at least 8 people in the area. One of the persons he had murdered was a younger brother of one of my clients. She had never gotten over the fact that he had cruelly murdered her brother and that the police could do nothing about it. Case 5 was cunning. If he thought that there was any chance that the person he was robbing could identify him, he killed his victim.

Eventually, he was apprehended for armed robbery. He is now serving time in prison and may be let out of prison in a few years.

Under the new law, once he was found guilty of armed robbery, the police could inform the jury of what they believed were his other crimes and why they believed it. Victims, such as my client, could then tell the jury of the horror she has felt and the cruel loneliness that has filled her and her parent's days since her younger brother was murdered. The probate court worker would be free to inform the jury about his juvenile record, which included several serious crimes.

Instead of receiving a sentence which would allow him to again return to society, the jury might well instead assign him a level four (confinement in prison until he presented no threat to society) or a level five (permanent removal from society).

Straightening out the sentencing and punishment side of our crime problem is however only half the battle. Sir Thomas More, a renaissance, English, Christian philosopher discussed the other side of the crime issue in his book on *UTOPIA*.[118] In the first chapter of his book, he quotes an imaginary conversation between two individuals in which a respected prosecuting attorney bragged that on that day they had hung twenty felons at one time in a public execution. The only thing that puzzled the prosecutor was that even though they were hanging felons at a goodly rate, there always seemed more felons available to take their place on the scaffold.

Sir Thomas More, who was later beatified by the Catholic Church, and is now one of the churches Saints cautiously criticized the powers that be by noting that hanging someone for simple thievery does not stop thievery and only encourages the thief since he is going to hang for simple theft anyway to go ahead and kill the witness to his theft. To More, the reasons for crime were such that he believed crimes would occur despite the punishments that were applied and that society had to get at the root causes of crime before crime would cease.

Sir Thomas More was beheaded in 1535 for refusing to recognize King Henry the VIII as the true vicar of the church. More elected to die rather than sacrifice his convictions about truth and justice. Let's review what he thought the root causes of crime were and compare those roots to our day. He believed that the source of crime came from two areas, the "useless" and the "useful." The useless were inherited nobility and mercenary soldiers. Once the inherited nobility and mercenary soldiers lost their source of income, they would not demean themselves by entering into common labor so they had no choice but to become robbers and thieves.

The Democrats have become expert at creating a class of "useless" people. It's called the "great society" and the "great society" has developed a class of people who depend on welfare for their existence. Their only duty is to vote "democratic" to continue their marginal existence and if possible to create more "useless" people by having children while on welfare. The "useless" in our day have little to keep them or their children occupied so it is normal for many of them to engage in the underground economy including drugs, prostitution, thievery, burglary, etc. The "useless" are also continually expanded so as to create more jobs for the welfare bureaucracy who also have to continue to vote "democratic" to keep their jobs.

More defined the "useful" as honest working people who were forced off of their jobs by the wealthy trying to become wealthier. More was writing at the time that English society was changing from an agrarian, share cropping society into an industrial society. Peasants were thrown off of their land and sent to live in squalid slums in the city, while their little farms were turned into grazing lands for sheep. Wealthy landlords could make more money raising sheep and producing wool than they could renting their lands to peasants.

The "useful" without home, land or income, also turned to crime to prevent their families from starving. In today's society, the Republicans have become adept at shipping "useful" jobs out of this country. Democrats, of course, have assisted the Republicans in their attack on "useful" jobs because they anticipate that the useful will then join the ranks of the useless.

While the crime rate of the useless is not news, the crime rate of the useful is often ignored. But Lawrence A. Greenfeld, acting director of the Bureau of Justice Statistics notes that one sixth of U.S. crime occurs at the job site. *The useful commit about one million violent crimes a year*.[119] These crimes include murdering their supervisors, aggravated assault, simple assault, theft, murder and rape. As jobs disappear, as the burdens of regulations continually increase from Washington, as taxes increase, employers flee to other lands.

The useful increasingly live under the constant awareness that they not only have little hope to see their jobs and income improve but that they can expect little job security for themselves or their children. Is it so surprising then that their anger, anxiety and insecurity turns many to crime?

In addition to More's two sources of crime, I would add a third source that did not exist in More's day. That is victimless crime. Politicians in their never-ending quest to get elected or re-elected continually find new scapegoats to attack. The administration's current crime bill contains 52 new laws, which are punishable by death along with new ways to keep prisoners in prison for life.[120]

A favorite scapegoat in the past for politicians has been alcohol and drugs. Now in addition to drugs, smoking, eating nachos, burritos and kung pao chicken are coming under fire.

Politicians are simply unable to keep their hands out of people's businesses. They have no ethics for distinguishing between existence and essence. It is the duty of government to deal with existence, i.e., the provision of roads, education, hospitals, common defense, public order, etc. It is not the duty of government to decide that we all should live forever and thus prohibit all harmful substances or acts which we engage in that could injure ourselves.

For instance, it is the duty of the government to arrest drunk drivers who drive and injure someone. It is not the duty of government to arrest citizens who get drunk in their own homes.

Organized crime gains power by convincing politicians to prohibit acts which are appealing to a percentage of the populace, i.e., gambling, prostitution and drugs. It then gains power and income by providing these services outside of the law. This type of crime was not widely evident in More's England but now accounts for half of the felons in prison.

To truly conquer crime, we must stop the Democrats in their drive to create more Useless people and the Republicans in their drive to steal jobs from the Useful. In addition, we have to set limits on the ability of politicians to continually define more acts as crimes.

Resolving welfare, creating infrastructure jobs, stopping the drug war and amending the constitution to deal with crime in a new way will go a long way to solving the issue of crime.

Remember that 7 percent of criminals commit 70 percent of the crimes. The useless and the useful commit the rest of the crimes. Crimes of the useless will go down as we reduce the number of people on welfare and crimes of the useful will decrease as we increase good middle-class jobs.

To resolve the issue of crime, we must vote against all incumbents until we have new elected officials who are willing to face the real issues of crime and how it is generated.

Insurance and the Cost of a Suing Society

"Liberty lies in the hearts of men and women; when it dies there, no constitution, no law, no court can save it; no constitution, no law, no court can even do much to help." Learned Hand[121]

Although I am not an attorney, my practice in medical psychology has forced me to become increasingly aware of the law and how it functions. Many of my patients have been the unfortunate victims of mishaps. And because I have participated in their care, my patient's attorneys often depose me or ask me to testify in court.

My experience with the court and legal system didn't start with my medical practice. It actually started when I first moved to Michigan and became the administrator of a small mental health clinic in Gladwin. Since I was the only "shrink" in town, the probate court frequently asked me to provide expert opinion in child and sexual abuse cases. As the attorneys in town got to know me, they sometimes asked me to act as an expert in their cases.

Since the town was quite small, I had the opportunity to become acquainted with the local probate judge, Alexander Strange, who at the age of 50 was the youngest probate judge in the state.

Gladwin had a particularly eccentric prosecuting attorney. One day while having coffee with one of the local attorneys, I asked him how the prosecutor had gotten his position. "Well, Martin it's this way," he said. "We make our money defending cases. We get a lot of drunk drivers in this area. So the better we do by them, the more money we make. We decided that we wanted a prosecutor in office that we could beat in court."

As an after thought, my attorney friend added, "Come to think of it, I don't think he's won a drunk driving case in the last ten years!"

Although I lack the temperament to be an attorney or a judge, I must admit that as a group, I like them better than many of the persons I have met in my own profession. Despite my natural affection for many of them, both judges and attorneys, I offer the following comments: If the middle class is to survive and expand, we must make some changes in the structure and practice of the law.

As Judge Hand (one of the greatest judges in American history[122]) asserted "a political community could not flourish or its citizens develop or improve their sense of moral responsibility, unless they participated in the community's deepest and most important decisions about justice."[123]

Unfortunately, I believe that we are becoming progressively more confused about justice and recompense. We are developing a "lottery" mentality, which has infused the average citizen. The lottery mentality seems based on two myths. The first myth is that we can place a money value on our injuries, the second myth is that when an insurer pays, it doesn't really "hurt anybody."

Myth #1

We can recompense you for your injuries by giving you money.

Several of my patients have won multi-million dollar awards due to their grievous injuries. After the first flush of victory and the congratulations they receive from their attorney, family and friends, they almost always go into a period of depression. Without realizing it, they had come to believe the myth of the lottery that the more injured they were, the more they deserved and the better they would feel when they got it. Nothing could be further from the truth! The experience of two of my patients illustrates this truth.

Case #1

A truck driven by a commercial firm struck B.J.. He sustained a skull fracture and was unable to return to work because of his head injuries. He had owned a successful machine shop. Four years after his injury, his case finally came to court. He received a judgement in excess of two million dollars.

I didn't see B.J. for two months after his suit was settled. Then he failed to keep his appointment. Later that day, he came to my office. He had become confused about the time of his appointment and had overslept. My secretary laughingly bawled him out, telling him he would have to pay a "no show" fee and reschedule his appointment.

Later that week, he managed to keep his appointment. As I had anticipated, he was depressed and tearful. "Man, I just don't understand it. I feel like shit! My head aches. I forget things. I didn't even remember to come here. Your boy (a high school student who works in the evenings) called to remind me about the appointment. (I make it a practice to call my head-injured patients, as they often forget their appointments)."

Then waving his hands, he added, "I just don't know what the f—is happening!"

"B.J. nothing new is happening," I told him. " You've had headaches since your accident. You've often felt like shit. The reason Brad called you is that you had a head injury and you're forgetful. Nothing has changed."

"Bull shit!" he countered. "I've got money up the ass! "I'm going to buy a converted Greyhound bus and tour the country!"

B.J. hesitated and added ruefully, "That is if I can find my way out of this f-ing city!"

"You got lost again?" I asked.

"Yeah, that's the other thing that pissed me off. I wanted to go to Flint to the mall and buy a gold chain for my son. He's playing outside linebacker for his school, the same position I played in school. But my wife wouldn't let me go by myself! I'm a f-ing millionaire and that b- wouldn't let me go!" Tears of frustration and anger rolled down his cheek.

"Well, she's probably a little anxious. The last time you went to Flint, you ended up in Canada." I reminded him.

B.J. laughed delightedly, "Yeah, I saw these two women who wore next to nothing in their convertible. So I kept them in sight in my truck, and everyone once in a while I'd pass them or let them pass me so I could get a good look. After a while, they even started waving and smiling at me. How did I know they were heading for Canada? You didn't tell my wife on me did you?" he asked.

"B.J. you know better than that. Whatever you say stays in this office unless you ask me to talk to someone," I reassured him.

A long silence settled over the office. Finally B.J. stated a truism that I have used with many other patients, clients, family and friends.

"You know doc, money is only important when you don't have it. If you have it, it don't mean shit!"

My own experience with many patients is that B.J.'s opinion has remained true over all the cases I've seen.

Case #2 is another example of this truism.

K. M. was a factory worker. He was on a scaffold attached to the interior of factory's building and the bolts that held the scaffold gave way. He tumbled several feet and landed on his head. When his suit was finally settled, he also received a settlement in excess of a million dollars. Three weeks after the suit was settled, he awkwardly came into my office on crutches.

Since K.M.'s suit was a product liability case, his suit had been long and protracted, settled about five years after he had been injured. "I hear your suit has been settled."

K.M. irritated replied, "I don't want to talk about it!"

"How come?"

"Because I'm a freak!" He hissed.

"What do you mean you're a freak?"

"I can't walk right and kids ask me why I'm on crutches."

K.M. had not only been a factory worker, he had also been a semi-professional hockey player. The idea that he was a cripple more than outweighed any settlement that he could have received.

Of all the patients that I have known who have received large settlements, none have been that much happier because of it! The fact is that we can't put a price on health. Health is a lot like money. It's only important when you don't have it! *Money and health can not be traded for each other!*

Myth #2

If the insurance company pays, it isn't really hurting anyone!

When I first started my practice in Michigan in 1971, I paid $90. a year for a million dollars of malpractice insurance. My bill this year was $2,482. A friend, an obstetrician, pays forty thousand dollars a year for his malpractice insurance. A local hospital recently closed its doors because it could not afford to pay its malpractice insurance premium of over two million dollars!

Patients frequently come into my office and seriously explain to me that they were a passenger in a car that their father, mother, brother, sister, close friend, husband, wife, daughter, son was driving. The driver was at fault in the accident, and they were suing the driver. After all, their attorney explained, you're not really suing them, you're suing the insurance company.

While a person should receive some recompense for their injuries, we have to remember that in the end it's the middle class that pays, not the insurance companies.

The Trial Lawyer's Association repeatedly claim to the public, "We have to get rid of the bad doctors that hurt people!" Then they parade a few patients who have had terrible experiences at the hands of their doctors. Of course, they are not as enthusiastic about "bad attorneys." Since they are making a killing off of bad doctors, one should also not be surprised that when the doctors try to set limitations on "bad doctors", attorneys rush to defend them. *After all, they reason, one should not kill the goose that lays the golden eggs!*

The Trial Lawyer's Association basically has it both ways. On the one hand, they convince the public that "bad doctors" have to be punished; i.e., fined large amounts of money, and, on the other hand, they protect the "bad doctors" so they can stay in business.

In reality, there are not as many bad doctors as there are "bad results" in medicine. Medicine is really much more of an art than a science! You can give the same so called "healing medicine" to one hundred people: seventy will get well, twenty-five will not respond to the medicine, and five will get worse. Doctors need to practice long enough and see enough people to get a "feeling" for the patient. Sometimes, he or she intuitively prescribes the right medicine. Other times, the doctor simply stumbles from one medicine to another until the right one is found.

The same thing happens with surgery. Given a specific procedure, such as a heart bypass, 90 out of 100 get well. Three die and seven have a poor response.

Perhaps some day medicine will have developed enough knowledge to move from an art to a science. Until then, every time you visit a doctor, take medicine, undergo surgery, you are taking a chance. Most of the time, chance is on your side, but sometimes-double zeros come up.

If doctors were sued every time double zeros surfaced, we'd soon have doctors only for the rich. The middle class and the poor would have no doctors who could afford the malpractice premiums necessary to practice.

This is not to imply that there are not ineffective doctors. As in any profession, there are some incompetent doctors. While I worked in my first job in Michigan, a surgeon in the area had a drinking problem. One night he came in and did emergency surgery while he was inebriated. He killed the patient. The vast majority of cases of which I am familiar, however, are more bad results than bad doctors.

If we continue to take the "lottery mentality" in America, we will increasingly deprive the middle class of both doctors and products. In many small cities in Michigan, there are no obstetricians. Increasingly, there are fewer hospitals, for the simple reason that there aren't enough patients with enough money to pay for malpractice insurance, let alone office expenses and staff.

Many products that could be of benefit to the middle class, including drugs, never come on line for the same reason. There is not enough money to be made to warrant the insurance expense of producing the product or medication.

To resolve the issue of malpractice and product liability, I offer a simple solution. We need a reasonable limitation on judgements. Once we reject the assumption that money can be traded for health, the issue becomes what is fair and just.

What is fair or just should be computed in one of two ways. In the case of a person who has been successfully working, what is fair is the amount of money that would have been earned until age 65. For instance, if a person is injured to the point that the person is permanently disabled, the annual earnings of the person are found to be $30,000 a year and the person is 40 years old. Thirty thousand would be multiplied by 25, which would be the maximum amount that the jury could award.

The judge could then add up to 50 percent of the jury award for pain and suffering. The judge should make this decision, as jury's do not have sufficient experience to fairly place pain and suffering in context.

In the case of unemployed persons, such as children, students, homemakers, etc., the figure used would be the median income for individuals that year. In the case of the elderly, i.e., those over 65, the cap would be set by the average earnings made during the person's life time, less social security times the expected life span of the person.

Having set a reasonable cap on awards, we next have to consider the issue of settling the lawsuit. Increasingly, claims adjusters are under pressure from their home office to deny claims—even legitimate ones.

A client of mine, who had a reputation for fairness in the community was fired from a large insurance company because his approach on how to settle the claim was based on what was fair and reasonable. His supervisor admitted she was firing him because of his "attitude." She said: "When you get a claim, *you* look for reasons to pay it, but your job is to look for reasons *not* to pay it!"

Trial lawyers, in the main, support the not-paying approach, because this requires persons to turn to attorneys for help because they can't get a fair shake from insurance companies on their own. And the insurance company also has to hire attorneys to defend them from the plaintiff. Each time someone is injured, the person has to go through the humiliation of proving they were really hurt and are not a "malingerer or crook." They have to spend years waiting for their case to be resolved. Many cases are open and shut in terms of liability and damages, but they are delayed simply because they *can* be.

One way to stop unnecessary lawsuits is to create a Citizen's Commission composed of a representative of plaintiffs, one of defendants, and a retired judge. This commission would have the power to hear complaints. If a plaintiff and his attorney believed that there action was "open and shut" with obvious liability and demonstrable damages and could prove that settlement was unreasonably delayed, they could submit their arguments to the commission. If the commission agreed, the defendant would have to pay the plaintiff's attorney fees, and the plaintiff's attorney would receive a twenty-five percent bonus. If the commission disagreed, the plaintiff and his attorney would have to pay a ten thousand-dollar fine.

In this kind of environment, defendants would risk having to pay an additional fifty percent over and above what the jury awarded, and plaintiffs would risk ten thousand dollars for spurious petitions.

Another type of case is that of attorneys who specialize in nuisance suits, without merit. In the past several years, I have had women in my office that were forced to turn over their children to their ex-husband. The husband hired an attorney to continually harass his ex-wife on spurious grounds. He could afford to pay his attorney's fees and she couldn't. Eventually, driven into poverty by legal fees and court costs, she gave up and quit fighting.

The commission in such cases would have the power to fine both the plaintiff's attorney and the plaintiff, double the attorney's fees and court costs so that the defendant would have some protection from suing individuals.

The carrot and stick approach, which rewards a quick and fair settlement and punishes a prolonged and unfair settlement could go a long way toward unclogging the court system.

There is another issue often ignored but which frequently comes to my attention. A client retires after working for General Motors for twenty-nine years. This person has heard that they could get more money on disability retirement as opposed to regular retirement.

The client wants me to establish that they have a stress-related disease due to conditions at work. Usually, such people can find an attorney to represent their claims. Increasingly, these claims clog the system and prevent persons who are truly in acute distress from being heard in court.

These people have set for themselves a perilous course, "proving that there is something wrong with them." They don't realize they will spend the next two to four years proving that they can't work or function. They will obsess about every symptom. They will be afraid to have fun, vacation, mow their lawn, or do any of the normal things that make life worthwhile. Instead, they will be constantly fearful of what they say, to whom they say it, and who may be watching them. Each person that drives down the street and stops near their house may be a private detective checking to see if they are really disabled.

Let's consider two real cases. L.H., was age 55 years. He had worked for General Motors for thirty years and had developed a case of ulcers. Each time he came to work, his ulcers acted up. Eventually, the company doctor suggested that he would be better off if he considered retirement. L.H.'s union representative told him that he should apply for disability. L.H. replied, "I never had to back up to a man to get my paycheck and I ain't starting now."

L.H. retired a few months later. L.H. loved to putz around in his basement with wood working equipment. His doctor to help him learn to relax referred him to me, hoping this would help his ulcers. In interviewing L.H., it seemed apparent he liked to be active. But he couldn't stand confined activity, such as working on the line at General Motors.

I suggested he consider a part-time job at a lumberyard. At first, L.H. resented my suggestion. "Why should I work for piddling wages when I used to make close to twenty bucks an hour?"

I replied, "Look, you like helping people and you love putzing with wood. This is just a second income to help you pay for trips up North and keep you busy. Try it and see if you like it."

L.H. applied for the job and eventually started working part time. To his surprise, he loved the work. His ulcers healed and he found himself not only enjoying his part-time job, but also working on his cabin up North. He lost weight, stopped drinking and smoking, and took in a foreign exchange student for the summer. L.H. found that he was happy on normal retirement from G.M. along with the freedom to earn additional monies.

In contrast consider B.K., 55 who developed a heart condition while working for General Motors. He had a triple bypass and seemed to be doing well enough. However, he still had problems with angina, and eventually decided to retire. His union representative also suggested that he apply for disability retirement.

B.K.'s wife worked at a local hospital and his two sons, ages 19 and 17, attended school. I told him that the ordeal of the process to collect disability would not be good for him, and suggested he consider part-time work. My suggestion enraged him. He declared, "I'm not going to work for no minimum wage job!"

I didn't hear from B.K. for several months. Finally, his wife made an appointment to see me. She was in the process of divorcing B.K. "He's totally changed! He won't go anyplace with me. We used to go up to Tawas and line dance. He was a lot of fun. Now all he does is sit at home. He won't mow the lawn nor do anything outside the house. He's afraid the Workman's comp carrier has a private detective that watching him if he does any kind of work."

She was clearly upset.

"While I'm at work, he draws the blinds and paces," she went on. "You can see the marks on the rug where he walks up and down. He drinks coffee after coffee. His nerves are on edge and he yells at the boys. They can't do anything right."

Tears came to her eyes, as she continued, "My oldest son just moved to Traverse City. I know it was to get away from my husband. "

I asked her why she had come here.

"My husband told me you told him not to apply for Worker's Comp. He said you told him he should consider taking a part-time job at Seven Eleven."

I nodded.

"I checked with an accountant and I found out that if he just took his retirement and worked part-time, he would do just as well as if he was getting disability retirement. When I told him that, he said I was right, but since he had started it, he couldn't stop now. Maybe he can't stop, but I can!"

The story of B.K. proves the truth of an old saying, "Every curse has its blessing, and every blessing has its curse." Insurance in certain circumstances can be either a blessing or a curse. It can provide peace of mind, or burden the mind. B.K. felt he was entitled to benefits under his plan due to the stress he had experienced over the years. Yet his struggle to "prove he was entitled" had more downside effects on him that any financial reward he received.

Judge Learned Hand's perceptive comment that liberty lies in our hearts is also true about truth, justice, fairness, love, concern, loyalty, and responsibility. We need to change our legal system to the extent that we no longer sponsor activities which lead to the degradation of the middle class and the continuance of the myth that there is a "free pot of gold" out there. Pots of gold are never free. Each pot has its price.

It is the nature of all of us to forget that "pots of gold" have a price. We seem inclined to throw money at persons who have sustained ill fortune. Thus, the patient who has a unfortunate experience in medical treatment is allowed to sue and win his judgement against the doctor. The result, however, is ever-higher medical costs for us all and fewer doctors willing to treat in rural areas or take risks in treatment that could be beneficial for their patients.

Perhaps, we need to add one penny to a national sales tax to insure citizens against "bad results" in medical practice and product liability. Thus, if a person is injured while being treated or is hurt while using equipment, a panel would first decide if the act was due to willful negligence or the random interaction of a particular person, a particular treatment, or a product. If the panel determined that it was not gross negligence on the part of the doctor or manufacturer, the person would be allowed to apply to the "bad result" fund.

You might ask, "Why should I pay one penny on a dollar for every purchase I make just so someone else can receive money for an unfortunate occurrence?" The truth is that you are now paying a *lot more* than one penny on each dollar you spend! It's time we dealt with the issue of malpractice and product liability in a more rational fashion.

Finally, I think we need to recognize that "work expands to fill a vacuum." As we move into the twenty-first century, with increasing need to improve and modernize our infrastructure and take care of an increasingly aged population, we need more engineers and health services workers and fewer attorneys.

It would be advantageous for the middle class to not only restrict the number of attorneys allowed to practice in court, but to also encourage current attorneys to enter other professions. When a society decides that it's advantageous to move persons from one profession to another, there is no reason why grants couldn't be offered to attorneys who want to switch careers.

An allied area for attorneys is to form citizen's councils, which deal with the issue of equity. By equity, I mean the "tension between raw power and just law."[124] The average middle-class citizen often has to throw up his hands and give up when faced with the power of unjust manufacturers and distributors of goods, unjust housing, unjust health care, unjust taxes, unjust government services, unjust occupational and environmental diseases, and corporate and bureaucratic abuses.

There is no reason why the middle class could not or should not develop municipal, state, regional and national councils whose sole purpose would be to listen to the problems of the middle class, and then present their problems to state and national legislatures to be heard and resolved.

The point made here is the same point made by Judge Gerber; "For too many attorneys, the accumulation of wealth has become the dominant focus of professional life, with little energy or commitment remaining for public service or pro bono work for those in need."[125] Judge Gerber believes that law schools spend too much attention to adversarial pursuits and train their students for combat and pay too little attention to the humane arts of negotiation, counseling, and conflict resolution.

Many of the clients I have seen who have struggled through the months and years simply to get their "just needs" taken care of have had many a tearful day or depressed period trying to understand why they couldn't do so. One client told me, "Dr. Shinedling, I didn't go up to a supermarket where there was a line that said Head Injuries Here, or Broken Backs there, or wheel chairs two for a dollar."

She continued, "I paid to have coverage for accidents. The insurance company was more than willing to take my money, but now all the red tape, delays, and you need to have a case manager. Do I need a case manager to come to my house and observe how I can't move my wheelchair up the porch steps, and do need a ramp?"

Furiously, she continued, "Am I a moron or something? I do a lot of things for myself. I could be charging the insurance company a lot more for the things I take care of myself. Why don't they believe me? I really don't need this aggravation in my life."

My response is the same old refrain, "It's not personal. They do this with everybody. They are not attacking you as a person, they are just trained to screen thoroughly all requests for services. Your claims adjuster has people continually looking over her back to make sure that she doesn't authorize services or pay for things they are not required to pay for."

She looked at me for a moment. "In other words, you're saying if they have an excuse not to help, then they won't help?"

I nodded. "True, but remember it's not personal."

"Well, maybe I ought to make it personal by blowing up the damn building!"

Several times a year, one of my clients threatens to kill their case manager, claims adjuster, or insurance representative. So far none have carried out the threat, but a few have come perilously close. On some occasions, I have had to notify the police or a particular agent that a patient was close to the edge of acting out. Whenever I did notify the agent or the police, I always told the patient that I was going to have to warn them. By the time the patient had reached the desperate stage of threatening murder or mayhem, they were often relieved by my intervention.

Is it really necessary, however, to take such an adversarial approach to the simple problems of just recompense for just injuries? I think not. At present, our system corrupts citizens and enriches attorneys.

My comments about the law, of course, are not new. Jesus had this to say about the lawyers of his time, "And he said woe unto you also, ye lawyers! For ye lade men with burdens grievous to be borne, and ye yourselves touch not the burdens with one of your fingers." Luke 11:46

Shakespeare was more precise when he wrote: "The first thing we do, let's kill all the lawyers." (*HENRY THE SIXTH, PART II*).

While I don't suggest that we heap woe unto all attorneys, we do need to compare our society to that of Japan. Per unit of population, Japan has one attorney for each 20 attorneys that exist in the United States.[126] When you consider that in the last year, Japan had a trade surplus of 143 billion dollars while the United States had a deficit of 115 billion dollars, one would have to ask the question, "Is having too many attorneys a drain on our economy?" If so, should we motivate our politicians (many of whom are attorneys) to do something about this by removing *all incumbents from office?*

Education—Recognizing We Are All Equally Different

We hold these truths to be self evident: that all men are created equal; that they are endowed by their creator with certain unalienable rights; that among these are life, liberty, and the pursuit of happiness.

Declaration of Independence, 4 July 1776

Because of an illness, a month was lost
For lack of a month, a semester was lost
For lack of a semester, a year was lost
For lack of a year, a student was lost
And a child gave up.

In 1990, America spent 377 billion dollars on education.[127] Eighty percent of the expenditures were substantially wasted. Before I explain why, I want to give you a challenge, go to your local school and ask for permission to observe a kindergarten class for one hour and then observe a 9th grade class for an hour. The truth of what I have just stated will become immediately obvious.

The reason for this truth however, is more complicated. Education, as practiced in America, is based on a delusion and an illusion. The delusion is that by using established educational principles we can change the happy, eager, optimistic and curious kindergartner into a successful, contributing member of society *USING STANDARD EDU-CATIONAL TECHNIQUES.* The illusion is that a high school or college diploma means something.

Although, I have thought for some time the monies spent on education were substantially wasted, I couldn't put my finger on why. It was not until I started studying Chaos Theory that my internal light bulb clicked on. Chaos theory is the study of non-predictable events, such as the ultimate course of a hurricane, the exact day, three years hence that an earthquake will occur, the exact place a tornado will appear and where it will strike.

These events are non-linear and the end of an action cannot be known by understanding the beginning.[128] Mathematicians and physicists once thought that if we had computers massive enough and fast enough and substantial measurement points, the mysteries of the weather could be predicted. Now they know that their belief is untrue. They also know that small differences in the beginning can result in massive disturbances at the end of a chaotic sequence. The poem I created about the effect of an illness on a child's life is one example of the long-term effect of a random event—being sick for one month and missing school.

Consider for a moment the kindergarten class you observed. The children differ in sex, health, height, weight, strength, activity level, familial background, race, religion, learning capacity, etc. They also differ in talents such as 1) linguistic skills, 2) musical skills, 3) logical-mathematic ability, 4) spatial visualization skills, 5) bodily-kinesthetic skills, 6) intrapersonal skills and, 7) interpersonal skills.[129] Some of their talents can be developed and others are naturally present and only have to be massaged into greater levels of perfection. In effect, one can never predict the exact composition of each new kindergarten class, hence each kindergarten class is an example of a normal non-linear event in nature, i.e., Chaos.

To deal with the Chaos of incoming students, American educators implement common courses, teaching methods, instructional periods, standardized subjects; all with the purpose and intent of changing the kindergartner into a thinking, productive adult. But, instead we find that the wonderful, excited kindergartners are now in the ninth grade, bored, disinterested and often hostile youth—that is, if they stayed in school. A substantial number have already dropped out. American educators explain their failure to educate by blaming the parents who are not supportive and government for not providing enough money. Others blame a society, which encourages teenage girls to have children and go on the welfare dole.

But could the explanation be simpler? After-all parents are with their children for far less time that the teachers in a typical day and isn't 377 billion dollars enough? The reality is that educational theory and practice is dead wrong! Instead of using common methods for chaotic students, educators should acknowledge that they are dealing with a fundamental fact of nature, i.e., and chaos in action, that is, children. And each child is equally different!

Sometimes the obvious is so obvious we ignore it. Perhaps that is why the adage "You can't see the forest for the trees" is so readily understood. But, it is usually the youth that brings us up short. Several years ago, I was invited to teach a Sunday school class. The subject came up that we are all created in the image of God. One thirteen year-old youth exclaimed, "He must be one strange looking dude!"

Although we accept the assertion that we are all created equal as a given truth, upon closer examination, we realize it's wrong. There are obvious differences in gender, race, and attributes (height, weight, hair color, strength, intelligence, artistic talent, athletic ability, curiosity, motivation, etc.). Of course, others might argue that we are not created equal, but we are created with equal *rights*.

Equal rights assumes America is a country that always asks critical questions such as "Is it just?" "Is it right?" "Is it fair?" And if something is not just, right, or fair, how can the law be utilized to make it so? In reality, the opposite happens. Lawyers argue against one or more of the issues of justice, rightness, fairness. Wealthy people especially can hire attorneys to evade justice or fairness in their defense. While prosecutors on the other hand, often persecute rather than prosecute—if it's to their political advantage. To the extent they are able, lawyers also lobby to put into effect laws which extend the power and influence of their clients, despite the fact that the laws are neither fair nor just.

In his book, *UNEQUAL JUSTICE*[130], Awerbuch documented how the major law firms in this country have been able to subvert the ideas of both justice and fairness. Judge Lois Forer[131] in her book on punishment, *A RAGE TO PUNISH*, demonstrates that since 1980 things have gotten worse not better. James Bovard (journalist and policy analyst) supports her conclusions in his book, *LOST RIGHTS*.[132] The fact is that the average middle-class person can neither afford to enforce the concept of fairness and justice in the courts, nor expect that statues written in Congress and the State legislatures will always consider their rights to be equal to the wealthy or powerful.

As Rousseau (1712-1778) noted in his treatise on freedom, "Man was born free and everywhere he is in chains."[133] And he added, "What good is freedom, if all you have is the freedom to starve."

The reality is, despite the protestations of politicians, bureaucrats and pundits, we are neither created equal nor do we have equal rights. There is one sense in which we are equal, we are all *Equally different!* Mathematician and statistician, B. J. Winer made a fairly good case of the principle of equal differentness[134] in his book *STATISTICAL PRINCIPLES IN EXPERIMENTAL DESIGN*. In fact, much of the foundation for social science statistics and research rests on the premise that we are equally different.

Education, on the other hand, continues to stress equality rather than equal differentness. Equality is emphasized in terms of federal and state bureaucrats, stipulating that the same programs be offered to all students. Most states have insisted that school districts must receive the same amount of money per student. And educators are continually measured by how well their students do under *standardized* testing.

Another impetus to the idea of equality came from American behaviorists such as John Watson.[135] He took the public stance that children were blank tablets upon which anything could be written—provided they were given the right training. His view that each child had the potential to become anything from President of the United States to a janitor in the local school, coincided with the Jeffersonian view that all of us are created equal.

But in an increasingly diverse and multi-cultural society, *"It just ain't so!"* Is it to the advantage of the middle class to participate in this "let's pretend" as children increasingly have poor educational performance and lessened opportunities? Or should we embrace the reality that each child is equally different?

Once we accept the idea that each child is equally different, it follows that we then must accept the truism that each child is entitled to an education that acknowledges the child's *differentness*. Children may be different in terms of the language spoken in the family home, in matters of health, learning capacity, future expectations, environmental constraints, inner motivation, social skills, and so forth.

Consider a small school in Wyoming vs. a school in the middle of a Greek enclave in New York City. Should children receive the same education in both schools? Should the Greek child be taught the basic elements of how to raise cattle, or climb mountains, treat a rattlesnake bite, or survive in the wilderness. On the other hand, should children in Wyoming be forced to be bi-lingual in Greek and English, or how to survive in the big city, or utilize the cultural and educational opportunities in New York City?

The answer is obvious. What is not so obvious is that tremendous amounts of money are being spent on federal and state bureaucracies who increasingly seek to obtain *uniformity* of education. This stress for uniformity pretends that children are "widgets" and that schools are factories. And the measure of a good factory is how many "widgets" it turns out, and how uniform in quality the "widgets" are. Schools are not and should not be factories, and children are not and should not be "widgets!"

LOCAL CONTROL

If the middle class is to improve education for its youth, it must first wrest control from the state and federal bureaucracies and return control to the parents in the community. The secret of success is both downsizing and participation in the school by parents and members of the community. Producing standardized curriculum which pretend that all children are the same (i.e. equal), is not the answer. The answer is to develop schools, which respond to the special needs of each community, while also providing children with basic learning tools!

Specifically, we need to consider a simple given. If a child has the basic skills of reading, writing, spelling , arithmetic, and rational/logical thinking, the child can elect to participate in any educational or vocational environment, which is consistent with the child's ability and interests. If children were not allowed to enter intermediate school (sixth grade) unless they had sixth grade reading, writing, spelling and arithmetic skills, the pressure would be on each school to work with each child to ensure a basic level of academic skills.

Of course, there are exceptions, such as children who have basic learning disabilities, brain injuries, health impairments, retardation, etc. But to pass them on, does them no favor. They increasingly feel isolated and hostile. Existing in an environment in which they continually fail, they often turn to anti-social activities, accepting their "classification as losers." Over seventy percent of the felons in prisons were the "losers and burn outs" in school.

Rather than allow them to go on to sixth grade, these special children, along with the underachievers, should be enrolled in enrichment programs to help them reach sixth grade level.. If they are not able to attain sixth grade level, they need to be enrolled in vocationally oriented apprentice programs, where they will have the opportunity to succeed rather than to continually fail.

The same strict criteria should apply to high schools and colleges. If the middle class insisted that children not be allowed to enter publicly funded intermediate schools, high schools, or colleges unless they have these requisite basic learning skills, and the middle class retained local control of each school, the continual interference of state and federal politicians and bureaucrats in school programs would soon be roundly rejected. Each local school district, its community, and parents would be intensely involved in seeing that their children first learned the basics, to whatever extent possible. Further, each of the schools would have teachers who would be allowed to teach rather than serve as disciplinarians and baby sitters.

Intermediate schools and high schools are difficult environments for teachers because of the frustration of dealing with students who are unable to follow the teacher because of deficient academic skills. These students are often the source of discontent and classroom disruption.

Of course, there would be fewer intermediate schools, high schools, and colleges if admissions are restricted to those who are able to learn. Some of the money saved would be used to fund alternative educational and vocational programs, to reduce classroom sizes, and the rest would result in reduced taxes.

In addition to focusing on basic academic skills, each school would be free to express its unique individuality. The school, which has a large Spanish-speaking population, for example, would be free to teach intensive English language training as well as supplemental

Spanish enrichment classes. Other schools would be free to teach range management, cattle management, mountain climbing, industrial skills, commercial skills, timber management, fishing and fisheries management, etc. Each local school could devise its own local curriculum. The only basic restriction would be that each child would have to learn basic academic skills before advancing to a new level of education. And each school district would have to pay part of the cost for enrichment programs for those students unable to continue to the next level of schooling.

Constitutional Amendment

After we freed up schools by returning local control, stressing basic academic skills, and acknowledging each region's diversity, we could still do even more! This would require a constitutional amendment. The middle class has a right to insist that each child has the opportunity to learn basic values and morality. The new Republican State Board of Education in Michigan adopted a mission statement in which they call on the schools to teach character and respect religion and morality.[136] Not to be outdone, Howard Simon, head of the Michigan chapter of the A.C.L.U. responded that the mission statement is the first shot in a new battle over secular education.

Although values and morality should be taught primarily in the home and at church, the reality is that we have an increasing number of dysfunctional homes, many with teenage mothers who have absolutely no foundation or ability to teach about what they themselves know very little. We have to ask ourselves, do we really want a value neutral society where children learn from their peers, single parents, alcoholics, drug addicts, workaholics, or parents who are simply uninterested in communicating basic values? Or do we want children to have an opportunity to learn basic values, which they can use to improve both themselves and society?

We may well need a constitutional amendment to do the following, which I believe is in the best interest of the middle class and children:

1) children should be exposed to texts in which basic moral issues are presented in story form, 2) children should be exposed to the moral thinking of the churches in their immediate community. Priests, pastors, ministers, rabbis, (and in localities in which there are Eastern or Near Eastern populations: Hindus, Buddhists, and Moslems) should be invited on a weekly basis to present discussions on issues of ethics and right living. 3) children should also be exposed to the values of community citizens, invited to present forums on what they believe is important in their lives, 4) children should be exposed to the police, therapists, and community drop-outs so that they can have an opportunity to understand the consequences of violating society's norms; 5) since we live in a society with single parents or no parent families, I suggest the following:

Teachers should be selected to follow each group of students from kindergarten through high school. In effect, they would serve as educational case managers whose primary duty would be to advocate for each child. As each child matures into the next grade, their teacher would stay with the group. The teacher's job would be not only to teach the student, but also to coordinate with each parent what the child needs in terms of education and training. As students spin off into their various pursuits, they would still have the same teacher for a homeroom base until they graduate high school or an equivalent vocational training program.

Assuming that each teacher who was part of this program began teaching at about 23 after an intensive grounding in chaos theory, the teacher would be able educate two classes of around 20 to 25 students in a twelve-year stint. After taking two classes through successive twelve-year stints, teachers could then complete their career by being specialists to assist other teachers to do as they have done.

The purpose of this dramatic change? To establish a bond between teacher and student, between student and student, so that the student's primary attachment after family, is to school, teacher and fellow students, instead of to gang.

If the Student Fails to Learn,
the Teacher has Failed to Teach

A popular excuse among educators (both administrators and teachers) is that the reason students are doing more poorly in our society is that the family has not been supportive. Since 1960, student S.A.T. scores have plummeted from an average of 975 to 900, while spending per student in constant 1960 dollars has doubled from $2,035 per student to $5,247 per student.[137] Claiming it's the parent's problem and not theirs is a huge copout. What has really happened? The truth is that schools have failed to change and adapt their teaching to the changed circumstances of the 90's.

Consider the following facts, 1) drug use and abuse is less now than it was in 1975. 2) Television viewing, however, is forty percent higher. 3) Social spending, means-tested welfare spending, and total expenditures on public elementary and secondary schools have all more than doubled. 4) Single parent homes, however, have tripled, children of divorce have doubled, teen suicide has tripled, and child abuse have tripled.[138]

The above unusual suggestion about changing how the schools teach is one way to improve the schools.

Let's consider another way, which is already working. One school district, which is adjacent to Saginaw, Michigan, has all the problems that many educators have used as reasons to defend their failures. It has a high proportion of Spanish-speaking students, black students, single-parent homes and homes, which are benefiting from means tested welfare.

Yet in the last four years they have moved from testing on the bottom when given standardized tests to being fourth highest in the district! What have they done? And why are they doing as well as many districts, which primarily serve middle class students?

It has the advantage of a superintendent who's willing to experiment, principals who are willing to risk, and teachers who are willing to teach, and a school board, which is student, oriented!

Let's look at what they are doing. First, they tossed out the summer vacation. Instead, they have nine weeks of school and three weeks off. In the interim three weeks of vacation, children can either stay home or take enrichment classes, such as 1) making up for any subjects in which they are deficient 2) music 3) art and 4) gymnastics, including karate, judo, etc.

The next thing they did was recognize that students are primarily visually oriented, thanks to thousands of hours of T.V. viewing. So in each classroom there is one computer to every five students. Teachers teach skills which are reinforced on the computer. Students have the opportunity to check out their academic skills directly on their computer. And each student has an access code so that the computer keeps daily track of his or her progress. Each student is allowed to go as far as he or she can.

In another modification, the district has tossed out grading. Instead, each student is given clusters of skills *They must learn before they can go on to a new cluster!* Instead of being passed along, as is currently done in many school districts, the students are not allowed to study a new subject until they have mastered the old.

Students, thus, are individually programmed and assessed. They are not allowed to compare themselves to others, but are constantly challenged to improve their own personal performance.

They are basically taught a fundamental truth that I have to continually emphasize to many of my clients; DIFFERENT IS JUST DIFFERENT, IT IS NEITHER BETTER NOR WORSE!

The result of this innovative program is a district, which should be on the bottom, but instead is one of the leaders.

When I was a student studying neuropsychology, the favorite expression of my mentor, Dr. Aaron Smith was "If the student disagrees with the book, *throw out the book!* Educational bureaucrats repeatedly have failed to throw out the book. Instead they force students to conform to their theory of education, then blame the students and their parents for their inability to teach.

The middle class is pouring hundreds of billions of dollars down a bottomless rathole in support of rigid educational bureaucracies and educational failures. In addition, we are forcing students to sit in classes in which they have no possibility of succeeding. This creates the anger, resentment, and hopelessness, which feeds delinquency, gang membership, drug use and crime.

To conquer this problem, we need to stop pouring money into bureaucracies which have not only failed to change, but have been part of the problem rather than part of the solution. The easiest way to change this situation is to cut in half both state and federal bureaucracies. Also, to examine the administrate overhead in each district, cutting it to the bone. Then to transfer the money to local school districts, which would be free to develop their own programs, including providing each pair of students with a computer.

Each school district would be assessed two ways: 1) the percentage of students who have developed basic competency in academics, i.e., grammar, arithmetic, and written expression; and 2) the extent to which students are able to go on and participate in their community upon graduation. Districts, which fail to produce competent students, would receive a penalty tax, which all members of the community would have to pay.

In other words, I am proposing the old carrot and stick approach. More money to be controlled by the local district, and more penalties for lack of performance. It is a simple truism that many districts are staff and administration heavy, but teacher and teacher-support light. I doubt that many school boards, superintendents, and administrators would be able to keep their position if the local district was penalized for their failure to innovate effectively. And if their failure was due to the unnecessary interference of politicians, local communities would soon band together to stop external interference.

One of the new factors in our society, which has impressed me, is the preponderance of educationally oriented visual materials that are available. Video presentations on philosophy, history, economics, art, music etc. are increasingly available. Students and teachers have the opportunity to have videocassette presentations by the best educators in our society to supplement each local teacher.

I'd like to close this chapter with two personal experiences. The first occurred while I was a graduate student at Brigham Young University. I was invited to do vocational testing with Indians who had applied to vocational rehabilitation services for employment help. I was surprised to find that if 8 Indians were scheduled, only one would appear. I discovered that on the particular Indian reservation where I was employed to serve there was one government employee for every two Indians!

One day while waiting for Indians to visit my office for assessment, I talked to a teacher who felt puzzled by a troubling fact. As they entered kindergarten, each of the young Indians were friendly, exuberant, and optimistic. They were excited to learn and fascinated by what the teacher had to offer. But by third grade, the Indian students were taciturn, quiet, moody, and inattentive. They weren't learning, and they didn't seem to care that they weren't learning. The teacher puzzled over how the Indians had changed, and how their families or culture must have poisoned them against the school. It never seemed to occur to her that the problem just might have been that the fault lay with the school system, which failed to change to elicit the very best in the Indian students.

It is a basic human fact that in all cultures through the ages, youth are initially optimistic and idealistic. If we change our school systems and our society to teach to the student's highest potential, we will succeed! Never underestimate our youth, and never overestimate our educational bureaucracies!

In the area of education, it's time we also threw out the incumbents who refuse to innovate! Let's replace them with persons who choose not to blame the students and their families as an excuse for their own failure to adapt!

The greatest resource America has is its youth. It is time we took on the mindless educational bureaucrats and politically posturing politicians, who too often use children as a foil to further their own interests. Instead as we move into the 21st century, we must downsize the educational bureaucracies and politicians that hold schools in chains. And we need to honor the fact that in education chaos reigns; and the job of each teacher and school is to make ways for each equally different student to move forward on their unique path.

War and Its Manifestations

Farewell the tranquil mind! Farewell content!
Farewell the plumed troops, and the big wars
That makes ambition virtue! O, farewell!
Farewell the neighing steed and the shrill trump,
The spirit-stirring drum, the' ear-piercing fife,
The royal banner, and all quality,
Pride, pomp and circumstance, of glorious war!
William Shakespeare 1564–1616, *OTHELLO*

There is many a boy here today who looks on war as all glory,
but, boys, it is all hell.
General William Tecumseh Sherman 1820–1891[139]

It is both human nature and the dilemma of humans to engage in conflict and abhor chaos. Thus war makes both perfect sense and perfect nonsense. Ancient Rome held out to conquered territories the promise of peace under Roman rule, yet never a year passed that a Roman legion was not engaged in conflict, either against barbarians or against another legion.[140]

Ever since civilized human beings first considered the need for order and the consequences of disorder, diverse theories as to what motivates

violence and what preserves order have surfaced.[141] Of all these theories, I identify most with that of Thomas Hobbes,[142] who lived in
England during the 17th century, during a time of civil disorder. As a
result no one was safe. Even the king of England had lost his head to the
Executioner. Hobbes became obsessed with the problem of how to create a safe and ordered society.

In today's society, Hobbes would have been diagnosed with an anxiety disorder. In his society, he was regarded as a person

Unusually sensitive to the anxiety of the age. He focused on what was
needed to preserve peace and safety. He theorized that man has a
natural tendency toward violence, which can only be stopped by fear of
greater violence. He thus penned the concept of the Leviathan or, in
other words, a greater governmental power, which if unleashed, could
destroy those who contributed to the disorder of society. He held that
the power of the Leviathan could or should only be released in defense
of the order of society and not in quest of conquering new territories or
engaging in wars outside the borders of the state. The express purpose
of the Leviathan would be to defend citizens from external aggression
or internal chaos. Hobbes was so intent on creating an ordered and safe
society, he was willing to give the ruler unlimited power so long as he
kept order, defended the natural borders of the land, and did not engage
in unjustified wars. He also considered wars outside the borders of his
country unjustified, if the conflicts were other than for defensive
purposes. But He lived in the seventeenth century. Today how does the
middle class protect both its resources (material and human) from
politicians engaged in unjust wars or interventions? Societies over the
centuries have developed a warrior class, which glorifies war, while
hiding their face from the casualties of war.

When Carl Von Clausewitz wrote his seminal work, ON WAR[143], he
wrote in hopes of a time when strong leaders could take the reigns of
their nation/state and move to the offensive when politics failed. But
this is a different time , one in which Clausewitz's ideas have to be

adapted to the realities of the 21st century. At least four types of wars will be possible in the next century:

1) Conventional war—organized conflict between states such as occurred between Western European nations and Iraq in the Gulf War.

2) Guerrilla warfare, now being conducted in many countries throughout the world.

3) State-sponsored international terrorism, where countries finance and equip terrorists to attack the populations of other countries or their material resources.

4) Civil war, either internal or external to the United States.

Given the diversity of conflicts which may rob you of your children, or spouse it seems to me that we must at least be sure that when our loved ones are put in harm's way, it is for a just cause and not to further the ambitions of politicians or international corporations. You, your mate, and your children are entitled to protection from the machinations of a government which often sees your life and those of your loved ones as resources to be expended to further their own interests.

When war or intervention occurs, who speaks for you? When the United States intervenes in Korea, Cuba, Vietnam, Nicaragua, Panama, Lebanon, Haiti, Rwanda, Macedonia or the Balkans, who speaks for the United States Soldiers who place life and limb in jeopardy?

At present, the answer is a resounding *NOBODY!*

Politicians are ever mindful of the currents of internal and external public opinion that wash over the land and bathe our country in the music of glory, responsibility, international stature, fairness, chaos, etc. And they move as public opinion moves.

A simple verification of this fact can be found in the book written by Bob Woodward titled *THE AGENDA*.[144] Mr. Woodward interviewed members of President Clinton's White House staff confidentially and recorded in his book the obsession the Administration has with public opinion polls. Of course, in this regard, I don't believe that President Clinton is different from other occupants of the White House. The fact is that Presidents live and die by the good opinion of the country. And it is the rare president who can rise above the tides of public opinion (Harry Truman was one who could!).

The media, especially the T.V. cameras that present the visual images of external or internal chaos, often shapes public opinion. In presenting information about Korea, Vietnam, Cuba, Lebanon, Macedonia, biases occur. Some argue that we should intervene, while others note that we have intervened before to no avail. What is the public to believe and to whom can we turn for support?

As I have often noted earlier, the first law of politics is to get elected, and the second law is to get re-elected. Each politician often stakes out a position on intervention based on what he or she believes can be presented to constituents in a 30-second sound bite on T.V. and what a potential opponent could attack in a 30-second sound bite.

My personal belief is that we can not trust politicians to act in our best interest when it comes to war. Vietnam is glaring proof of this assertion. Who then can we turn to? Certainly the news media can not be trusted! It was the news media who glorified the French in their epic battle at Diem Bien Phu in Viet Nam?[145] Sob stories by the media which covered the tragic battle of Diem Bien Phu and how French forces were surrounded and destroyed by the evil Communists, inspired intensified efforts by the United States to create and then protect South Vietnam and the rest of Indo-China from the Communists.

The media supported American intervention and then, typical of their fickleness, supported the youth who *opposed* the Vietnam war.

In turning to the media for an opinion, remember that the specialize in *presenting* the news. Ordinary and common things are not news. How often have you read articles or seen T.V. news commentators tell you that there is sand on the beach, or that the sun sets in the West and rises in the East? The media specializes in presenting for our entertainment the unusual and striking. In that sense, they are natural adversaries of what is usual or customary, and in that capacity they do great service! But in no way should they be allowed to decide if you or your spouse or loved ones should be placed in harm's way.

Yet that is exactly what happens! Vietnam was not the first armed intervention encouraged by the media. Political leaders in the United States were blatantly pushed into war with Spain and conquered Cuba because of the incendiary articles in the media, which forced politicians to send our youth into war.

We can neither trust the politicians nor the pundits to protect our youth or us. Who then can we trust? Can we turn to the Chief's of Staff of the Armed Forces? Of course not! Even if they have an opinion, they can not ethically express it while they are in uniform. Can we turn to think tanks? I hope not! Foundations or corporations support think tanks and this affects who they employ and the information they present to the public.

What then should the middle class do? The answer has already been solved in another area. This same debate was presented and resolved when it came to protecting the financial stability of the United States. Since it was acknowledged that neither politicians nor the media could be trusted to protect our financial stability, twelve Federal Reserve Banks were formed with a board of governors, which make up the Federal Reserve Board. Board members serve for twelve years and thus are mostly independent of a particular governmental administration.

The current chairman of the Federal Reserve, Alan Greenspan, has one primary job, to do as much as possible protect the financial integrity of the United States.

If we are willing to establish an independent board to protect the financial integrity of the United States, why not institute another board to protect the youth of America?

While we can't take away the President's job or his ability to be the commander and chief of the United States Armed Forces or Congress's ability to declare war, we can create a body which will have as its responsibility the requirement to inform us if they believe that intervention is just and appropriate.

My suggestion is to create a board of governors with staggered terms so that no one president in a four-year term could appoint more than three of the governors. The board should consist of people who know the glory and the bitterness of war. Three of the board members should be wounded veterans. Three should be citizens who have lost their spouse or children in combat. Three should be retired military commissioned or noncommissioned officers. And the final three should have backgrounds of specialization in the military industrial complex.

The board of Governors, called the Federal Defense Board, should receive the same pay and benefits now received by Federal Reserve Board Members. The Federal Defense Board should also receive the same intelligence reports provided to the Administration. Their staff should be large enough to assist them in examining the pros and cons of involving American troops in the various hot spots around the world.

Each time the United States intervenes militarily outside the borders of the United States, the Federal Defense Board's obligation would be to present a 30 minute monthly broadcast to the American people about the reasonableness and justification to place U.S. troops in harm's way. Consider for a minute our current problems in the Balkans. President Clinton used our Air Force to attack positions of the Serbs. Once he actually engages our forces in combat, the Federal Defense Board would make a presentation to the American people about their assessment of the situation and if they believed American intervention was justified.

So as not to take the President unawares, he would have the right to ask the Federal Defense Board for its opinion about intervention in the Balkans or elsewhere. The President would not be controlled by the Federal Defense Board's opinion, but as the Board gained credibility, the Administration would have to think twice before engaging in unwise, media-driven interventions.

Consider what would have happened if there had been such a board at the time of Vietnam. The Federal Defense Board could have presented to the American people a honest assessment of the situation. Thus, they would have acted as a foil which Presidents Eisenhower, Kennedy, Johnson and Nixon could have used to either not engage in a useless war or disengage from it once it began. Instead of having 57,000 dead and 250,000 wounded, plus millions of damages souls, the Federal Defense Board could have created a political climate which would have severely limited our losses.

The Federal Defense Board would have had access to the C.I.A.'s initial assessment, which indicated that we could not win in Vietnam. In their presentation, they could have described the hostile climate and the inevitability of a decades long struggle.

Having developed a Federal Defense Board, the middle class also needs to decide how to respond to the four types of war which are currently possible. Let us first consider conventional warfare. Conventional warfare in its bloodiest form first started in America during the Civil War. During the Civil War, 650,000 Americans died in the battle—more that the sum of Americans killed in World War I, World War II, Korea and Vietnam![146] Germany, England, and other major powers sent observers to observe the new style of conflict the Civil War represented. They learned a new technology by studying the mass movements of soldiers on railroads, and from their observations of both the North and the South adapted the new technology of war.[147] Steel-hulled ships and rifled cannons were built to rule the oceans, while railroads were constructed to move troops. And they learned how important trench warfare had become.

In addition, nations began to vie for power and influence. England dominated the seas while Russia, Germany, and France struggled for supremacy on the continent.[148] Struggles for dominance on the European and Asian continents have resulted in arms races and also in the gradual impoverishment of the major adversaries. Russia's demise was an economic demise, not a military demise.

Intervention by the United States and its allies in Iraq was despite the protestations of the governments involved, economically driven to protect oil resources and not to save the innocent inhabitants of an oil rich monarchy.

Given the demise of Russian power, the middle class needs to re-think what it should do about American forces stationed around the world. Historically, powerful nations defended their resources and citizenry by extending their borders and placing armies near their borders. Two inevitable things occurred. 1) The financial drain on the nation eventually led to its economic collapse (i.e. Rome and the modern day Soviet Union) and 2) Placing armies near their borders eventually led to teaching their opponents how to fight them.[149]

The American middle class spends tens of billions of dollars maintaining units of armed forces around the world. Isn't it time we changed a policy which never worked and tried something different? What if we brought our forces back home and did the following: Divide the Army into two types of units, small and large. The small, mobile elite force would specialize in rapid movement, be trained and equipped in continually improving weapon systems. Units organized around concepts similar to the Navy Seals, Marine Reconnaissance Units or Army Special Forces.[150]

The larger force would devote its energies to improving America's infrastructure. American youth would be drafted into the Army for two years. They could compete to join the combat arm or become part of the infrastructure arm. Those on welfare too long and illegal immigrants would also be drafted into the larger infrastructure army.

This infrastructure force would be assigned huge tasks, such as building new high-speed railroads, water purification plants—water moving canals and pipes which take water from where it is surplus and move it to where it is needed—and re-renewing and re-building the infrastructure of the cities. Further, reliable members of the larger force would be used to protect citizens from lawless elements.

One particularly interesting project would be to build huge launching rails in isolated areas of the West, where small capsules containing the waste of Atomic Energy Plants and dangerous chemicals could be sent into parking orbits in space.

The main function of the larger infrastructure force would be to continually improve the infrastructure of the United States. Instead of being a professional force, which continually takes without contributing, as has been true throughout history for standing armies, it would contribute to the health of America's economy and citizens.

The second area we must consider is guerilla warfare, where America's hands are bloodstained. Although most people think of the United States as a victim of guerrilla warfare, such as in Vietnam, the truth is quite different. The fact is that America has been an imperious trading nation. For example, we've taken lands and countries, which have not belonged to us, such as the Philippines and Cuba, and we have subverted many of the governments in Central and South America.

American financial corporations have diverted monies to rulers of these lands and then aided in forcing the poorer classes to work for them in producing goods for America. This tendency to subvert the upper classes and use the lower classes is particularly evident in countries such as Guatemala. Here children are forced to work in factories, which have replaced American workers in this country. Unless we stop this process, more and more middle-class jobs will be exported to quasi-slave labor plants throughout Latin America.

To aide in the stability of each nation, "formally called protecting the Western Hemisphere from Communism," our country has taught the military and police of Latin America how to respond to and suppress internal opposition. In fact, many of the current leaders of Western Hemispheric police states were trained by U.S. personnel.[151]

The defense of the Democratic and Republican administrations, which help Latin American despots, has been manifest in the form of "better the devil we know than the devil we don't know." The implication is that if we don't help the despotic governments of the Western Hemisphere something worse will take their place. This posture continually places a nation, which loves freedom, justice, and opportunity in the position of supporting despots who abhor freedom, justice, and opportunity.

The middle class must take a different stance. Consider the consequences of forbidding American agencies from assisting police and Latin American Armies to act against their own citizens. Imagine instead an America which called for a conference of American countries from North, South and Central America which proposed the following: Each and every country in the Americas had to demonstrate their legitimacy by submitting at least once every four years to a plebiscite of its citizens. Each country would have to allow its citizens to vote on one question: "Shall the present government and its constitution stay in force?" If more than 65 percent of citizens voted against the government continuing in power, a constitutional convention and a new government would be formed under the observation of members of the other countries in the Americas. Nations which refused to submit to the vote of their citizens would be called outlaw nations which could legally be invaded or attacked by any other nation or group of nations in the Americas.

Using this profile, Cuba or any other nation would be recognized as long as it was willing to demonstrate its legitimacy by submitting to a plebiscite of its citizens. Each government in the Americas would know that ultimately they would have to submit to a plebiscite once every four years. Their knowing would thus act as a brake to prevent flagrant abuses of its citizenry and help all of the countries in the Americas to make freedom a fact, not just a hope. And special interests within America would not be able to use American resources to manipulate and control nations within the Americas.

The third type of force that America has to face is state-sponsored international terrorism. And in this area, I am a definite supporter of Hobbes. Each passing year increases the danger that terrorist groups financed by countries such as Iran, Syria, Libya, North Korea, and Iraq, may arrange to place in terrorist hands catastrophic weapons either nuclear, chemical, or biological. The ability of humans to destroy humans increases in efficacy and efficiency each year. Because of the impending proliferation of nuclear bomb-producing nations, mutually assured destruction has become mutually assured temptation.[152]

Consider the following scenario: A terrorist unit is formed from disaffected members of a country, which then receives further training in Libya. The unit is supplied with funds from Iraq, Iran or Syria. North Korea sells them a transportable bomb, which they place in a location in New York or California. Then they make a demand that the United States can't meet. For example, they insist that the United States conquer Israel and ship its occupants to Siberia. The United States refuses, and a major American city is destroyed.

The terrorists are then captured. Do we punish or execute 20 terrorists in exchange for four million Americans? If we do, we simply invite the destruction of more American cities. Any nation can find a few suicidal persons to engage in mass destruction. Witness the bombing of the soldiers in Lebanon by a suicidal teenage girl. The answer has to be a Hobbesian one! If we lose a city due to atomic destruction, chemical warfare, or biological warfare, we must act not only against the terrorists but also against the nations that made it possible.

If terrorist sponsoring nations knew for a certainty that we would act aggressively against any nation or international corporation that had helped the terrorists—and we'd use our nuclear, chemical, or biological weapons to wreak havoc and retribution on the culprits—then nations around the world would think twice about sponsoring well-financed, terrorist-weapons attacks on the United States!

In this increasingly dangerous age of more and better producers of death, the "doctors of death" must know that the United States will respond on the basis of, "If you cut off a finger, I will take off your hand; if you cut off a hand, I will take off your arm; and if you cut off an arm, I will take off your head." If the United States is to survive in an increasingly dangerous world, it must become the incarnation of Hobbe's Leviathan! The United States can no longer take the ostrich position and hide its head in the sand, pretending that dangerous super weapons don't exist. It must take a proactive position. Let terrorist groups and countries around the world, particularly countries in the flashpoint zone,[153] know that we will not tolerate having their wars exported to our borders.

The final thing we have to consider is civil disorder. Having lived fifteen miles South and East of Watts during the 1965 riots, I shared the frustrations that residents of Greater Los Angeles felt as they perceived the weakness and inadequacy of California's political leaders. Many of my fellow students thought that Governor Brown was reluctant to act for fear of being perceived as anti-black. He was well aware of the fact that he had been elected governor of California because of the 90 plus percentage of Blacks who voted for him.

Frustration with government, politicians and race relations erupted again in 1968 following Martin Luther King's assassination. One hundred twenty-five cities experienced civil disorder.[154]

Reagan's successful election bid to be governor of California was generated by many formerly Democratic voters who were disgusted with Brown's ineptitude and indecisiveness. Governor Brown's inaction was not unique to him. In fact, his behavior is typical of self-serving politicians who consider their futures before that of the safety of the population. Remember the mob behavior in South Los Angeles following the Rodney King verdict? I believe both the media and inherent political weakness were the culprits. The media kept asking: "Will the people riot following the jury's verdict?" Neither the police nor the National Guard was evident following the verdict. It was as if the population of South Los Angeles was invited to engage in insurrection and lawless behavior.

Having been invited by the media and sensing the deliberate evacuation of the police and the National Guard, the rioters took advantage of the opportunity. Lawless behavior and mob violence became the issue of the day. After mobs succeeded in destroying their own community, they headed for Korea Town. As they approached the community with the intention of burning and pillaging, they were stopped. But not by police or the Guard. They were stopped by ordinary citizens who stationed themselves on the rooftops of stores with assault rifles.

The riots in Watts and South Los Angeles are not unique. Similar lawless behavior of mobs have occurred throughout the history of the United States. In my senior year at Phoenix Union High School, I took a class in Southwestern history. During the class, our teacher described several instance where Indians had been encouraged to disarm in the interest of civil disorder and peace, only later to be attacked, murdered, and raped by lawless mobs and soldiers.

The Indians are not the only victims of civil disorder. Early Mormon settlers moved to Missouri to escape persecution in the East. But Missouri was a slave state and the residents viewed with great suspicion and distrust the increasing population of anti-slavery Mormons. In 1844, Governor Boggs persuaded the Mormons to disarm in the interest of peace and harmony.[155]

Three days later, lawless mobs attacked the defenseless Mormons, killing the men, raping their wives-often to the point of death, burning their homes, and stealing their livestock. While they attacked, the Governor of the state did absolutely nothing to interfere! He chose to not stop the killing and rapine, because he believed that the people who had voted him into office, would have voted him out of office.

History does not only include the actions of cowardly politicians. President Lincoln was also faced with the lawless actions of mobs in

New York. Newly arrived immigrants to America were being drafted into the Civil War, many being killed and wounded. They finally erupted into a raging mob, which chose as the focus of its anger inno-cent blacks and places of commerce. The mob attacked any black it could find. Many were hanged from lampposts, burned alive, or kicked and beaten to death.[156]

President Lincoln supported local militia generals in stopping the mobs at any cost. The General entered New York with his cannon and fired grapeshot on the mobs. The spine of the insurrection was imme-diately broken, and New York again became a safe and secure city, but only after 1000 citizens had been killed.[157]

There are few politicians like President Lincoln who would have the courage to fire cannon on American citizens engaged in looting, murder, and rapine. Those who did have the courage to defy public opinion were assassinated (Lincoln), or voted out of office (Truman). Unfortunately, there are more politicians like Governor Boggs or Governor Brown than like Abraham Lincoln. To protect ourselves, we need to make sure that all middle-class citizens have the right to bear arms.

Some members of Congress however, would prefer otherwise. In the "crime bill" assault rifles are banned. These are the same rifles the Korean-American citizens used to stop the mobs in Los Angeles. The arguments against assault rifles is that mentally deranged persons might fire them on American Citizens or the children of American Citizens. Another argument against assault rifles is that they are often used by lawless elements—particularly in the drug culture. While a ban on manufacturing and selling assault rifles could keep them out of the hands of individual unbalanced individuals, it is unlikely that the crim-inal element would be stopped.

If we can't stop tons and tons of cocaine, heroin and marijuana from entering the United States, is it conceivable that criminals could be stopped from acquiring assault rifles?

What we need to consider is the scenario of what might happen if lawless mobs or criminals, knew that the middle class was disarmed. The response of the anti-gun lobby in Congress is "You still have rifles and pistols." The National Rifle Association has been able to propagandize many of its members into believing that the anti-gun lobby's response is not honest. Most members of the middle class are well aware of the *salami theory* that Congress and the anti-gun lobby takes. Once they get one bill in they quickly move to another.

The N.R.A. has tried its best to make its members and other U.S. citizens believe that the ultimate goal of the anti-gun lobby in Congress is to substantially disarm American Citizens. In this instance, middle-class citizens are on the horns of a dilemma. In the old West, many of the little towns were fed up with the continuing uncertainty and anxiety brought on by gun-toting citizens. At the same time, they wanted to carry their own weapons to protect themselves from other gun-toting citizens. It was not until an effective sheriff was employed to protect the peace that they felt safe giving up their weapons.

In today's society, ask yourself these simple questions? How safe do you feel walking the streets of your city at night? How safe do you feel in your own home? How safe do you feel when you go shopping at a nearby mall? How safe do you feel taking mass transportation at odd times of the day or night? If we were to take substantial numbers of personnel from the larger force of soldiers and place them at key points around the city, the need to carry weapons of any kind would be vastly reduced. In other words, a police officer on every corner and a deputy on every bus, train and trolley would go a long way to changing the atmosphere of fear that encourages White flight and a disabled city.

Forbidding guns is not the real issue for the middle class. The real issue is providing for peace and safety. Once that is accomplished, banning assault rifles becomes a moot point. The middle class could vote out of office just the incumbents in Congress which were part of the anti-gun lobby. But there are many members of Congress who are willing to defend the middle class's right to bear arms but also are hostile to other middle-class interests.

Reality would suggest that the middle class should continue to vote out all incumbents, then work to either include guarantees to the middle class that they can keep their weapons or establish an independent American party which endorses the right of Americans to bear arms. Reality would also suggest that once fear no longer permeates the citizenry of our country, the only demand for weapons will be in the area of shotguns, deer rifles and pistols.

Political Parties—the Need for a Third Party

"For forty years after 1930, the gap between the rich and the poor in America narrowed. Since the end of the 1960's it has been widening, and is greater now than at any time since the creation of the modern welfare state." *The Economist,* P. 13. November 5th to 11th, 1994.

Constituents often asked Senator Paul Coverdall why the two parties cannot quit their partisan squabbling. Coverdall replied to this question by asserting that the differences between the parties are irreconcilable. They have a profound philosophical disagreement about the role and nature of government. The Democrats want more and bigger government and the Republicans want less government and more freedom. And when constituents ask Coverdall "When are they going to hear us in Washington?" His reply: "They hear you, they just don't agree with you."[158]

November 8, 1994 was the day the voters let Congress know they didn't agree with Washington. But the reason they don't agree with Washington does not seem to be perceived by either political party or the so-called political pundits. The reason the Democrats suffered a catastrophic loss is not that America has moved right but rather that the middle class is increasingly fearful. And middle-class fear relates to job security and economic inequality. Inequality in America narrowed between 1929 and 1969. But from that point on, inequality expanded dramatically. In 1992, the income of the top 20% in America was **eleven times greater than the bottom 20%.** In Britain the gap has widened from a factor of four to a factor of seven. The major difference between Britain and America is that in Britain both the bottom 20% and the top 20% have gained while in America, the bottom 20% have suffered an eleven percent drop in real income.[159]

Democrats were defeated in the 1994 election because the public did not approve of the job Clinton was doing as President (50%), did not like Democratic programs (24%) and supported Republican programs (12%). But at the same time, despite the defeat the Democrats suffered most people think "there will be a continuation of politics as usual (63%).[160] The reasons for this bleak outlook among U. S. citizens is readily apparent when you know that forty percent of young men can not earn enough money to support a family of four and that sixty percent of the work force have seen their real wages fall by twenty percent since 1973. And the new jobs being created are in the area of knowledge work and services that most Americans are not trained to do. In a "postindustrial society" security does not come from being employed but from being employable.[161] The day after the Democratic debacle, President Clinton addressed the nation and expressed his hope that he could work together with the Republican Party. His major hope is he can convince Congress to pass GATT. If GATT does nothing else, it will certainly place more lower middle-class jobs at risk. President Clinton is not the only enemy, Congress is also! While the major parties fight over philosophical differences, income inequality continues to exacerbate and neither party even mentions it in their contentious debates.

Income inequality and recent events, which have swept Washington, such as the debate over taxes, crime, and health care, make it clear that the President advises and Congress (under the influence of the special interests) disposes. We are no longer a Republic or a Democracy.

Republics are countries where citizens feel a "special bond between themselves and their country." This spirit of loyalty usually surfaces during crises such as fires, floods, earthquakes and wars.

President Kennedy said, "Ask not what your country can do for you, rather ask what you can do for your country." This question reflects the true spirit of a Republic where country comes before self. Americans had that spirit in 1776 when they rebelled against England. Both the North and the South had that spirit during the American Civil War, when 650,000 lives where lost. And that spirit surfaced again during World Wars II and II. The spirit of the Republic which the Republican Party claims to defend by its original stance against the spread of International Communism abroad and the ever increasing burden of a government in size, cost and bossiness has fled. The force of International Communism has dissipated and Republicans have caved in to big government. They fear the tongue-lashing of the liberal media and posture Republicanism while they quietly give in to an ever increasing and dominating governmental bureaucracy.[162] As Senator Bob Smith stated when he switched from the Republican Party to being an Independent, I'm tired of going to leadership meetings and being told what the pollsters say about positions on issues.

It's my observation that when it comes to increasing government, the Democrats beat their breasts and offer more and bigger, while the Republicans yell no and then behind the barn throw in the towel. As a result of the loss of the vision of a Republic by both major parties in America, American citizens are becoming increasingly dependent and corrupt. We are losing the true spirit of a Republic and moving more rapidly toward the spirit of dictatorship.[163]

Although we pretend to be a Democracy, the same powerful monied interests support both major parties.[164] Thus we have become an oligarchy, a nation invisibly ruled by the privileged few while still pretending to represent Americans. As Juliet said in *ROMEO AND JULIET,*

"What's in a name? That which we call a rose By any other name would smell as sweet." The converse is also true, That which we call an oligarchy, by any other name would stink as badly! The Reform Party Governor Jesse Ventura deals with the special interests by tweaking their noses. The Jesse Ventura for President committee has an interesting choice of three posters you can order which on two of them show Ventura in a wrestling ring body slamming the special interests. You can obtain a copy of these posters by sending a check for $15. To the Draft Jesse Ventura for President Committee, 10723 S.W. 104 Street, Miami, Florida, 33176.

Just as Republicans have given up on controlling the size, cost, and dictatorship of government, so the Democrats have given up on their original pledge to promote equality, justice, and fairness.[165] Instead of promoting equality, they promote racial conflict. Instead of justice, they promote arbitrary criminalization of citizens at all levels; and for diverse reasons and instead of fairness, they promote quota systems and rigid bureaucratic rule.[166]

Americans were born free yet everywhere we see bureaucratic dictatorship, tax slavery, and the looming chains of fear! I am not an unrealistic idealist. Realism compels me to say that neither the Democratic nor the Republican party can be saved. Both are the willing servants of the monied interests of America! Throughout this book, I have proposed voting out all incumbents, regardless of political affiliation, sex, race, age, personality or intelligence.

I then suggested that by voting against the incumbents in three successive national elections, at least one of the major parties would awaken and start to defend and expand the middle class. While certainly it is a possibility that Americans can cause change from within either or both political parties, reality compels me to state that in the interest of what is Right, Just, and Fair, a third political party is both necessary and inevitable. Despite the prevailing opinion of leaders in government, politics and the media, the appearance of a third political party which has power is not impossible.

Once the false hope of the Republican's Contract With America is demonstrated, a third-party climate will ripen. Consider for a moment this simple fact, eighty percent of nothing is still nothing! The Republicans can cut the cost of government and reduce taxes, *but if there is no high-paying industrial base to provide more high paying jobs what good will come of it?* Americans are not forever fools! If they continue to see their neighbors or themselves downsized out of a job and no new jobs being available are they likely to think that all is well with the world? Are they likely to support political parties that do nothing to protect this land from 20 cents an hour slave labor?

I feel compelled to state that the real race is not between the Republican and Democratic Parties but between a viable third party and dictatorship. Unless a third party is formed which will attempt to rectify the disenfranchisement of the middle class which is now taking place, a revolt will inevitably begin to occur. The revolt, as Christopher Lasch states,[167] will probably come from the upper and not the middle class. When only twenty percent of the population is in an upwardly mobile track, what is the other eighty-percent likely to do?

Entitled or not entitled the eighty-percent may well demand more for them and seek a leader who promises more. The upper class will then have to choose between giving up what they believe they have earned or opt to control the masses through intimidation. Thus America will have to choose between establishing a new, viable, third party or follow the road of Latin American and Asian countries which chose a dictatorship.

Third parties have tried and failed to gain control of political life in America since the Civil War. But I believe we can now overcome these failures. Let's consider the six major reasons why third party movements have failed.

1) For parties to win, they must endorse Lockean Liberalism, the simple concept that each American has the right to pursue life, liberty, prosperity, and the pursuit of happiness. New parties have traditionally come from an extreme position, which tended to negate one or more of those virtues. Consider Ross Perot's bid for power.[168] Perot basically ran on a platform espousing the American Dream, which is a Lockean liberal dream, and he won 19 million votes.

Perot could have won more votes if he had not shot himself in the foot by revealing a side of himself, which suggested emotional instability and paranoia. While many Americans believed in his goals, his program appeared to be one of doing things more efficiently. But, if you are running in the wrong direction, going faster just leads you further from the goal! I voted for him because he recognized programs could be wrong and that if they were, "We'll just fix it." In other words, he was not afraid to change his mind.

Both Democrats and Republicans claim to be Lockean Liberals, and use the language of Lockean Liberals, but their actions suggest otherwise. The truth is there is no major political party that actually endorses and promotes Lockean Liberalism. The middle class has truly lost its power![169]

2) National prosperity has also been a core reason why third parties have not been successful. When things are going well, reasonable persons do not want to rock the boat. But since 1973, America has increasingly lost its industrial base. Nine out of ten jobs the economy creates pay less than $14,000 a year and seven out of ten new jobs pay less than $7,000 a year.[170] The fact is that roast beef and apple pie have been replaced with dog food and a twinkie. The wage difference between the upper forty-percent of Americans and the lower forty-percent has become truly astounding!

The argument, "Don't rock the boat!", has little meaning when it is already swamped and under water.

3) A third reason why third parties have failed is that the major parties have promoted the idea of upward social mobility. In this respect, they

speak with forked tongues! On the one hand, they ennoble American individualism, but on the other, they seek to destroy our right to make personal decisions about our health (banning substances or foods because they know better), our safety (striving to ban American's right to have weapons without considering the consequences of disarming the American people), our opportunity (by laying such heavy costs on small business that it is becoming increasingly impossible to start and maintain your own business),[171] and our children's future (by encouraging the rampant export of middle-class jobs).[172]

During the Great Depression in the thirties, Marxist Parties and Socialist Parties never gained control, because most Americans blamed themselves for their losses.

The two-edged sword of pretending that Washington can solve everything has created a mind-set in America which can surface at any time things go wrong. If our economy worsens, Americans are now conditioned not to blame themselves, but instead to blame Washington. 4) The myth of Horatio Alger has also acted as a block to third parties. Horatio Alger stories portray the simple American spirit of working hard, studying hard, and being virtuous as the keys to success. The implicit belief was that everyone has an opportunity to get a piece of the pie and that failure to do so rests on the individual not the system.

The Democratic Party has abandoned this fundamental American belief. Instead, the Democratic Party increasingly espouses the idea that the American economy is a zero-sum game. In other words, the pot is only so big and whenever you take a bigger share you are depriving someone else of a portion of his or her share. America is not an ever-expanding, limitless country. It is now a limited, declining country! The Democratic party has shifted from equal opportunity, justice, prosperity, and fairness to class *conflict*. To wit: If you are not doing well, it is because you are Black, Latino, Asian, Female, Old, Young, A Child of A Single Parent, Don't Have a Degree From Harvard University, Don't

Live in a Sociable Suburb, or Don't Belong to the Right Athletic Club, Sorority or Fraternity.

Republicans on the other hand, also endorse the idea of a zero-sum game. In the interest of paying their C.E.O.'s more, they find ways to increasingly destroy middle-class jobs.

In the last election, Perot was the only contender who honestly voted for the Horatio Alger Story. Problematically, he was not able to verbalize in clear form how Americans could remove the spiritual, moral, intellectual and governmental blinders that darken their way.

5) The language of assimilation. Once one of the major parties realize that the other party or a smaller party has grabbed onto a gut issue for the American people, they quickly try to assimilate it or pretend to assimilate it in their political posturing. When Reagan won election by a landslide, the Democratic Party produced the "New Democrat." This "New Democrat" was supposed to be for lower taxes (Ha! Ha!), smaller government (Ha! Ha!) and a less dictatorial bureaucracy (Ha! Ha!). President Clinton was one of the Governors who was head of the caucus of "New Democrats." The only thing new about the "New Democrats" is the name!

6) The final reason that third parties fail in America is that in contrast to Europe, we have not had a class-consciousness. American society has no feudal tradition where citizens divided themselves into Royalty, Religious Classes, Military, Townspeople, and Peasants. The heterogeneity of our population created a diverse and classless society. All Americans had the right and the hope to partake in the American Dream. But that dream is rapidly failing. Due to the collusion of both parties, the middle class is dying! Instead, it is being fragmented into the welfare poor, lower working class, salaried middle class and the wealthy.

I was really shocked by the following incident. My literary agent asked me to put together a book proposal, which would include comments from leaders who have expert knowledge in some of the areas dealt with in this book. Most did not respond to my request for endorsement. I was not surprised by this fact. Most of us are buried in paper and simply don't have the time to read unsolicited mail.

What really shocked me however, was the hostile and superior attitude revealed in a communication received from a political scientist at Princeton University. In criticizing my book, he made the bald faced assertion that factory workers were "simply not middle class and that I wanted a fail-safe guarantee for them." His statement dumbfounded me, just as I was dumbfounded when President Clinton debunked the idea of job security. Living in middle America, it never occurred to me that the factory workers I saw in my practice who worked at General Motors and Dow Chemical did not have the right to consider themselves middle class, or that they had no right to protect their jobs from export to slave labor camps in China or other countries where workers have no rights.

His assertion was made without apology or argument; it was a stated as simple fact. Apparently, he believes factory workers have no right to be part of the American dream! The disenfranchisement of American unions and the export of high-paid American jobs under the aegis of the "Global Economy" that both parties worship is accepted as a given fact of life. Senator Kennedy talked on C-span about the Health-Care Bill. He spoke in response to the Republicans, who pointed out that the Health-Care bill includes fines and jail time for businesses or doctors who violate the bill's regulations. He stated that fines and jail time was necessary for Health Care just as it had been for Social Security, Minimum Wage and other worker's improvements. He pointed with pride to how Congress had improved the quality of life for factory workers in shoe factories. (Factories that are now closed and whose owners are employing children in foreign lands.)

What Kennedy did not offer an explanation for was his support of N.A.F.T.A. and the "global economy." This fork-tongued Senator espouses the causes of laborers and then sends their jobs overseas to slave labor camps, child laborers, and lands with no unions, social security, minimum wage, worker's compensation or occupational health and safety standards. The health care legislation that he supports will add to the hemorrhaging of American jobs unless these jobs are protected with a social tax (which only Ross Perot supported).[173]

Because the middle class, and in particular, the high paying factory workers (which also have a right to be part of the American Dream) is under constant threat from both the Democrats and the Republicans, a middle-class class consciousness is forming and the fall of both parties will be exceedingly great.

If a new third party adopts middle-class, Lockean-Liberalism, eventual victory is inevitable! This party would not be acting from the extreme right or left, but would co-opt the center of American philosophy with not only the language of Lockean-Liberalism, but also with practical programs to advance and expand the middle class.

Before you say, it can't be done, let me remind you that it already has been done both in America and abroad. In America, the Republican Party formed because the dominant parties of the time could not resolve the important problems of the day.

In this era in Denmark, people took matters in their own hands in 1973. The citizens of Denmark, increasingly tired of rampant pornography, sex shops, out of control taxes, and an ever-increasing bureaucracy with its parasitic power base in welfarism rebelled. Denmark has proportional representation. That is, each party receives seats in their national assembly based on the number of votes cast for the party in national elections. In 1973, five parties were in power: Social Democrats, Radical Liberals, Agrarian Liberals, Conservatives, and the Socialist People's Party.

Just as in America today, these parties accommodated each other to share power. The citizens of Denmark, however, were not satisfied by their informal agreements to rule. So in 1973, without warning or fanfare, Denmark's citizens voted them out. The ruling parties went into the election controlling all 175 seats in the Government. And when the election was over, they collectively lost 60 seats. New parties gained power! The newly formed Progressive Party gained the most power, going from zero seats in the previous election to 28 seats in the new government.[174]

All of the old parties lost an average of 27 to 48 percent of their seats. They were dumbfounded. How could this have happened? Could it be because they had abandoned the citizens of Denmark?

Not only Denmark has shown the way, but Canada as well. In a recent national election in Canada, the ruling Progressive-Conservative Party went from over 150 plus seats to four seats in the new Parliament. If Denmark and Canada could do it, why not Americans?

Removing Democrats and Republicans from power is the easy part, the hard part is preventing the newly formed third party from becoming dominated by the rich and monied interests of America who have paid the hundreds of millions of dollars it costs to run campaigns.

There is a way to avoid domination from the oligarchic interests that have progressively destroyed the American Dream for the middle class.

If we are going to make war on the special interests that govern America, we must take the same approach I suggested in the chapter on the Drug War. The German genius of Carl Von Clausewitz[175] can be applied to political parties as well as to war between states or nations. On of Clausewitz's main principles for winning was to direct efforts at the center of gravity of the opposing state or nation. This center of gravity could be a state's capitol, its army, or its resources.

Fortunately, Hitler did not truly understand this concept. America, England, and Russia escaped Hitler's clutches, because he did not truly understand the necessity of directing an all-out effort at our center of gravity which was transporting goods, men and materials overseas. He also did not understand the necessity of destroying England's Air Power or Russia's Armies. Allied Forces could have greatly shortened the war by concentrating more efforts on destroying German petrol-chemical factories and oil wells. Even the great Tiger Tanks of World War II Germany can't run if they have no fuel.

Fuel fed the great Panzer Armies of Germany, and monies feed the politicians in Washington! Special interests not only contribute to the major political parties, they also contribute to the individual campaigns of Senators and Congresspersons. Thus many Senators and Congresspersons can defy their own party and its leader, the President, because they have the power base and monies at home to run despite the anger of the President or their political party.

For the middle class to gain back its power, we must attack the center of gravity, which allows oligarchic interests in America to maintain power regardless of whether there is a Democratic or Republican Administration. The *key* to attacking the money and influence of the oligarchic interests of America is to limit the influence of the Lobbyists. As Sir Thomas More said in his book, *UTOPIA*, laws are not meant to create justice, but are devised by the wicked and powerful to *escape* justice. More restrictions on lobbyists will do nothing more than create an illusion with no substance.[176] Smarter lobbyists and more crooked politicians will inevitably be the result of taking the tack of regulating lobbyists. There is a simpler solution!

The solution rests in the simple American Dream of life, liberty, prosperity, and the pursuit of happiness! A new party must have the courage to campaign on this platform and back it up with behavior as well as words! Because both the Democratic and Republican Party have abandoned the American Dream, they instead engage in personal polemics. Bush gained election the first time because he was able to tie Willie Horton to his opponent's coat tails. Bush was defeated in re-election because he could not successfully tie draft-dodger and womanizer to Clinton's image.

President Clinton got the message by avoiding personal polemics (which he would have probably lost) and responded with issues the declining middle class understood, "It's the economy, stupid!"

Unfortunately, President Clinton's campaign was not matched by subsequent actions, which are leading toward ever-increasing taxes, more governmental bureaucracy, and reduced opportunities for the middle class.

What is the answer? The answer is obvious and necessary. We must change from a party, which emphasizes individual contests and personal mudslinging, as well as outright deception, to one that emphasizes platforms and ideas! We must move the political agenda from one, which involves a fight between heroes of the left or right, to one, which endorses argument in the market place of ideas.

To do this is simple. Let's start with a relatively simple scenario. Let's assume the middle class awakens, feels its power, and votes out each and every incumbent. A visibly distraught and shaken Congress forms, which is comprised of newcomers in the House of Representatives and many newcomers in the Senate.

A new independent American party forms and invites the current members of Congress to attend an informal gathering to see if they wish to join the new party. To join the new party, a simple contract is needed. Firstly, they must endorse the party platform (which includes specific proposals to increase and expand middle-class life, liberty, prosperity, and pursuit of happiness). Secondly, they must agree not to campaign personally for re-election or to accept campaign funds to get re-elected. Instead, the new independent American party will present to the American people its platform and will ask Americans to vote a straight party ticket.

Instead of voting for the individual, Americans will be asked to vote for the party platform, and to donate a small amount of money to the national party. The party, in return, will inform the American public of its goals and how it will take actions to reduce the size, cost, and ever expanding power of the bureaucracies as well as deal with issues such as crime, welfare, infrastructure, loss of American jobs, etc. As monies come in, past campaign debts incurred by members of Congress when they were Democrats or Republicans will be paid. Most importantly, *NO NEW CAMPAIGN DEBTS WILL BE ALLOWED!*

In the next election, the only campaign will be that conducted by the new independent American party. The Party will campaign first on what it can and will do. Next, on the issue that their opponent's election campaign material are being paid for by special interest groups which want their jobs, or their money by increasing their taxes. Members of the new independent American party will be expected to stay in Washington and solve the problems that former Administrations have created.

The American people will then vote on how successful the current party has been and not on the personal attractiveness of Congresspersons. Party discipline and focus on what is important to middle-class Americans will be maintained by party membership. If a Congressperson gets too involved with money, pleasure, drugs, special interests, etc., they will simply lose their party identification, and a new person will be encouraged by the party to take his place.

America's democracy has been in force for over two hundred years. It started as a Republic but has now become a degenerate form of democracy, which for all intents and purposes is not unlike the oligarchic governments that control many of the Latin-American countries. The choice is ours. We can continue down the road of impoverishing the many to enrich the few, or we can return to the ideals of the Republic. Our founding fathers started this country on the model of the Roman and Greek Republics not on the model of a Roman dictatorship.

It's time we caught our second wind and moved to ever-greater levels of American life. Let us join hands with each other and form a new Republic!

Living in the 21st Century

Societies that allow themselves to be governed by
politicians whose only qualification is that they
won an election will go from failure to failure and eventually
pass from the scene.[177]

As I spent several weeks thinking about this chapter, I realized that Americans speak three languages and politicians speak a fourth. The three languages Americans speak are 1) Biblical, 2) Lockean Liberalism and 3) Republican. Biblical language enters our consciousness when we consider issues of morality, sin, right, wrong, and individual and group responsibility. Just prior to the Civil War, Biblical language conflicted with Lockean Liberalism. Many of the spokespersons of the East and North took a biblical approach to slavery, claiming it was not right, and to own another person was a sin.

Southerners protected the "peculiar institution" by using the language of Lockean Liberalism. They stated their fundamental right to be free of governmental interference in their pursuit of life, liberty, prosperity, and pursuit of happiness. When Lincoln was elected, both sides spoke the language of Republicanism. Lincoln abhorred the idea of a civil war. He stated that rather than see the Union divide however, he would go to war. Jefferson Davis also abhorred the idea of war, but stated rather than continue in the Union, he would fight to end it. Both Lincoln and Davis appealed to the spirit of the Republic, which placed country before self, and patriotism before self-interest. Robert E. Lee, the grandson of George Washington, spoke the language of the Republic of Virginia, when he resigned his commission and placed his loyalty to Virginia above his loyalty to the Union.

In America today, we also have a conflict between Biblical language and Lockean Liberalism. Many leaders throughout the Union protest against millions of abortions that have been performed in the language of the bible, calling it a sin and murder. Other leaders uphold the language of Lockean Liberalism, asserting that a woman has the right to control her own body, including her reproductive decisions.

Fortunately, the conflict has not risen to the point of war. Both sides (with a few tragic exceptions) are willing to speak the language of the Republic. They are willing to try the issue in the courts and in the voting arena. Politicians, on the other hand, speak both languages, but mean neither. Just as in the days before the Civil War, politicians try as best they can to avoid taking sides. So they say words which they hope will appeal to both sides.

To the middle class words mean things. You are either for a woman's right to control her own reproductive decisions or you are against abortion. Politicians, however, don't believe words mean things. They pretend they are for both reproductive freedom and against abortion.

Lincoln however, believed that you can not be for two diametrically opposed things. A house divided can not stand. He also believed that nations and peoples are punished for great sins. He believed that the terrible price in carnage Americans suffered during the Civil War, where almost every family of America lost a loved one or had a loved one return disabled was the just due of a just God. He felt that Divine Providence had decreed that Americans, both slaveholders and those who permitted slavery, should be wrung through a divine wringer for America's toleration of slavery.

President U.S. Grant also believed in the Biblical language of individual and collective sin. He felt, however, that the Civil War was the just retribution of a just God because our nation had stolen land from a weak nation. He believed that our war with Mexico resulted in the catastrophe of the Civil War.

DURING THE ERA OF THE AMERICAN CIVIL WAR, WORDS MEANT THINGS AND BEHAVIOR MEANT THINGS!

In this era, we have lost our way. Words don't mean things and behavior is rapidly becoming irrelevant. A President such as Lyndon B. Johnson could campaign against Barry Goldwater on a peace platform, knowing that he intended to expand our Armed Forces in Vietnam ten-fold.

A President such as Richard Nixon could campaign on justice and law and order yet endorse criminal acts. A President such as Jimmy Carter could campaign on reducing inflation and increasing jobs and do the opposite. A president such as Ronald Reagan could campaign on a populist program of reducing the size of government yet negotiate in secret to expand the government. A President such as George Bush could campaign on "no new taxes" and then cave in to congressional pressure and pass new taxes. And the list goes on and on and on. A President such as Bill Clinton could campaign on a crime bill that has virtually no hope of actually reducing crime.

The language of politics has increasingly deserted Biblical language, Lockean Liberalism, and Republicanism. Instead, political language uses Machiavellian deceit, using words with no intention to validate them. Politicians in Washington, as well as state and local municipalities, have becomes experts in using symbols without substance.

For these reasons I advocated again that we remove all politicians who have learned the fourth language, replacing them until we can elect people who no longer speak the language of Machiavellian deceit.

After removing Machiavellian deceit, what then? What ought to be the America of the 21st century? This book and the ideas therein are not only about improving the quality and quantity of jobs in America. It's not only about having affordable housing and transportation without living in fear. It's not only about being able to walk the streets during daylight or darkest night. And it's not only about having a good future for our children. It is about creating a renewed society, which will allow us to move from existence to essence.

Existence is about the day to day activities that have to happen to survive. Working streetlights, decent roads, reduced crime, medical treatment, etc. On a personal level, existence refers to simple acts like brushing your teeth, taking a bath, wearing clean clothes, etc. Many individuals and many societies never get beyond issues of existence. America can and should pursue greater goals. To do so however, we need to make some hard choices. Let me list a few.

1. We need to give back to ourselves the right to manage our own pain through prescribing our own pain medication and in the process cut $200 billion dollars from the health budget.

2. We need to stop the drug war and allow persons inclined to self-destructive behavior the opportunity to kill themselves on drug using reservations and in the process save $200 billion dollars.

3. We need to set limits on international trade and protect the middle class from having to compete with slave labor which will may the cost of some products and protect the future of our children.

4. We need to reduce the cost of government by providing incentives for bureaucrats to reduce rather than expand government which will save at least another $200 billion dollars.

5. We need to go to a flat tax, which takes equally from all and does not punish capitol formation and job creation. There is absolutely no reason why we can't move toward a flat tax of 10% from income of any type with no exceptions except the direct cost of production.

6. We need to completely restructure welfare so that we truly operate under the rubric of an ounce of prevention is worth a pound of cure. We need to free our people from welfare slavery and our government from being controlled by welfare bureaucracies. This will save at least $200 billion dollars a year.

7. We need to take the homeless off the streets. This will cost money but in a just society we can not allow the mentally ill to roam the streets as they did in the middle ages and hurt themselves as well as afflict the middle class.

8. We need to build our infrastructure and prepare for the 21st century. We need to renew the cities of America, build high-speed railroads, subways, improved mass transportation, and improved water purification, launch radioactive and dangerous contaminants into parking orbits in space, provide for the elderly and improve our environment. Of course doing this will require hundreds of billions of dollars. But, these billions will multiply as America charges into the 21st century and will provide the jobs and the quality of life the middle class needs.

10. We need to take crime out of the hands of the politicians and return justice to the people and the judges.

11. We need to set limits on lawyers and legal judgements. We can not continue to be a lottery society where rapacious attorneys lay in wait to destroy products and corporations in their own pursuit of unearned wealth. A person should be recompensed for injury but not to the extent it becomes a lottery for self-serving lawyers.

12. We need to re-evaluate education and stop functioning under the delusion that we are all equal and we can all arrive at the same goal through the same training. By realistically dealing with education, we can save at least $100 billion dollars a year.

13. We need to develop a national defense board, which functions to protect our youth from the machinations of politicians and the media. We need to only enter military actions when it is in the best interest of

our country to do so. And not to placate the press or build the popularity of a particular politician or politicians.

14. Finally, we need a third party, which represents the middle class and not the special interests of America.

In considering our future we also have to remember the story that the Lord used in his metaphor of the wheat and the tares. In this story a farmer plants wheat. While the farmer is asleep an enemy creeps into his field and plants weeds among the wheat. The farmer's employees find out what has happened and suggests that they should go into the field and root up the weeds. The farmer wisely says no, don't do it because in rooting up the weeds, you could also destroy a lot of wheat. He councils them to wait till the wheat is grown to the point that the plants can survive the destruction of the weeds.

Unfortunately, well meaning Americans have not learned this lesson well and we are paying for it. The United States spends over 300 billion dollars a year on non-profit agencies such as Volunteers of America, Catholic Relief Services, United Cerebral Palsy Association, CARE, etc. This is not to say these organizations are bad, but we have to remember that for them to exist they must have someone to service. For the prison to stay open it must have prisoners. For charities to function they must have someone in need. And if there are too many charities with too many resources they can actually function to choke out the opportunities the poor need to advance into the middle class.

Consider for a moment that in New York City, the New York Social Services economy employs more persons than Wall Street.[178] Community Planning Boards have arisen which are often staffed by members from social service organizations, which in New York often give preference to social agencies over businesses in taking new properties. Think for a moment what this means. Each time a piece of property is given to a charitable organization rather than a business, the property goes off the tax roles. The tax burden on the remaining private properties rises which encourages them to leave and creates the opportunity for new properties to be assigned to charitable organization. Thus the poor get poorer with no hope for the future while the charitable organizations actually strangle the poor they are supposed to serve.

We need to change this. Programs I have suggested will do so but the axe that gets gored (charitable organizations) will howl in the wilderness. It will take great courage and determination for the middle class and a new third party to hold its course.

If America is to retain its position of being a first class nation, it must have a third party with a viable ideology. A belief system that the middle class can support. And it must find a way to deal with the postindustrial world. If we allow the majority of our citizens to become unemployable, we invite an inevitable conflict between the have and have-nots; between the professional/technical class and the rest of America who are forming a hard core of unemployables.

As both Christopher Lasch[179] and Patrick Kennon[180] assert the conflict between the have and have nots will dramatically affect the course of America in the twenty-first century. Unless a third party develops that can produce an ideology with hope and is positioned so as to command the loyalty of the middle class[181], America's decline is inevitable. We have to rethink economics and economic theory. If multi-national corporations can shift factories to China where workers work for twenty cents an hour, why not the next step and employ robots who work for nothing but their cost of maintenance and development? And if products, i.e. material goods can be produced by fewer and fewer workers and lower and lower costs, how then does an economy expand to employ all of its citizens?

A third party must be formed which redesigns the postindustrial world so that jobs are available to all of its citizens. If jobs are not available in factories, it will make them available maintaining and improving the infrastructure of the country. Instead of the continuing course of the more and more of our citizens having less and less, we can look forward to an economy, which produces more and more and also improves its land.

Instead of struggling to survive, we will be able to devote our energies to defining both what we can give to life and what we want from life. What is the point of correcting the ills of our society if we are unwilling to chart a new course with a new society? The overall focus and emphasis is about re-creating a whole new truly democratic society, which recognizes that we are all equally different.

In thinking about a new course, much can be learned from Hegel, the German philosopher who believed in a God very much involved in the affairs of humans. He thought that studying history could apprehend the Grand Designs of God. God acted to change humanity by favoring nations, which would best forward God's programs.

Hegel's idea of *historical determinism* was used heavily by both the Communists and the Fascists. Both Marx and Hitler, knowingly or unknowingly, used many of Hegel's basic ideas as they formed their governments. But neither Marx nor Hitler nor Hegel himself fully understood or supported one of the basic principles that Hegel taught. And that principle was the issue of existence vs. essence.

Existence vs. Essence, one of the enlarging principles that Hegel taught, states society has two choices: One is take care of the day-to-day activities that can make or break a society—such as hurricanes, earthquakes, tidal waves, roads, bridges, railroads, airports, crime, national defense, social security, etc. The more effectively a society deals with daily existence, the more powerful it will be.

Existence, on a national or personal basis, deals with taking care of the normal or extraordinary emergencies a nation or person faces. But there are also issues of essence, which is the degree to which a nation or person is able to fulfill its potential. Often leaders talk about potential when they talk about purpose. What is the purpose of the United States for instance? Essence is found in the American Pledge of

Allegiance, which states that we are a nation united under God with liberty and justice for all.

Communists and fascists co-opted Hegel's ideas. In the process of adopting his ideas, they confused existence with essence. Both Stalin, Hitler and Mussolini believed that they could dictate programs or policies, which would force citizens to fulfill the dictator's dreams of conquest. Millions of Jews and Slavs died as Hitler strove to have his people become the super race. Millions of middle-class landholders died in Communist lands, as Stalin formed huge farming cooperatives, which never fulfilled their potential. Why? Workers within the cooperative lacked enthusiasm or investment in the Communist dream. Fascism also failed to flourish in part because of the passive resistance of many citizens of both Italy and Germany.

In America, neither the Conservatives nor the Democrats have made an attempt to distinguish between existence vs. essence. In a participative democracy, citizens must participate in the details of existence and be held accountable for their participation, or lack thereof. But it is not the privilege nor right of the state to *dictate* issues of essence. It is, however, the right of a state to insist that citizens of the state *respect* the property and persons of others. Those who take other's property or harm other persons should be held responsible for their actions.

But a state should not attempt to *dictate* the personal decisions of citizens when it comes to issues of personal choice involving health or death. A citizen has a right to drink alcohol but does not have a right to drive and drink, which affects other citizens. A citizen has the right to use drugs to control emotional or physical pain, but does not have the right to endanger others by performing a task, which requires a clear head. A citizen has the right to use mood and mind-altering drugs, but only in a place where his impaired mind will not place others at risk.

In the mid twenty-first century, education should deal with both existence (basic tools of learning such as language, mathematics, science, philosophy, history, etc.) and essence (issues of ethics, morality, and spirituality), with one major difference. Government should involve itself only in existence and invite members from the local community to discuss essence. The local community should provide resources so that students can learn to develop their potentials to the fullest within an ethical framework.

The basic principle to learn and be taught throughout society in the mid-twenty-first century must be that *change comes from within* and not from without. Government has neither the right nor the power to dictate change within a citizen's own heart. Choices, which produce change, must come from *within*.

Thus, with respect to the issue of abortion, governments and local communities can and should encourage basic respect for a person's body, and encourage and support a higher level of morality than is currently expected from our youth. In my own practice, I've seen that youth are far more idealistic and moral than their elders are are. Further, a state can and should hold a citizen responsible for irresponsible parenting. But a state should not attempt to control a woman's body or make her choices for her. This has to be a personal and not a state decision, a private and moral decision, not a political one.

Finally in the mid-twenty-first century, citizens will have learned that behavior has consequences. Each time a state or a person supports a basically unethical act, a price has to be paid. Citizens of the United States paid a heavy price for slavery and for taking lands from a weaker nation. Society will inevitably pay a price for ignoring ethical morality. And all of us are paying a price, and will pay a heavier price, by electing and re-electing politicians who support legalized thievery.

In the past, politicians have gained power by promising to give to one group by taking from another group. This has led to the increasing impoverishment of America. Eighty percent of Americans now face a bleaker future, while twenty percent are doing better.

The time has come for Americans to totally force out of office any politician who *PROMISES TO GIVE US SOMETHING, WHICH WE*

DON'T HAVE TO PAY FOR! How can we expect any sense of dignity, honesty, or integrity when we elect politicians who haven't the slightest sense of injustice or immorality when they offer free services? Citizens in the mid-twenty-first century will know that the freest services have the highest cost.

At the same time however, we do not have to be a land, which ignores its aged population. Citizens who have spent their lives toiling in America. As we cut the waste and re-engineer our society, it's also time we stopped stealing from the social security program. We can and should increase social security benefits and also do away with Medicare and replace Medicare with good, private insurance. Insurance just as good as the person receives who works for General Motors, Chrysler, Ford, etc. As we cut programs we don't need and increase programs we do need such as improving the infrastructure and providing for the aged, America will truly become a beacon for the world.

When Martin Luther King spoke his famous words, "I have a dream," he wasn't talking only about black and white equality. He envisioned a just society in which *all* citizens had access to opportunities for progress at all levels. He dreamed of rebuilt cities, quality education, and quality jobs for all.

When my son and I survived an accident in which a drunk driver struck our car and caused our vehicle to roll over twice, I regained consciousness with a wonderful feeling of exhilaration. I was still alive! Americans can all share in the feeling of aliveness! I believe America can still be the "land of opportunity in the highest sense." We can not only fulfill the American Dream of individual freedom, safety, financial opportunity, and quality transportation, we can also become a country which encourages (without dictating to them) all citizens to develop their potentials in all walks of life to the fullest, best, positive extent possible.

About the Author

Dr. Shinedling has practiced medical psychology for over 30 years. Medical psychology is a field in which patients who have suffered some sort of catastrophic illness or injury need psychological counseling to help them overcome their problems. His experience with normal people trying to survive led him to understand the pitfalls in our society. Reluctantly, he also came to the conclusion both major parties are blind to the needs and concerns of the middle class. Giving up on the major parties, he briefly joined the Perotistas, Libertarians, New Party and the Reform Party. Dissatisfied with them all, he decided to invent a party which really would appeal to the concerns, hopes and desires of the middle class.

Dr. Shinedling, ever a romantic and an optimist believes in the future. He also believes that the future will eventually lead to a better society and a more relevant political party.

Endnotes

1. Berke, Richard L. The Swing Vote has Dim View of Both Parties, *The New York Times*, March 27, 1995.

2. Benedeto, Richard Voters want independent in race. *USA TODAY,* August 11-13, 1995.

3. *ibid.*

4. *ibid.*

5. *ibid.*

6. Smith, Page *TRIAL BY FIRE,* McGraw-Hill, New York, 1982.

7. *PUBLIC OPINION QUARTERLY VOL 56, #4,* Winter, 1992.

8. Barta, Carolyn *PEROT AND HIS PEOPLE,* The Summit Group, Fort Worth, 1993.

9. Bartlett, Donald L. and Steele, James B. *AMERICA: WHAT WENT WRONG?* Andrews and McMeel, Kansas City, 1992.

10. Gross, Martin L. *A CALL FOR REVOLUTION,* Ballentine Books, New York, 1993.

11. Beatty, Jack "Who Speaks for the Middle Class?" *ATLANTIC MONTHLY,* May, 1994.

7. *CONGRESSIONAL QUARTERLY,* January 23, 1993.

12. Bartlett, *op. cit.*

13. Beatty, *op. cit.*

14. *ibid.*

15. Locke, John *A Letter Concerning Toleration Concerning Civil Government, Second Essay An Essay Concerning Human Understanding* in *Great Books Enclyclopaedia Britannica,* 1952.

16. Jack Beatty, "Who Speaks for the Middle Class?" *ATLANTIC MONTHLY,* May, 1994.

17. Peterson, Wallace C. *SILENT DEPRESSION,* W. W. Norton and Company, 1994.

18. Duke, Steven B., and Gross, Albert C. *AMERICA'S LONGEST WAR,* G. P. Putnam's Sons, 1993.

19. Vienneau, David, "Court puts child's life ahead of religion." *The Saturday Star,* Metro Editon, Toronto, January 28, 1995.

20. Barta, Carolyn *PEROT AND HIS PEOPLE,* The Summit Group, Fort Worth, 1993.

21. Arendt, Hannah *THE ORIGINS OF TOTALITARIANISM,* Harcourt Brace Jovanovich, New York, 1951.

22. Trueheart, Charles, "Canada's era of good feeling with Chretien." *The Washington Post National Weekly Edition,* January 16-22, 1995.

23. Gross, Martin L. *A CALL FOR REVOLUTION,* Ballentine Books, New York, 1993.

24. ibid; also see Bibby, John F. *POLITICS, PARTIES, AND ELECTIONS IN AMERICA,* Nelson-Hall, Chicago, 1987.

25. *BALLOT BOX,* P. D8, Saginaw News, March 14, 1994, Saginaw.

26. *ibid.*

27. Howard, Philip K. *THE DEATH OF COMMON SENSE,* Random House, New York, 1994.

28. *ibid.*

29. Peterson, Wallace C. *SILENT DEPRESSION,* W. W. Norton and Company, New York, 1994.

30. Gross, Martin L. *A CALL FOR REVOLUTION,* Ballentine Books, New York, 1993.

31. Lambro, Donald "Republicans need a sharper knife." *Conservative Chronicle,* August, 23, 1995.

32. Sternhell, Zeev with Sznajder, Mario and Asheri, Maia *THE BIRTH OF FASCIST IDEOLOGY*, Princeton University Press, Princeton, 1994.
33. Bovard, James *LOSING RIGHTS*, St. Martin's Press, New York, 1994.
34. Bellah, Robert N. *HABITS OF THE HEART*, Harper and Row, New York, 1985.
35. Barta, Carolyn *PEROT AND HIS PEOPLE*, The Summit Group, Fort Worth, 1993.
36. Duke, Steven B., Gross, Albert C. *AMERICA'S LONGEST WAR*, G. P. Putnam's Sons, 1994.
37. Howard, Philip K., *op.cit.*
38. Machiavelli, Nicolo *THE PRINCE*, Great Books, Encyclopedia Britannica, Chicago, 1952.
39. Merida, Kevin "And in this corner, in the Democratic Trunks..." *Washington Post National Weekly Edition*, January 16-22, 1995.
40. Bibby, John F. *POLITICS, PARTIES AND ELECTIONS IN AMERICA*, Nelson Hall, Chicago, 1987.
41. Rosin, Hanna *ACTION JACKSON*, The New Republic, March 21, 1994.
42. Bibby, John F. *op.cit.*
43. *ibid, p.266.*
44. *ibid.*
45. Barnes, Fred "Health Care Costs are Going Down", *THE AMERICAN SPECTATOR*, February, 1994.
46. *ibid.*
3. Bovard, James "Double-Crossing to Safety," THE AMERICAN SPECTATOR, January, 1995.
47. *ibid.*
48. *ibid.*
49. Gaylin, Willard "Faulty Diagnosis" *ADVANCE*, Winter, 1994.
7. *ibid.*
50. Friedman, Lawrence M. *CRIME AND PUNISHMENT IN AMERICAN HISTORY*, Basic Books, New York, 1993.

51. Duke, Steven B. and Gross, Albert C. *AMERICA'S LONGEST WAR*, G. P. Putnam's Sons, New York, 1993.

52. Clymer, Adam "The Hidden Atagonists of Clinton's Health Plan", *THE NEW YORK TIMES*, June 19, 1994.

53. Hyman, Robin *DICTIONARY OF QUOTATIONS*, National Textbook Company, Lincolnwood, 1985.

54. U. S. Department of Justice, Office of Justice Programs, Bureau of Justice Statistics, November, 1991.

55. U.S. Department of Justice, Office of Justice Programs, Bureau of Justice Statistics, "Drugs, Crime and the Justice System", December, 1992.

56. Friedman, Lawrence M. *CRIME AND PUNISHMENT IN AMERICAN HISTORY* Basic Books, New York, 1993.

57. U.S. Department of Justice, Office of Justice Programs, December, 1992, *op. cit.*

58. *CRIMINAL VICTIMIZATION IN THE UNITED STATES, 1991* U. S. Department of Justice, Office of Justice Programs, Bureau of Justice Statistics, 1991.

59. Duke, Steven B. and Gross, Albert C. *AMERICA'S LONGEST WAR* G. P. Putnam's Sons, New York, 1993.

60. *CRIMINAL VICTIMIZATION IN THE UNITED STATES*, op. cit.

61. Talan, Jamie "Painkillers of the future are much more powerful." *Saginaw News,* January 13, 1995.

62. "Dangerous Drugs," *U. S. News and World Report,* January 9, 1995.

63. Duke, Steven B., *op. cit.*

64.Bovard, James *LOST RIGHTS*, St. Martin's Press, New York, 1994.

65.Forer, Lois G. *A RAGE TO PUNISH*, W. W. Norton and Company, New York, 1994.

66. Herbert, Bob, "In America", *The New York Times,* Sunday, June 19, 1994.

67. "Financial Indicators", *The Economist,* August 13-19, 1994.

68. "Economic Indicators", *The Economist,* January 7th-13, 1995.

69. *ibid.*

70. Rothstein, Richard, "Continental Drift: NAFTA and Its Aftershocks," *The American Prospect,* Winter, 1993.

71. Wu, Harry, Op. Ed. section, *The New York Times,* October 3, 1993.

72. Chen, Chi Kwan, Op. Ed. section, *The New York Times,* October 3, 1994.

73. Schlafly, Phyllis, "The Secret Media Subsidies in WTO/GATT." *Conservative Chronicle,* October 26, 1994.

74. Crutsinger, Martin, "Despite promised U.S. aid, Mexico's future bleak." Associated Press, January 14, 1995.

75. Buchanan, Pat, "Is the United States becoming Two Countries?" October 14, 1994, PJB Enterprises Inc.

76. Hollings, Ernest F. "Reform Mexico First," *Foreign Policy,* Winter, 1993-1994.

77. "New Democrats, Old Cynicism", *The New York Times,* Thursday, June 23, 1994.

78. Drucker, Peter F. "Really reinventing government." *The Atlantic Monthly,* February, 1995.

79. Pear, Robert "President decides to limit, not cut, federal deficit." *The New York Times,* February 5, 1995.

80. *ibid.*

81. Drucker, *op. cit.*

82. Kudlow, Lawrence. "Middle Class Tax Hike." *National Review,* June 13, 1994.

83. Bartlett, Donald L., and Steele, James B. *AMERICA: WHO REALLY PAYS THE TAXES?* A Touchstone Book, New York, 1994.

84. Olaskey, Marvin, *THE TRAGEDY OF AMERICAN COMPASSION,* Regnery Gateway, Washington, D.C., 1992.

85. Rasberry, William, *Detroit News,* July, 19, 1989.

86. Beck Joan, "The Huge difference between a good dad and a no-good bum." Chicago Tribune, June 19, 1994.

87. Olaskey, *op.cit.*

88. Murray, Charles, *LOSING GROUND: AMERICAN SOCIAL POLICY 1950–1980,* Basic Books, New York, 1984.

89. Beck, *op.cit.*

90. Olaskey, Marvin, *THE TRAGEDY OF AMERICAN COMPASSION,* Regnery Gateway, Washington, D.C., 1992.

91. Rasberry, William, *Detroit News,* July, 19, 1989.

92. Beck Joan, "The Huge difference between a good dad and a no-good bum." Chicago Tribune, June 19, 1994.

93. Olaskey, *op.cit.*

94. Murray, Charles, *LOSING GROUND: AMERICAN SOCIAL POLICY 1950–1980,* Basic Books, New York, 1984.

95. Beck, *op.cit.*

96. Dalton, Dennis, *FREEDOM, THE PHILOSOPHY OF LIBERATION,* The Teaching Company, Springfield, 1994.

97. Jencks, Christopher *THE HOMELESS,* Harvard University Press, Cambridge, 1994.

98. *ibid.*

99. *ibid.*

100. Olasky, Marvin *THE TRAGEDY OF AMERICAN COMPASSION,* Regenery Gateway, Washington, D.C., 1992.

101. Duke, Steven B. and Gross, Albert C. *AMERICA'S LONGEST WAR,* A Jeremy P. Tarcher/Putnam Book, New York, 1993.

102. Bovard, James *LOST RIGHTS,* St. Martin's Press, New York, 1994.

    1. Shaw, Peter "Let a Hundred Cities Bloom" *National Review,* July 11, 1994.

    2. Reich, Robert B. *THE NEXT AMERICAN FRONTIER,* Penguin Books, New York, 1983.

    3. Woodward, Bob *THE AGENDA,* Simon and Schuster, New York, 1994.

    4. Reich, *op. cit.,* p. 279

103. Forer, Lois G. *A RAGE TO PUNISH,* W. W. Norton, New York, 1994.

104. Bovard, James *LOST RIGHTS,* St Martin's Press, New York, 1994.

105. *ibid, p. 51.*

106. *ibid, p. 50.*

107. Friedman, Lawrence M. *CRIME AND PUNISHMENT IN AMERICAN HISTORY,* Basic Books, New York, 1993.

108. Forer, *op.cit.*

109. Van Den Haag, Ernest "How to Cut Crime" *National Review,* May 30, 1994.

110. *ibid.*

111. Starr, Oliver "The Case of Richard Davis" *National Review,* May 30, 1994.

112. Staloff, Darren, "More's Utopia: Reason and Social Justice", *GREAT MINDS PART II: The Age of Faith to the Age of Reason,* The Teaching Company, Springfield, 1993.

113. "About a Sixth of U.S. Crime Is at Job Site" *The New York Times,* July 25, 1994.

114. Van Den Haag, *op. cit.*

115. Hand, Learned *THE SPIRIT OF LIBERTY,* Knopf, New York, 1952.

116. Gunther, Gerald *LEARNED HAND: The Man and the Judge,* Knopf, New York, 1994.

117. Dworkin, Ronald "Mr. LIBERTY" *The New York Review of Books,* August 11, 1994.

118. Nader, Ralph and Green, Mark *VERDICTS ON LAWYERS,* Thomas Y. Crowell Company, New York, 1976.

119. Gerber, Rudolph J. *LAWYERS, COURTS, AND PROFESSIONALISM,* Greenwood Press, New York, 1989.

120. Spangler, Eve, *LAWYERS FOR HIRE,* Yale University Press, New Haven, 1986.

121. *THE AMERICAN ALMANAC,* The Reference Press, Austin, 1993-1994.

122. Gleick, James *CHAOS,* Penguin Books, New York, 1987.

123. Herrnstein, Richard J. and Murray, Charles *THE BELL CURVE,* The Free Press, New York, 1994.

124. Auerbach, Jerold S. *UNEQUAL JUSTICE*, Oxford University Press, New York, 1980.

125. Forer, Lois G. *A RAGE TO PUNISH*, W. W. Norton and Company, New York, 1994.

126. Bovard, James *LOST RIGHTS*, St. Martin's Press, New York, 1994.

127. Hyman, Robin *DICTIONARY OF QUOTATIONS*, National Text Book Company, Lincolnwood, 1988.

128. Winer, B. J. *STATISTICAL PRINCIPLES IN EXPERIMENTAL DESIGN*. McGraw Hill, New York, 1962.

129. Watson, John B. *BEHAVIORISM*, W. W. Norton, New York, 1924.

130. Foren, John "Board: Teach Morality." *The Saginaw News,* January 20, 1995.

131. Bennett, William J. *THE INDEX OF LEADING CULTURAL INDICATORS*, The Heritage Foundation, Washington, D.C., 1993.

132. *ibid.*

133. Hyman, Robert *DICTIONARY OF QUOTATIONS*, National Textbook Company, Lincolnwood, 1985.

134. Keegan, John. *A HISTORY OF WARFARE*, Sanford J. Greenburger Associates, Inc., New York, 1993.

135. Wrong, Dennis, *THE PROBLEM OF ORDER*, The Free Press, New York, 1994.

136. Hobbes, Thomas *LEVIATHAN*, Encyclopedia Britannica, Inc. Chicago, 1952.

137. Howard, Michael and Paret, Peter. *ibid.*

138. Woodward, Bob *THE AGENDA*, Simon and Schuster, New York, 1994.

139. Simpson, Howard R. *DIEM BIEN PHU*, Brassey's Inc., Washington, 1994.

140. Keegan, *op. cit.*

141. Keegan, John, *op. cit.*

142. Massie, Robert K. *DREADNOUGHT*, Random House Inc., New York, 1991.

143. Keegan, John, *op. cit.*

144. Dockery, Kevin *SEALS IN ACTION*, Avon Books, New York, 1991.

145. Asprey, Robert B. *WAR IN THE SHADOWS*, William Morrow and Company, Inc., New York, 1994.

146. Burrows, William E. and Windrem, Robert. *CRITICAL MASS*, Simon and Schuster, New York, 1994.

147. Dupuy, Col. Trevor N. *FUTURE WARS*, Warner Books, New York, 1992.

148. *THE LINCOLN LIBRARY OF ESSENTIAL INFORMATION*, The Frontier Press, Columbus, 1985.

149. Hill, Donna. *JOSEPH SMITH*, Doubleday and Company, Inc. Garden City, 1977.

150. Catton, Bruce. *NEVER CALL RETREAT*, Doubleday and Company, Inc. New York, 1965.

151. Iver Bernstein, *THE NEW YORK CITY DRAFT RIOTS*, Oxford University Press, New York, 1990.

152. Charen, Mona, "Party Differences are irreconcilable." *Conservative Chronicle*, Vol 9. No. 43, October 17, 1994.

153. "For richer, for poorer.", *The Economist*, November 5th-11th, 1994.

154. Stacks, John F. "Stampede," *TIME*, November 21, 1994.

155. Zuckerman, Mortimer B. "Who Does Feel Your Pain?" *U.S. News and World Report*, December 26, 1994/January 2, 1995.

156. Frum, David, *DEAD RIGHT*, A New Republic Book, New York, 1994.

157. Bovard, James, *LOST RIGHTS*, St. Martin's Press, New York, 1994.

158. Gross, Martin L., *A CALL FOR REVOLUTION*, Ballentine Books, New York, 1993.

159. Heineman, Robert, *AUTHORITY AND THE LIBERAL TRADITION*, Transaction Publications, New Brunswick, 1994.

160. Olaskey, Marvin, *THE TRAGEDY OF AMERICAN COMPASSION*, Regenery Gateway, Washington, D.C., 1992.

161. Lasch, Christopher, *THE REVOLT OF THE ELITES*, W. W. Norton and Company, New York, 1995.

162. Barta, Carolyn, *PEROT AND HIS PEOPLE*, The Summit Group, Fort Worth, 1993.

163. Peterson, Wallace C. *SILENT DEPRESSION*, W. W. Norton and Company, New York, 1994.

164. Karp, Walter, *LIBERTY UNDER SEIGE*, Franklin Square Press, New York, 1988.

165. Barlett, Donald L. and Steele, James B. *AMERICA: WHO REALLY PAYS THE TAXES?* A Touchstone Book, New York, 1994.

166. Batra, Dr. Ravi, *THE MYTH OF FREE TRADE*, A Robert Stewart Book, Charles Scribner's Sons, New York, 1993.

167. Perot, Ross with Choate, Pat, *SAVE YOUR JOB, SAVE OUR COUNTRY*, Hyperion, New York, 1993.

168. Lawson, Kay and Merkl, Peter H. *WHEN PARTIES FAIL*, Princeton University Press, Princeton, 1988.

169. Howard, Michael and Paret, Peter, *CARL VON CLAUSEWITZ ON WAR*, Princeton University Press, Princeton, 1984.

170. Limbaugh, Rush, *THE WAY THINGS OUGHT TO BE*, Pocket Books, New York, 1992.

171. Kennon, Patrick E. *THE TWILIGHT OF DEMOCRACY*, Doubleday, New York, 1995.

172. Tucker, William, "Sweet Charity," *American Spectator*, February, 1995.

173. Lasch, Christopher, *THE REVOLT OF THE ELITES*, W. W. Norton, New York, 1995.

174. Kennon, *op. cit.*

175. Hinich, Melvin J. and Munger, Michael C. *IDEOLOGY AND THE THEORY OF POLITICAL CHOICE*, University of Michigan Press, Ann Arbor, 1994.

compliance